Mastering Fortran Programming

From Basics to Expert Proficiency

Contents

Introduction

Fortran, short for Formula Translation, holds a significant position in the history of programming languages. Developed in the 1950s for numerical and scientific computing, it continues to be a critical tool for researchers, engineers, and scientists worldwide. This book, 'Mastering Fortran Programming: From Basics to Expert Proficiency', aims to impart a comprehensive understanding of Fortran, from its fundamental principles to advanced topics, ensuring that readers develop both theoretical knowledge and practical skills.

As the first high-level programming language, Fortran was designed to allow easy translation of mathematical formulas into code. Over the decades, it has undergone numerous revisions, each adding more capabilities. Fortran's legacy editions include Fortran 66, Fortran 77, Fortran 90, Fortran 95, Fortran 2003, Fortran 2008, and the recent Fortran 2018. Each version has introduced innovations that enhance the language's power and usability while maintaining backward compatibility.

Understanding Fortran's syntax and unique constructs is integral to mastering the language. This book will guide readers through the intricacies of Fortran's data types, control structures, and modular programming capabilities. Starting from the basics, we will explore how to set up a Fortran development environment and write simple programs. Further chapters will delve into complex topics like arrays, file handling, and memory management.

Input and output (I/O) operations are crucial for any programming task. Fortran provides robust mechanisms for file handling and data management, which will be discussed in detailed chapters focused on I/O operations and file handling.

Functions and subroutines are fundamental building blocks in Fortran, allowing for modular and reusable code. This book will cover the creation, usage, and best practices for functions and subroutines, ensuring that readers can write efficient and maintainable code.

Arrays and array operations are core components in scientific computing. Fortran's array handling capabilities are extensive and powerful. We will examine single and multi-dimensional arrays, dynamic memory allocation, and intrinsic array functions in depth.

Modules and packages facilitate modular programming and code organization in Fortran. The various aspects of module creation, usage, and advanced features will be thoroughly covered. This section of the book will enable readers to manage dependencies and organize code effectively.

Memory management, including the use of pointers, is an advanced topic that will be addressed comprehensively. Efficient memory management is essential for high-performance computing, and readers will learn best practices to avoid common pitfalls like memory leaks.

Optimization is a critical aspect of programming, especially in scientific computing, where performance is paramount. This book will guide readers through profiling programs, applying compiler optimization techniques, and writing efficient Fortran code. Optimization strategies such as loop unrolling, vectorization, and minimizing computational complexity are discussed to improve the performance of Fortran applications.

With each chapter building on the previous, "Mastering Fortran Programming: From Basics to Expert Proficiency" is designed to be a definitive resource. This structured approach will equip readers with both foundational knowledge and advanced skills, enabling them to tackle complex computational problems using Fortran effectively.

By the end of this book, readers will have a thorough understanding of Fortran programming and will be well-prepared to address challenges in scientific and numerical computing. They will gain confidence in writing optimized, maintainable, and high-performance Fortran code, ensuring Fortran's continued relevance and utility in modern computing.

Chapter 1

Introduction to Fortran

Fortran is a pioneering high-level programming language developed for numerical and scientific computing, achieving widespread use since its creation in the 1950s. This chapter provides an overview of Fortran's history and evolution, the various standards it has gone through, and sets the stage for learning by introducing essential concepts such as setting up the development environment, writing basic programs, and understanding the language's syntax and conventions. Readers will also familiarize themselves with compiling and running Fortran programs, as well as common terminologies and development tools essential for effective Fortran programming.

1.1 History and Evolution of Fortran

Fortran, an acronym derived from **For**mula **Tran**slating System, was developed in 1957 by IBM for scientific and engineering computations. It is recognized as one of the oldest high-level languages still in use today. The primary motivation for Fortran's development was to reduce the complexity and increase the speed of programming in the context of numerical and scientific computations, which were predominantly performed using assembly language at the time.

The first version, known as Fortran I, introduced revolutionary concepts including variables, loops, and conditional statements. These features significantly decreased the time needed for program development and debugging, setting the stage for the widespread adoption of high-level programming languages.

Following the initial release, Fortran underwent a series of updates to address growing computational demands and to incorporate advances in programming language theory and practice:

- **Fortran II (1958)**: Introduced subroutines and functions, enhancing code modularity and reusability. The inclusion of these features allowed programmers to encapsulate code segments for specific tasks, promoting better program structure and maintainability.
- **Fortran IV (1962)**: Improved upon its predecessors by introducing explicit type declarations, logical IF statements, and formatted input/output. This version became the basis for a formal standard, culminating in the publication of the **ANSI X3.9-1966** standard, commonly referred to as Fortran 66.
- **Fortran 66**: Defined further refinements and provided a standardized version of the language that could be universally adopted, enhancing portability of Fortran code between different computer systems.
- **Fortran 77**: Marked a significant step forward by incorporating structured programming constructs like DO loops with end labels, block IF, ELSE IF, and string handling capability. This made the language more powerful and expressive.
- **Fortran 90**: Introduced modern programming concepts such as array operations, module systems for better namespace management, and recursion. Additionally, it embraced dynamic memory allocation, user-defined data types, and more sophisticated control constructs. This version was backward-compatible with Fortran 77 but offered extensive enhancements to promote more efficient and readable code.
- **Fortran 95**: Primarily an incremental improvement over Fortran 90, it incorporated some relatively minor updates and performance enhancements, such as FORALL and WHERE constructs for array processing, and the PURE and ELEMENTAL procedure attributes.
- **Fortran 2003**: Introduced object-oriented programming features, enabling the definition of type-bound procedures (akin to meth-

ods in other object-oriented languages) and inheritance. Additionally, it included support for the IEEE floating-point arithmetic standard and interoperability with the C programming language, significantly broadening Fortran's applicability.

- **Fortran 2008**: Included enhancements such as coarray parallel programming capabilities, submodules for improved module management, and enhancements to input/output features. This extension was designed to address the need for high-performance computing by facilitating more advanced parallelism approaches.
- **Fortran 2018**: Continued to refine and expand the language, introducing features like improved interoperability with C, enhanced array handling capabilities, and additional parallel computing facilities. This version aimed to further modernize the language by catering to the evolving needs of the scientific computing community.

The evolution of Fortran reflects an ongoing effort to balance backward compatibility with the incorporation of new programming paradigms and high-performance computing requirements. Despite the introduction of several powerful modern languages, Fortran remains unparalleled in certain domains of scientific and engineering computation. The robust ecosystem, extensive libraries, and community of dedicated users ensure its continued relevance and usefulness in solving complex computational problems. Understanding Fortran's history and evolution provides valuable context for appreciating its current capabilities and ongoing development.

1.2 Overview of Fortran Standards

Fortran, originally developed in the 1950s, has undergone multiple revisions and updates to address the evolving needs of scientific and numerical computing. Each version introduces new features, improves syntax and performance, and often provides backward compatibility. Understanding these standards is crucial for leveraging Fortran's full potential and maintaining legacy codebases. This section delves into the key Fortran standards, emphasizing their enhancements and implications.

FORTRAN I (1957): The original version, developed by IBM, was designed to optimize numerical computations and reduce the need for manual coding in machine language. Key features included arithmetic operations, assignment statements, and basic control structures like DO loops. It lacked more advanced structuring and data formatting capabilities found in later versions.

FORTRAN II (1958): Building on its predecessor, FORTRAN II introduced procedural programming elements, such as subroutines and functions, allowing for code modularity and reuse. It included the COMMON statement for sharing variables among program units, enhancing its usability in larger programs.

FORTRAN IV (1961): Standardized by the American National Standards Institute (ANSI) as ANSI FORTRAN, it introduced new constructs for more sophisticated programming, including the BLOCK DATA statement for initializing data and improved input/output control.

CODE

```
BLOCK DATA
COMMON /BLOCK/ X, Y, Z
DATA X, Y, Z /0.0, 0.0, 0.0/
END BLOCK DATA
```

FORTRAN 66 (1966): As the first standardized version (ANSI X3.9-1966), FORTRAN 66 brought consistency across implementations. Its key features supported fixed-format code, structured control statements, and the capability to handle real and complex arithmetic.

FORTRAN 77 (1978): This version, identified as ANSI X3.9-1978, incorporated enhancements for better programming efficiency and readability. It introduced structured programming constructs like IF-ELSE blocks and the DO WHILE loop, as well as efficient input/output handling.

CODE

```
CHARACTER*20 NAME
PRINT*, 'ENTER YOUR NAME:'
READ*, NAME
PRINT*, 'HELLO, ', NAME
```

Output execution:

```
ENTER YOUR NAME:
John Doe
HELLO, John Doe
```

Fortran 90 (1991): Representing a major overhaul, Fortran 90 introduced free-format source input and modern programming constructs such as recursion, dynamic memory allocation, and array operations.

It provided extensive enhancements to modularity through modules, enhancing reusability, and maintainability.

```
MODULE MOD
  INTEGER :: I
END MODULE MOD
```

Fortran 95 (1997): Building on Fortran 90, Fortran 95 offered minor revisions for further optimization and introduced new intrinsic functions for numerical operations and array processing. It added the capability for processing pointers and the FORALL construct for array assignment.

```
REAL, ALLOCATABLE :: A(:)
ALLOCATE(A(100))
FORALL(I = 1:100)
  A(I) = I**2
ENDFOR
```

Fortran 2003 (2004): A significant step towards object-oriented programming, Fortran 2003 included support for classes, inheritance, and polymorphism. It also enhanced interoperability with C and introduced features for improved concurrent execution.

```
TYPE :: POINT
REAL :: X, Y
CONTAINS
    PROCEDURE :: DISPLAY
END TYPE POINT
```

Fortran 2008 (2010): This revision emphasized parallel processing capabilities and expanded the standard to include coarrays, enhancing Fortran's utility in high-performance computing (HPC).

```
REAL :: A[*]
A = THIS_IMAGE()
SYNC ALL
PRINT*, 'Image ', THIS_IMAGE(), ' holds ', A
```

Output execution:

```
Image 1 holds 1
Image 2 holds 2
...
```

Fortran 2018 (2018): The latest standard focuses on further refining parallel and concurrent programming features, enhancing usability and performance in modern computing environments.

Precise understanding and application of these standards enable developers to write efficient, maintainable, and portable Fortran programs. This historical context highlights how each incremental update contributes to the robustness and versatility of Fortran in scientific computing.

1.3 Setting Up the Fortran Development Environment

Setting up an effective development environment is crucial for Fortran programming. A well-configured environment will streamline the coding process, minimize potential errors, and allow efficient debugging and execution of programs. This section delineates the steps involved in configuring the Fortran development environment on various operating systems. It assumes that the reader has a basic understanding of their operating system's functionalities.

Required Software:

- A Fortran compiler
- An integrated development environment (IDE) or a text editor
- Additional tools for debugging and performance analysis (optional)

Popular Fortran Compilers:

- GNU Fortran (gfortran): Part of the GNU Compiler Collection (GCC), highly popular and open-source.
- Intel Fortran Compiler (ifort): Optimized for Intel processors, offers high performance.
- PGI Fortran Compiler: Known for performance and support for parallel computing.
- NAG Fortran Compiler: Focuses on comprehensive standards support and debugging features.

Integrated Development Environments (IDEs):

- Eclipse with the Photran plugin
- Code::Blocks
- Visual Studio Code with appropriate extensions

- JetBrains CLion
- Emacs with Fortran mode

Installation on Linux:

To install gfortran on a Debian-based system (such as Ubuntu), use the package manager apt:

```
sudo apt update
sudo apt install gfortran
```

Once the installation completes, verify the installation by executing:

```
gfortran --version
```

The expected output will resemble:

```
GNU Fortran (Ubuntu 10.2.0-5ubuntu1) 10.2.0
```

For other distributions, the package manager might differ. For instance, on Fedora, use dnf:

```
sudo dnf install gfortran
```

Installation on macOS:

To install gfortran on macOS, it is advisable to use a package manager such as Homebrew. First, install Homebrew (if not already installed):

```
/bin/bash -c "$(curl -fsSL https://raw.githubusercontent.com/Homebrew/install/
      HEAD/install.sh)"
```

Then, install gfortran:

```
brew install gcc
```

Note: gfortran is included in the GCC package.

Verify the installation:

```
gfortran --version
```

Installation on Windows:

For Windows users, a straightforward method is to install MSYS2, a collection of GNU utilities.

First, download and install MSYS2 from https://www.msys2.org/.

Open the MSYS2 terminal and update the package database:

```
pacman -Syu
```

Install gfortran:

```
pacman -S mingw-w64-x86_64-gcc-fortran
```

Verify the installation:

```
gfortran --version
```

Setting Up an IDE:

Visual Studio Code (VS Code) is a highly customizable and popular text editor. Here's a brief guide to configuring VS Code for Fortran development:

1. Install VS Code from https://code.visualstudio.com/ 2. Launch VS Code and navigate to the Extensions view by clicking the square icon in the sidebar or pressing Ctrl+Shift+X. 3. Search for Modern Fortran and Fortran IntelliSense, and click Install. 4. Configure VS Code to recognize your Fortran compiler by adding the following settings to the settings.json file:

```
{
    "fortran.compiler": "gfortran",
    "fortran.linter.compiler": "gfortran",
    "fortran.formatting.formatter": "findent"
}
```

Compiling and Running Fortran Programs:

With the development environment set up, you can proceed to compile and execute your Fortran programs.

Create a simple Fortran program, hello.f90:

```
program hello
    print *, "Hello, Fortran!"
end program hello
```

Compile the program:

```
gfortran -o hello hello.f90
```

Run the executable:

```
./hello
```

The expected output will be:

```
Hello, Fortran!
```

A meticulously configured development environment significantly enhances productivity and programming efficiency, providing a robust foundation for learning and mastering Fortran.

1.4 Basic Structure of a Fortran Program

A Fortran program consists of a series of statements that are executed in a sequential manner. The basic structure of a Fortran program includes several key components: program units, program structures, declaration and execution sections, and comments. Each of these components plays a crucial role in ensuring that the program runs correctly and efficiently.

Program Units

A Fortran program can consist of one or more program units. The primary program unit is the "main program", and it may contain other program units such as subroutines and functions. The standard way to denote the beginning and the end of a program unit is to use the PROGRAM and END PROGRAM statements, respectively.

```
PROGRAM Example
  PRINT *, 'Hello, World!'
END PROGRAM Example
```

In the example above, Example is the name of the program. The PRINT statement is used to output text to the console, and the END PROGRAM statement marks the end of the program unit.

Program Structure

The structure of a Fortran program can typically be divided into three main parts: the declaration section, the execution section, and the termination section.

- **Declaration Section:** This section includes the declaration of variables, constants, and other data items. It is essential to declare all variables before using them in the execution section.

- **Execution Section:** This section contains the executable statements that define the logic of the program. This is where the actual computation and processing take place.

- **Termination Section:** This section gracefully terminates the program by releasing any resources that were allocated during execution.

```
PROGRAM Sample
  INTEGER :: a, b, sum

  a = 10
  b = 20
  sum = a + b

  PRINT *, 'The sum is:', sum
END PROGRAM Sample
```

In this example, the declaration section declares the variables a, b, and sum as integers. The execution section assigns values to a and b, calculates the sum, and prints the result. The termination of the program is implicit with the END PROGRAM statement.

Declaration and Execution Sections

The declaration and execution sections are integral parts of any Fortran program. The declaration section must be placed before the execution section.

```
PROGRAM ComputeArea
  REAL :: radius, area
  REAL, PARAMETER :: pi = 3.14159

  radius = 5.0
  area = pi * radius * radius

  PRINT *, 'The area of the circle is:', area
END PROGRAM ComputeArea
```

In the ComputeArea program, the declaration section declares the variables radius and area as real (floating-point) numbers. It also declares pi as a parameter with a constant value. The execution section calculates the area of a circle using the formula πr^2 and prints the result.

Comments

Comments are non-executable statements used to enhance the readability of the code. In Fortran, comments are denoted by an exclamation mark !. Comments can be placed on a new line or at the end of an executable line.

```
PROGRAM CommentExample
  ! This is a comment
  INTEGER :: x

  x = 25 ! Assign the value 25 to x
  PRINT *, 'The value of x is:', x
END PROGRAM CommentExample
```

In the above code, ! This is a comment and ! Assign the value 25 to x are comments. They provide information about the program without affecting its execution.

Understanding the foundational structure of a Fortran program is essential for writing effective and efficient code. The clear demarcation between declaration and execution sections, and the use of comments, make Fortran programs easy to read and maintain.

1.5 Compiling and Running Fortran Programs

Fortran, a highly efficient language for numerical and scientific computations, leverages its compilation process to translate human-readable source code into machine-executable binaries. The process of compiling and running Fortran programs involves several vital steps, including preparing the source code, invoking the compiler, and executing the resultant program. This section will walk through these steps in detail to ensure a comprehensive understanding of the compilation process.

Preparation of Source Code

Begin by preparing the source code file. A basic Fortran source file typically has a .f90 or .f95 extension. Consider the following example, saved as hello_world.f90:

```
program hello
  print *, "Hello, world!"
end program hello
```

Invoking the Compiler

The next step is to compile the source code. Fortran has several compilers available such as gfortran, ifort, and flang. The GNU Fortran Compiler (gfortran) is widely used due to its open-source nature and robustness.

The general command structure to compile a Fortran program using gfortran on the terminal is:

```
gfortran -o output_executable source_file.f90
```

Applying this to our example:

```
gfortran -o hello_world hello_world.f90
```

This command instructs gfortran to compile hello_world.f90 and produce an executable named hello_world. If no errors occur during compilation, the executable file will be generated in the current directory.

Handling Compilation Errors

Compilation errors, often syntax-related, need to be resolved for successful compilation. Errors are reported with file names and line numbers indicating the error's location. For instance, if a semicolon is missing,

```
hello_world.f90:2.10:

   print *, "Hello, world!"
         1
Error: Syntax error in PRINT statement at (1)
```

This indicates that a syntax error exists in line 2. Correct the error in the source file and recompile.

Running the Executable

Once compiled, the executable can be executed from the terminal. For instance, running our hello_world program can be done using:

```
./hello_world
```

This would generate the following output:

```
Hello, world!
```

Compiler Options

Fortran compilers offer various options to optimize, debug, and specify the behavior of the compilation process. These options can alter the optimization level, generate debugging information, or specify standards:

- -O0, -O1, -O2, -O3: Control optimization levels.
- -g: Generate debugging information.
- -std=f95, -std=f2008: Enforce compliance with a specific Fortran standard.

A compilation with optimization and debugging information may look as follows:

```
gfortran -O2 -g -o optimized_debug_hello hello_world.f90
```

Using Makefiles

For larger projects with multiple source files, Makefiles can simplify the compilation process. A Makefile describes how to derive one or more targets, typically executable programs, from source files. Here is an example of a simple Makefile for our hello_world program:

```
# Makefile for hello_world program
FC = gfortran
FFLAGS = -O2 -g
TARGET = hello_world
SRC = hello_world.f90

$(TARGET): $(SRC)
	$(FC) $(FFLAGS) -o $(TARGET) $(SRC)

clean:
	rm -f $(TARGET)
```

To build the program, navigate to the directory containing the Makefile and run:

```
make
```

To remove the executable, use:

```
make clean
```

Leveraging Makefiles automates the compilation process and is invaluable in large-scale development.

Ensuring an acute understanding of these fundamental concepts in compiling and running Fortran programs equips developers to effectively manage and execute their projects, laying a solid groundwork for mastering more advanced topics in Fortran programming.

1.6 Fortran Syntax and Conventions

Fortran, a language designed with a focus on numerical computation and scientific applications, possesses a set of syntax rules and conventions that determine the structure and interpretation of programs. Understanding these rules is fundamental to writing clear, efficient, and error-free code. This section elucidates the essential elements of Fortran's syntax and conventions, covering topics such as variable naming, data types, control structures, and code organization.

Variable Naming Conventions
Variable names in Fortran must adhere to specific rules. They may contain up to 31 characters, starting with a letter followed by alphanumeric characters. Underscores are allowed but other special characters are not. Here is an example demonstrating valid and invalid variable names:

```
! Valid variable names
real :: temperature
integer :: count1
character(len=10) :: first_name

! Invalid variable names
real :: 1st_temperature ! Starts with a number
integer :: count$ ! Contains a special character
character(len=10) :: first&name ! Contains an invalid special character
```

Data Types
Fortran supports several fundamental data types, each with specific application in scientific computation. The primary types include:

- INTEGER: Represents whole numbers.
- REAL: Represents floating-point numbers.
- DOUBLE PRECISION: Represents double-precision floating-point numbers for higher accuracy.
- CHARACTER: Represents strings of characters.
- LOGICAL: Represents boolean values (TRUE or FALSE).

Here is an example illustrating the declaration and initialization of these data types:

```
integer :: i = 10
real :: x = 3.14
double precision :: y = 2.718281828459
character(len=20) :: name = 'John Doe'
logical :: is_valid = .true.
```

Control Structures
Fortran provides various control structures to manage the flow of execution within a program. These include conditional statements, loops, and case constructs.

Conditional Statements

The IF statement and its variants (IF-ELSE, IF-ELSEIF) are used to execute code based on conditions.

```
if (x > 0.0) then
    print*, 'x is positive'
else if (x < 0.0) then
    print*, 'x is negative'
else
    print*, 'x is zero'
end if
```

Loops

Fortran supports various looping constructs to execute code repeatedly. The DO loop is one of the most commonly used looping structures.

```
integer :: i

! Simple DO loop
do i = 1, 10
    print*, 'Iteration ', i
end do

! Nested DO loop
do i = 1, 3
    integer :: j
    do j = 1, 2
        print*, 'i = ', i, ' j = ', j
    end do
end do
```

Code Organization

Proper organization of code enhances readability and maintainability. Fortran uses subprograms (functions and subroutines) to encapsulate functional units of the program.

Subroutines

Subroutines perform operations and can modify the arguments passed to them.

```
subroutine increment(value)
    integer, intent(inout) :: value
    value = value + 1
end subroutine increment
```

Functions

Functions return a value and are often used in expressions.

```
integer function factorial(n)
    integer, intent(in) :: n
    integer :: i

    factorial = 1
    do i = 1, n
        factorial = factorial * i
```

```
    end do
end function factorial
```

Integrating these elements correctly within a program ensures that the Fortran code is both efficient and comprehensible, adhering to the language's standards and maximizing its robust capabilities for scientific computing.

1.7 Writing Your First Fortran Program

To write your first Fortran program, begin by setting up the development environment as outlined in the preceding sections. Ensure you have a Fortran compiler installed, such as gfortran, and a text editor or an Integrated Development Environment (IDE) suitable for coding in Fortran.

Fortran programs typically consist of a series of statements that perform arithmetic calculations, data manipulations, and input/output operations. Programs in Fortran are contained within a program unit, and the standard structure is as follows:

```
program MyFirstProgram
  implicit none

  ! Variable declarations
  integer :: a, b, sum

  ! Program logic
  a = 5
  b = 10
  sum = a + b

  ! Output the result
  print *, "The sum of ", a, " and ", b, " is ", sum

end program MyFirstProgram
```

This program adds two integers, a and b, and prints their sum. Let us dissect each part of the program for clarity:

- program MyFirstProgram: This line denotes the start of the program and gives it the name MyFirstProgram.

- implicit none: This statement is recommended to be included in every Fortran program to avoid implicit typing of variables. It ensures that all variables must be explicitly declared.

- integer :: a, b, sum: This line declares three integer variables, a, b, and sum.
- a = 5: This statement assigns the value 5 to the variable a.
- b = 10: This statement assigns the value 10 to the variable b.
- sum = a + b: This statement computes the sum of a and b, storing the result in sum.
- print *, "The sum of ", a, " and ", b, " is ", sum: This line prints the message to the console. The asterisk (*) serves as a format specifier for default output formatting.
- end program MyFirstProgram: This statement marks the end of the program.

To compile the program, save the code in a file named MyFirstProgram.f90. Use the terminal or command prompt to navigate to the directory containing the file and run the following command:

```
gfortran MyFirstProgram.f90 -o MyFirstProgram
```

This command invokes the gfortran compiler, specifying the source file and the -o flag to name the executable MyFirstProgram. Upon successful compilation, execute the program with:

```
./MyFirstProgram
```

The expected output will be:

```
The sum of 5 and 10 is 15
```

This simple example demonstrates fundamental components of a Fortran program: variable declaration, computation, and output. Next, consider expanding functionality by incorporating basic input operations using the read statement:

```
program SumTwoNumbers
  implicit none

  ! Variable declarations
  integer :: a, b, sum

  ! Input from user
  print *, "Enter two integers separated by space:"
  read *, a, b

  ! Program logic
```

```
  sum = a + b

  ! Output the result
  print *, "The sum of ", a, " and ", b, " is ", sum

end program SumTwoNumbers
```

In this revised program, the print statement prompts the user to input two integers, which are then read using the read statement. The rest of the program logic remains the same, adding the two integers and printing their sum.

Following compilation and execution, the program will interactively request user input and respond accordingly based on the provided integers. The pseudo code for the expanded functionality can be described as follows:

Algorithm 1: Pseudo Code for SumTwoNumbers Program

Data: User inputs two integers
Result: Outputs the sum of the two integers

```
Print "Enter two integers separated by space:"
Read two integers into variables a and b
Compute sum = a + b
Print "The sum of ", a, " and ", b, " is ", sum
```

By examining and running these examples, readers are encouraged to experiment by modifying variable values, adding more operations, or introducing new variables to enhance their familiarity with Fortran programming basics.

1.8 Common Terminologies in Fortran

Understanding the terminology in Fortran is crucial for anyone aiming to achieve proficiency in this programming language. Familiarity with these terms will not only enhance comprehension of Fortran literature but will also aid in the efficient writing, debugging, and optimization of Fortran programs.

Program Unit: A program unit is either a main program, a module, or a subprogram. The structure and organization of a Fortran program revolve around these units.

Main Program: The main program is the entry point of a Fortran application. Execution starts here after all necessary compilation and linking steps:

```
PROGRAM MainProgram
    ! Declarations and statements
END PROGRAM MainProgram
```

Module: Modules are software units containing procedures and data definitions that can be shared across different program units:

```
MODULE MyModule
    INTEGER :: x
CONTAINS
    SUBROUTINE MySubroutine
        ! Procedure implementation
    END SUBROUTINE MySubroutine
END MODULE MyModule
```

Subprograms: Subprograms are divided into two types: subroutines and functions. Subroutines perform tasks and can modify their arguments, while functions return a value and are more restrictive in their usage.

Subroutine: A subroutine is a block of code that performs a specific task but does not return a value:

```
SUBROUTINE MySubroutine(arg1, arg2)
    INTEGER, INTENT(IN) :: arg1
    INTEGER, INTENT(OUT) :: arg2
    arg2 = arg1 + 10
END SUBROUTINE MySubroutine
```

Function: A function returns a value and is used in expressions:

```
INTEGER FUNCTION AddTen(arg)
    INTEGER, INTENT(IN) :: arg
    AddTen = arg + 10
END FUNCTION AddTen
```

Type: Fortran supports intrinsic and derived data types. Intrinsic types include integer, real, complex, logical, and character. Derived types are user-defined structures:

```
TYPE :: Person
    CHARACTER(LEN=50) :: name
    INTEGER :: age
END TYPE Person
```

Variable: Variables in Fortran must be declared with a type. Variable names should be indicative of their purpose and follow the language's naming conventions, avoiding special characters and reserved keywords.

Array: Arrays are collections of data items of the same type. They can be one-dimensional or multi-dimensional, often used for handling numerical datasets:

```
INTEGER, DIMENSION(10) :: oneDArray
REAL, DIMENSION(5, 5) :: twoDArray
```

Pointer: Pointers hold the address of a variable and can be associated with arrays or scalar variables:

```
REAL, POINTER :: ptr
REAL, TARGET :: var = 3.14
ptr => var
```

Intent: The intent attribute specifies the intended use of subroutine or function parameters:

- INTENT(IN): The argument is read-only.
- INTENT(OUT): The argument is write-only.
- INTENT(INOUT): The argument is both readable and writable.

Intrinsic Functions: These are built-in functions provided by Fortran for common mathematical, character, and array operations, such as SIN, COS, SUM, and LEN.

Control Constructs: Control constructs enable decision-making and repeating execution flow:

- IF-THEN-ELSE: Conditional branching.
- DO loops: Iterative looping.
- SELECT CASE: Multi-way branching based on the value of an expression.

```
IF (condition) THEN
    ! Conditional code
ELSE
    ! Alternative code
END IF

DO i = 1, 10
    ! Loop code
END DO

SELECT CASE (i)
    CASE (1)
        ! Code for case 1
    CASE (2)
```

```
        ! Code for case 2
    CASE DEFAULT
        ! Default code
END SELECT
```

Compilation and Linking: Fortran source code (*.f90, *.f95, etc.) must be compiled into object files and then linked to create an executable. Common Fortran compilers include GNU Fortran (gfortran) and Intel Fortran (ifort).

Executable Statement: These are statements that are executed at runtime, including assignment statements, arithmetic operations, and I/O operations.

Non-executable Statement: These are used to declare types, variables, and provide documentation in the form of comments, which are ignored during program execution.

Familiarity with these common terminologies will facilitate your learning of Fortran and allow you to write more efficient and effective programs. Each term introduced here is essential for tackling more complex concepts and applications in subsequent chapters.

1.9 Fortran Development Tools and IDEs

The effectiveness of programming in Fortran, or any language, can be greatly enhanced with the appropriate development tools and integrated development environments (IDEs). These tools aid in writing, compiling, debugging, and optimizing code, providing a more efficient and streamlined workflow. This section explores the various Fortran development tools and IDEs that are widely used in the programming community.

Compilers

A compiler is a fundamental tool required to transform Fortran source code into executable programs. There are several Fortran compilers available, each with distinct features and optimizations:

- **GNU Fortran (gfortran)**: Part of the GNU Compiler Collection (GCC), gfortran supports many Fortran standards, including Fortran 77, 90, 95, 2003, and 2008. It is widely used due to its open-source nature and broad platform support.
- **Intel Fortran Compiler (ifort)**: Known for its performance opti-

mizations, especially on Intel hardware, ifort is favored in high-performance computing environments. It supports various Fortran standards and integrates well with Intel's development tools.

- **PGI Fortran Compiler (pgfortran)**: Provided by NVIDIA, pgfortran is optimized for CUDA and heterogeneous parallel computing environments. It is suitable for systems leveraging NVIDIA GPUs.
- **NAG Fortran Compiler**: The Numerical Algorithms Group (NAG) Fortran Compiler is known for its robust support for the latest standards and identifying potential issues within code. It is often used for academic and research purposes.

Debuggers

Debugging tools are essential for identifying and resolving errors or unexpected behavior in Fortran programs. Key debuggers include:

- **GNU Debugger (gdb)**: The gdb can be used to debug Fortran programs compiled with gfortran. It provides a command-line interface for setting breakpoints, inspecting variables, and controlling program execution.
- **Intel Debugger (idb)**: This debugger is designed for use with Intel compilers and provides an extensive range of features for debugging Fortran programs.
- **Allinea DDT**: A powerful parallel debugger used for debugging complex MPI, OpenMP, and hybrid parallel programs. It provides a GUI and supports debugging of Fortran code across multiple nodes.

Integrated Development Environments (IDEs)

IDEs combine the functionalities of code editing, compiling, and debugging within a single interface. Below are some popular IDEs for Fortran development:

- **Eclipse with Photran Plugin**: Eclipse, a widely used open-source IDE, becomes a full-featured Fortran development environment with the Photran plugin. It provides syntax highlighting, code completion, and integrated debugging.

- **NetBeans with Fortran Plugin**: Another versatile open-source IDE, NetBeans supports Fortran development through extensions, offering features like smart code editing, project management, and debugging.
- **Microsoft Visual Studio with Intel Fortran Integration**: For developers using Intel compilers, Visual Studio provides comprehensive support with features like advanced debugging, performance analysis, and code optimization tools.
- **Code::Blocks**: A lightweight, open-source IDE that supports Fortran through additional plugins. It is known for its simplicity and ease of use.
- **JetBrains CLion**: Although primarily designed for C/C++, CLion can be configured to support Fortran through custom toolchains and plugins, offering a modern development environment with powerful features.

Editors with Fortran Support

For developers who prefer lightweight text editors over full-fledged IDEs, there are several options that support Fortran syntax highlighting and basic features:

- **Visual Studio Code**: A popular, highly customizable code editor, VS Code offers an array of extensions for Fortran development, including syntax highlighting, linting, and integration with compilers and debuggers.
- **Sublime Text**: Known for its performance and versatility, Sublime Text provides Fortran support through community-developed plugins, making it a favorite among many programmers.
- **Emacs**: A powerful, extensible editor, Emacs has modes specifically tailored for Fortran. Its robust customization options make it a choice editor for many experienced developers.
- **Vim**: Similar to Emacs, Vim offers extensive customization and powerful editing features. Various plugins are available to enhance Fortran development within Vim.

Build Systems

Automating the build process is crucial for managing complex Fortran projects. Several build systems are widely used in Fortran development:

- **CMake**: A cross-platform build system that uses CMakeLists.txt files to define the build configuration. It simplifies the management of multi-platform builds and is compatible with most Fortran compilers.
- **Make**: The traditional Makefile system is still prevalent in Fortran development. It offers simple yet powerful build automation capabilities.
- **SCons**: An alternative to Make, SCons uses Python scripts for build automation. It provides more flexibility and is easier to configure for complex builds.

Version Control Systems

Version control systems are indispensable for tracking changes and collaborating on Fortran projects. The most commonly used version control systems include:

- **Git**: A distributed version control system that enables local repositories and branching/merging workflows. GitHub, GitLab, and Bitbucket are popular platforms utilizing Git.
- **Subversion (SVN)**: A centralized version control system that provides robust capabilities for version tracking and collaboration, suitable for both small and large projects.
- **Mercurial**: Another distributed version control system similar to Git, Mercurial is known for its simplicity and performance.

These tools and environments collectively form the backbone of a productive Fortran development process. Understanding their features and capabilities can significantly enhance the efficiency and quality of coding practices within Fortran development. The selection of tools often depends on specific project requirements, team preferences, and compatibility with existing workflows. As technology evolves, staying informed about updates and new tools remains essential for maintaining proficiency in Fortran programming.

Chapter 2

Basic Data Types and Variables

This chapter delves into Fortran's fundamental building blocks: data types and variables. Readers will learn about the different data types available in Fortran, such as integer, real, complex, character, and logical types, and how to declare and use variables. The chapter also covers type conversion and casting, variable scope and lifetime, naming conventions, and the use of constants and parameters, providing a thorough understanding of how to manage and manipulate data within Fortran programs.

2.1 Understanding Fortran Data Types

Fortran, an acronym derived from "Formula Translation," is a high-level programming language that primarily serves scientific and engineering computation needs. One of the foundational aspects of writing effective Fortran programs is understanding its data types. Data types define the nature of data that can be stored and manipulated within a program. In Fortran, these types explicitly determine the kind of operations that can be performed on the data and the memory storage implications.

Fortran natively supports several data types: INTEGER, REAL, DOUBLE PRECISION, COMPLEX, CHARACTER, and LOGICAL. Each of these types is tailored to handle specific forms of computation and data manipulation.

1. INTEGER Data Type

The INTEGER type is used to represent whole numbers, both positive and negative. The syntax for declaring an integer variable is straightforward:

```
INTEGER :: variable_name
```

For example, the following line declares an integer variable named count:

```
INTEGER :: count
```

Fortran uses a default integer size; however, the size can be specified to ensure portability and compatibility across different systems. This is achieved by using KIND parameters, as illustrated below:

```
INTEGER(KIND=4) :: count
```

2. REAL Data Type

The REAL type represents floating-point numbers, which include values that have fractional parts. This is essential in scientific calculations where precision is critical. Declaring a REAL variable:

```
REAL :: temperature
```

For higher precision, Fortran provides the DOUBLE PRECISION type, often specified as follows:

```
DOUBLE PRECISION :: precise_var
```

Similarly, the precision and range of floating-point numbers can differ based on the system. Using KIND parameters allows control over this:

```
REAL(KIND=8) :: high_precision_temperature
```

3. COMPLEX Data Type

The COMPLEX data type is used to represent complex numbers with both real and imaginary parts. This is commonly required in advanced scientific computations, including electrical engineering and quantum physics problems. Declaring a complex variable is done as follows:

```
COMPLEX :: z
```

Operations can then be performed on these complex variables, such as addition, subtraction, and multiplication, reflecting the mathematical rules governing complex numbers.

4. CHARACTER Data Type

The CHARACTER type in Fortran is utilized for handling strings of text. A character string variable can store sequences of characters, such as words or sentences. Declaring a CHARACTER variable requires specifying the length of the string:

```
CHARACTER(LEN=20) :: name
```

In this declaration, name can store up to 20 characters. When the length is not specified, a default length of one character is assumed.

5. LOGICAL Data Type

The LOGICAL data type represents Boolean values, typically .TRUE. or .FALSE.. This type is especially useful in control structures and conditional statements. Declaring a logical variable is done as follows:

```
LOGICAL :: is_valid
```

This variable is_valid can be used to store and evaluate Boolean expressions.

Understanding and using these basic data types effectively is crucial in Fortran programming. It allows for appropriate memory management and ensures that the operations on variables are consistent with their represented data styles. For more advanced data manipulation and program efficiency, knowing when and how to use each type, along with their respective kind parameters, is essential.

2.2 Declaring Variables

Variables in Fortran are declared to store data that the program will manipulate. The declaration specifies the type of data the variable will hold and optionally sets an initial value. This section will discuss the syntax and rules for declaring variables in Fortran, ensuring code clarity and correctness.

Variable declarations in Fortran begin with the type specifier followed by the variable name. For instance, to declare an integer variable named counter, we use:

```
INTEGER :: counter
```

Variables can be initialized at the time of declaration by including an equal sign and the initial value:

```
INTEGER :: counter = 10
```

Fortran supports multiple type declarations, including REAL, COMPLEX, CHARACTER, and LOGICAL. Each type has its specific syntax rules which will be illustrated below.

To declare a REAL variable for storing floating-point numbers:

```
REAL :: temperature
REAL :: pressure = 101.3
```

For COMPLEX numbers, which store pairs of real numbers representing the real and imaginary parts:

```
COMPLEX :: impedance
COMPLEX :: voltage = (120.0, 0.0)
```

CHARACTER variables for storing strings require a length specification. For example:

```
CHARACTER(LEN=20) :: name
CHARACTER(LEN=10) :: code = 'AB1234'
```

LOGICAL variables represent boolean values (true or false):

```
LOGICAL :: flag
LOGICAL :: is_valid = .TRUE.
```

Multiple variables of the same type can be declared in a single statement separated by commas:

```
INTEGER :: x, y, z
REAL :: a = 1.0, b = 2.5
```

Fortran allows the use of the DIMENSION attribute for arrays, which will comply with the multi-dimensional nature of scientific computations. Declaring an array involves specifying the type, name, and dimensions:

```
REAL, DIMENSION(10) :: vector
INTEGER, DIMENSION(3, 3) :: matrix
```

Associating initial values with arrays can be done as follows:

```
REAL, DIMENSION(3) :: vector = (/1.0, 2.0, 3.0/)
```

Fortran provides the option of using the PARAMETER attribute for constants, which facilitates the declaration of named constants. This improves code readability and maintainability:

```
REAL, PARAMETER :: pi = 3.14159
INTEGER, PARAMETER :: max_length = 256
```

Implicit typing is discouraged in modern Fortran programming due to the potential for errors arising from default type inference. Therefore, using the IMPLICIT NONE statement is essential. This statement ensures all variables must be explicitly declared, promoting safer and more reliable code:

```
PROGRAM example
  IMPLICIT NONE
  INTEGER :: i, j
  REAL :: x = 0.0, y = 1.0

  ! ...rest of the program
END PROGRAM example
```

The IMPLICIT NONE statement is particularly important in large projects or collaborative environments where the risk of typographical errors and unintended type mismatches can lead to significant issues.

By convention, variable names in Fortran should be descriptive and follow a consistent naming pattern. Variable names must start with an alphabetic character and can be followed by any combination of letters, digits, and underscores. Variable names are case-insensitive in Fortran:

```
INTEGER :: Temperature_Reading
REAL :: average_pressure
LOGICAL :: flag_status
```

Following these conventions and guidelines will lead to clearer, more maintainable code, which is an essential practice for both novice and experienced Fortran programmers.

2.3 Integer Data Types

Fortran provides comprehensive support for integer data types, a fundamental aspect in programming for performing arithmetic operations, looping structures, indexing arrays, and more. The integer data type in Fortran is defined to hold whole numbers, both positive and negative, without any fractional component. This section delves into the properties, declaration, and manipulation of integers in Fortran.

Properties of Integers:

In Fortran, integers are stored using a fixed amount of memory, typically 4 bytes, although this can vary based on the implementation and system architecture. The range of allowable integer values depends on the number of bytes allocated. As per the Fortran standard:

- Default integer: Usually occupies 4 bytes (32 bits), with a typical range from -2,147,483,648 to 2,147,483,647.
- Integer(1): Occupies 1 byte, with a range from -128 to 127.
- Integer(2): Occupies 2 bytes, with a range from -32,768 to 32,767.
- Integer(4): Standard 4-byte integer.
- Integer(8): Occupies 8 bytes (64 bits), with a range significantly larger, from -9,223,372,036,854,775,808 to 9,223,372,036,854,775,807.

Declaring Integer Variables:

To declare an integer variable, Fortran uses the integer keyword followed by the variable name. One can assign specific kinds of integers by appending a kind=selector or a kind parameter. Example declarations are illustrated below.

```
program IntegerExample
  implicit none
  ! Declaration of integer variables
  integer :: i
  integer(kind=1) :: smallInt
  integer(kind=2) :: int2Bytes
  integer(kind=8) :: largeInt

  ! Assignment of values
  i = 2147483647 ! Maximum of 4-byte integer
  smallInt = 127
  int2Bytes = 32767
  largeInt = 9223372036854775807

  print*, 'Default integer:', i
  print*, '1-byte integer:', smallInt
  print*, '2-byte integer:', int2Bytes
  print*, '8-byte integer:', largeInt

end program IntegerExample
```

```
Default integer:     2147483647
1-byte integer:             127
2-byte integer:           32767
8-byte integer:  9223372036854775807
```

Operations on Integers:

Integer operations include basic arithmetic such as addition, subtraction, multiplication, and division, which strictly adhere to integer arithmetic rules. Any fractional part from division is truncated.

```
program IntegerOperations
  implicit none
  integer :: a, b, sum, difference, product, quotient

  ! Assign values
  a = 10
  b = 3

  ! Perform arithmetic operations
  sum = a + b
  difference = a - b
  product = a * b
  quotient = a / b

  print*, 'Sum:', sum
  print*, 'Difference:', difference
  print*, 'Product:', product
  print*, 'Quotient:', quotient

end program IntegerOperations
```

```
Sum:          13
Difference:   7
Product:     30
Quotient:     3
```

Integer Constants and Parameters:

In Fortran, integer constants (literals) can be specified directly in the code, often with an optional kind parameter. Integer parameters, declared with the parameter attribute, define constants which cannot be altered during the execution of the program.

```
program IntegerConstants
  implicit none
  integer, parameter :: maxValue = 100
  integer, parameter :: minValue = -100

  print*, 'Maximum Value:', maxValue
  print*, 'Minimum Value:', minValue

end program IntegerConstants
```

```
Maximum Value:        100
Minimum Value:       -100
```

Integer Intrinsic Functions:

Fortran includes several intrinsic functions for integer operations. Commonly used functions include:

- abs(int): Returns the absolute value of an integer.

- mod(int, div): Computes the remainder after division.
- sign(a, b): Transfers the sign of b to a.

```
program IntegerIntrinsic
  implicit none
  integer :: val, negVal, remainder

  val = -15
  negVal = abs(val) ! Absolute value
  remainder = mod(15, 4) ! Modulus operation

  print*, 'Absolute value of', val, ':', negVal
  print*, '15 mod 4:', remainder

end program IntegerIntrinsic
```

```
Absolute value of      -15 :  15
15 mod 4:              3
```

Understanding and using integer data types proficiently ensures that Fortran program performance and accuracy are optimized. Mastery of integer declarations, operations, and intrinsic functions equips programmers to handle a variety of computational tasks effectively.

2.4 Real Data Types

Fortran provides a robust and precise way to handle real numbers, or floating-point values, through its real data types. These types enable programmers to perform computations involving non-integer numbers, which are crucial in many scientific and engineering applications. A real data type in Fortran represents a value that contains a decimal point, allowing for the expression of fractions and high-precision numbers.

In Fortran, the default real type is declared using the keyword real, which can be specified as follows:

```
real :: a, b, c
```

The precision and range of a real type can vary depending on the compiler and the system. Fortran allows for more precise control over the precision of real types using the kind parameter. By default, the real type usually provides single precision, which ensures approximately six to seven decimal digits of accuracy. However, Fortran also supports double precision, which significantly extends the range and precision.

To declare a real variable with double precision explicitly, the double precision keyword is used:

```
double precision :: d, e, f
```

Alternatively, one can use the kind parameter to specify the precision more flexibly. The kind parameter is often used in conjunction with the selected_real_kind intrinsic function, which allows the programmer to request a real kind based on the desired precision and/or range.

```
integer, parameter :: dp = selected_real_kind(15, 307)
real(kind=dp) :: g, h, i
```

In this example, selected_real_kind(15, 307) requests a kind type that provides at least 15 decimal digits of precision and a range of 10^{-307} to 10^{307}.

Real constants are usually written with a decimal point in Fortran. For instance, 2.0, -3.14, and 6.022e23 (which uses scientific notation) are all valid real constants. When specifying real constants with different kinds, a kind suffix can be appended:

```
1.0_dp
```

This guarantees that the constant 1.0 is interpreted as double precision.

Arithmetic operations involving real numbers include addition, subtraction, multiplication, division, and exponentiation. Here is an example demonstrating basic real arithmetic operations:

```
real :: x, y, z
x = 10.5
y = 3.2
z = x + y ! z is now 13.7
z = x - y ! z is now 7.3
z = x * y ! z is now 33.6
z = x / y ! z is now 3.28125
z = x ** y ! z is now approximately 5963.6
```

Real data types are also subject to intrinsic functions which perform various mathematical computations. Some key intrinsic functions for real numbers include:

- sqrt(x): Computes the square root of x.
- exp(x): Computes the exponential function of x (e^x).
- log(x): Computes the natural logarithm of x.
- sin(x), cos(x), tan(x): Compute the sine, cosine, and tangent of x, respectively.

Here is an example using some of these intrinsic functions:

```
real :: a, b
a = 9.0
b = sqrt(a) ! b is now 3.0
b = log(a) ! b is now approximately 2.197
b = exp(a) ! b is now approximately 8103.08
```

Handling real data types with appropriate precision is critical, especially in applications where numerical precision can significantly impact results. Thus, understanding and correctly implementing real data types ensures computational accuracy and efficiency in Fortran programs.

2.5 Complex Data Types

Fortran provides robust support for complex data types, enabling the representation and manipulation of complex numbers. A complex number, as understood in mathematics, comprises a real part and an imaginary part. In Fortran, these two parts are typically represented by two real numbers, with the imaginary unit i satisfying the equation $i^2 = -1$.

complex is the primary keyword used to declare complex variables. Complex numbers are inherently useful in various scientific computations, especially in fields like engineering, physics, and applied mathematics.

To declare a complex variable in Fortran, use the complex keyword as shown below:

```
program example
  complex :: z
end program example
```

This code snippet declares a complex variable z. By default, complex variables in Fortran conform to a specification of complex*8, meaning each part (real and imaginary) is stored as a 4-byte real number.

Initialization of a complex variable in Fortran can be done in two principal ways:

1. Using the (,) notation:

```
program example
  complex :: z
  z = (3.0, 4.0)
end program example
```

2. Using the cmplx intrinsic function:

```
program example
  complex :: z
  z = cmplx(3.0, 4.0)
end program example
```

In both examples, z is initialized as $3.0 + 4.0i$.

Fortran supports various arithmetic operations on complex numbers, including addition, subtraction, multiplication, and division:

```
program operations
  complex :: z1, z2, result
  z1 = (3.0, 4.0)
  z2 = (1.0, -2.0)

  result = z1 + z2 ! Addition
  result = z1 - z2 ! Subtraction
  result = z1 * z2 ! Multiplication
  result = z1 / z2 ! Division
end program operations
```

Mathematical functions operating on complex numbers can be performed using Fortran's intrinsic functions explicitly designed for complex arithmetic. Some commonly used intrinsic functions include:

- abs(z): Computes the magnitude of a complex number z.
- aimag(z): Retrieves the imaginary part of z.
- real(z): Retrieves the real part of z.
- conjg(z): Computes the complex conjugate of z.
- exp(z): Computes the exponential of the complex number z.

Example usage of these functions is illustrated below:

```
program intrinsic_functions
  complex :: z
  real :: magnitude, real_part, imaginary_part
  complex :: conjugate, exponential

  z = (3.0, 4.0)
  magnitude = abs(z)
  real_part = real(z)
  imaginary_part = aimag(z)
  conjugate = conjg(z)
  exponential = exp(z)
end program intrinsic_functions
```

Here, abs(z) will compute the magnitude of $3.0 + 4.0i$, which is 5.0. aimag(z) will return 4.0, the imaginary part, and real(z) will return 3.0, the real part. Using conjg, the complex conjugate of $3.0 + 4.0i$ will be $3.0 - 4.0i$. exp(z) will compute the exponential of the complex number.

It is worth noting that complex variables can be used as components of other derived data types. Consider the following derived type definition:

```
program derived_types
  type :: Particle
    complex :: position
    complex :: velocity
  end type Particle

  type(Particle) :: electron
end program derived_types
```

In this example, the derived type Particle has two components: position and velocity, both of which are complex variables. This feature enables the modeling of multidimensional attributes that require both real and imaginary components.

Furthermore, complex numbers are often utilized within arrays and passed to functions or subroutines:

```
program array_complex
  complex, dimension(5) :: z_array

  call initialize_complex_array(z_array)

contains
  subroutine initialize_complex_array(arr)
    complex, dimension(5), intent(out) :: arr
    integer :: i
    do i = 1, 5
      arr(i) = cmplx(i, -i)
    end do
  end subroutine initialize_complex_array
end program array_complex
```

In this program, z_array is a complex array initialized within the initialize_complex_array subroutine, where each element receives a complex value.

Utilizing complex data types in Fortran allows for comprehensive and efficient handling of computations involving complex numbers, effectively broadening the scope of numerical and scientific programming the language can achieve.

2.6 Character Data Types

Character data types in Fortran are essential for handling textual data. This section covers the declaration, manipulation, and usage of character types, which are unique compared to numerical types due to their nature of storing strings. Understanding character types is crucial for tasks such as reading and writing text files, and processing user input.

Fortran uses the keyword CHARACTER to define character variables. A character variable can store a sequence of characters, with the length specified either at the time of declaration or dynamically during program execution. A simple declaration of a character variable is shown below:

```
CHARACTER(LEN=10) :: word
```

Here, word is a character variable capable of holding a string up to 10 characters long. If the length is not specified, Fortran assumes a default length of 1.

To assign a value to a character variable, you use the assignment operator =:

```
word = 'FORTRAN'
```

In this example, the string 'FORTRAN' is assigned to the variable word. It's important to note that Fortran strings are space-padded to their declared length. Thus, if word has a length of 10, the value assigned would be 'FORTRAN ' (with three trailing spaces).

You can also declare character arrays similarly to other data types, enabling the handling of multiple strings in a single structure:

```
CHARACTER(LEN=15) :: names(5)
```

This declaration creates an array called names consisting of 5 character strings, each with a maximum length of 15 characters. You can then assign values to elements in the array similarly:

```
names(1) = 'Alice'
names(2) = 'Bob'
```

Fortran supports dynamically allocated character lengths using the LEN=* syntax, allowing lengths to be determined at runtime by the context of their use:

```
CHARACTER(LEN=*) :: dynamicString
```

In this case, dynamicString assumes the length based on the string assigned to it later in the program. This flexibility is particularly useful in situations where the length of strings cannot be determined a priori.

Concatenation of character strings is performed using the double slash operator //. This operator combines two strings into one:

```
character(LEN=20) :: fullName
fullName = names(1) // ' ' // names(2)
```

The result stored in fullName would be 'Alice Bob', demonstrating the concatenation of names(1) and names(2) with a space in between.

Fortran also provides intrinsic functions to manipulate character strings efficiently. Key functions include LEN, TRIM, and ADJUSTL / ADJUSTR. The LEN function returns the declared length of the character variable, while TRIM removes trailing spaces from a string. The ADJUSTL and ADJUSTR functions adjust the string by shifting characters to the left or right respectively, filling the remaining positions with spaces.

```
PRINT *, LEN('FORTRAN') ! Outputs: 10
PRINT *, TRIM('FORTRAN ') ! Outputs: 'FORTRAN'
PRINT *, ADJUSTL(' FORTRAN') ! Outputs: 'FORTRAN '
PRINT *, ADJUSTR('FORTRAN ') ! Outputs: ' FORTRAN'
```

Substring operations are also a fundamental aspect of handling character data. Substrings in Fortran can be referenced using a parenthesis with starting and ending indices.

```
character(LEN=10) :: word
word = 'FORTRAN'
PRINT *, word(1:3) ! Outputs: 'FOR'
```

In this snippet, word(1:3) extracts the substring containing the first three characters of word.

Additionally, Fortran allows for the comparison of character strings using relational operators like ==, /=, <, >, <=, and >= based on lexicographical ordering:

```
IF ('Alice' == 'Bob') THEN
    PRINT *, 'Strings are equal'
ELSE
    PRINT *, 'Strings are not equal'
ENDIF
```

Understanding the operations and functions available for character data types in Fortran empowers a programmer to handle text effectively in diverse applications. This forms the foundation for more complex string manipulations and input-output operations in Fortran programming.

2.7 Logical Data Types

Logical data types are a fundamental aspect of Fortran, enabling programs to make decisions based on true or false conditions. The logical data type in Fortran is primarily used for control flow statements and is essential in implementing conditional logic. The logical type can take on two values: .TRUE. or .FALSE.. These values are represented internally in the computer's memory, but from a programming perspective, they simplify the process of writing conditional statements.

Logical variables are declared using the LOGICAL keyword. Below is an example of how to declare logical variables in Fortran:

```
LOGICAL :: isPositive, isZero, isNegative
```

In this example, three logical variables are declared: isPositive, isZero, and isNegative. By default, Fortran does not initialize these variables, so they must be assigned a value before use. Assigning values to logical variables can be done directly or through conditional statements. For example:

```
isPositive = .TRUE.
isZero = .FALSE.
```

Fortran provides a variety of logical operators that can be used in expressions with logical data types. These operators include .AND., .OR., .NOT., .EQV. (equivalence), and .NEQV. (not equivalence). Below are examples demonstrating the use of these operators:

```
LOGICAL :: a, b, result

a = .TRUE.
b = .FALSE.

result = a .AND. b ! result is .FALSE.
result = a .OR. b ! result is .TRUE.
result = .NOT. a ! result is .FALSE.
result = a .EQV. b ! result is .FALSE.
result = a .NEQV. b ! result is .TRUE.
```

These logical operations allow for complex conditional logic to be expressed succinctly. For instance, logical operators are commonly used in conjunction with IF statements to direct program flow based on multiple conditions.

Here is an example of an IF statement utilizing logical variables:

```
LOGICAL :: isEven, isPositive
INTEGER :: number

number = 4

isEven = MOD(number, 2) == 0
isPositive = number > 0

IF (isEven .AND. isPositive) THEN
    PRINT *, 'The number is a positive even number.'
ELSE
    PRINT *, 'The number is either not positive or not even.'
END IF
```

In this example, the logical variables isEven and isPositive are used to determine characteristics of the variable number. The IF statement then uses the logical AND operator to check if number is both positive and even.

Fortran ensures that logical expressions are evaluated in a manner consistent with mathematical logic. This means that logical expressions involving .AND. and .OR. will short-circuit evaluation as needed. For instance, in an expression involving .AND., if the first operand evaluates to .FALSE., the entire expression is .FALSE., and the second operand is not evaluated. Similarly, for .OR., if the first operand evaluates to .TRUE., the expression evaluates to .TRUE. without evaluating the second operand. This can be crucial for performance optimization and avoiding unnecessary computations or potential errors (e.g., division by zero).

Logical data types are also used extensively within loops to control iteration, especially with the DO WHILE construct:

```
LOGICAL :: continueLoop
INTEGER :: counter

continueLoop = .TRUE.
counter = 0

DO WHILE (continueLoop)
    PRINT *, 'Counter = ', counter
    counter = counter + 1

    IF (counter >= 5) THEN
        continueLoop = .FALSE.
    END IF
END DO
```

In the loop example above, the logical variable continueLoop controls the execution of the DO WHILE loop. The loop continues to execute as long as continueLoop is .TRUE.. Once counter reaches 5, continueLoop is set to .FALSE., and the loop terminates.

Logical variables and operations underpin the control structures of Fortran programs, providing the foundation for making decisions and controlling program flow based on conditions. Their usage in IF statements, logical expressions, and loops are essential for writing clear, efficient, and correct Fortran code.

2.8 Type Conversion and Type Casting

In Fortran programming, type conversion and type casting are essential operations that allow programmers to manipulate data types effectively. These operations ensure that values of different types can interact smoothly within expressions and assignments. Understanding type conversion and type casting is crucial for robust and error-free coding, especially when dealing with mixed-type arithmetic operations and function calls.

Type conversion in Fortran can be implicit or explicit. Implicit type conversion occurs automatically when Fortran determines that conversion between types is necessary. On the other hand, explicit type conversion requires the programmer to intentionally perform the conversion using intrinsic functions.

Implicit Type Conversion

Fortran performs implicit type conversion in expressions involving operands of different types. For example, when an integer is used in a real arithmetic context, Fortran automatically converts the integer to a real value before performing the operation.

```
program implicit_conversion
    implicit none
    real :: x
    integer :: y
    x = 10.5
    y = 3
    x = x + y ! y is implicitly converted to real
    print *, 'The value of x is: ', x ! Output: 13.5
end program implicit_conversion
```

In the above code, the integer y is implicitly converted to a real type to perform the addition with the real variable x. The result of the expression is then assigned to x.

Explicit Type Conversion

Explicit type conversion, also known as type casting, requires the use of intrinsic functions to convert from one type to another. The main intrinsic functions for type conversion in Fortran are REAL, INT, DBLE, CMPLX, and CHAR.

- REAL(A): Converts its argument A to a real type.
- INT(A): Converts its argument A to an integer type.
- DBLE(A): Converts its argument A to a double-precision real type.
- CMPLX(A): Converts its argument A to a complex type.
- CHAR(A): Converts its argument A to a character type.

Example of Explicit Type Conversion

```
program explicit_conversion
    implicit none
    real :: a
    integer :: b
    double precision :: c
    complex :: d
    character(len=10) :: e

    a = 5.7
    b = INT(a) ! Explicit conversion from real to integer
    c = DBLE(a) ! Explicit conversion from real to double precision
    d = CMPLX(a, b) ! Explicit conversion to complex type
    e = CHAR(97) ! Explicit conversion of ASCII code to character
    print *, 'Value of b (INT(a)): ', b ! Output: 5
    print *, 'Value of c (DBLE(a)): ', c ! Output: 5.7
    print *, 'Value of d (CMPLX(a, b)): ', d ! Output: (5.7, 5.0)
    print *, 'Value of e (CHAR(97)): ', e ! Output: 'a'
end program explicit_conversion
```

Explicit type conversions are especially useful in ensuring that variables of different types can be used together without causing type mismatch errors.

Type Conversion in Function Calls

When passing arguments to functions in Fortran, it is sometimes necessary to ensure that the argument types match the function's parameter types. This often requires explicit type conversion.

```
program function_conversion
    implicit none
    real :: result
    integer :: n
```

```
    n = 10
    result = sqrt(REAL(n)) ! Explicit conversion to match sqrt function requirement
    print *, 'Square root of n is: ', result ! Output: 3.16228
end program function_conversion
```

In the above example, the integer n is explicitly converted to a real type using the REAL function to match the parameter type required by the sqrt function.

Avoiding Type Conversion Pitfalls

Incorrect type conversions can lead to unexpected results or runtime errors. For example, converting a real number to an integer will truncate the fractional part rather than rounding it. This behavior must be accounted for when performing type conversions involving real and integer types.

```
program conversion_pitfalls
    implicit none
    real :: r
    integer :: i
    r = 8.9
    i = INT(r) ! Truncates the fractional part
    print *, 'Truncated value of r is: ', i ! Output: 8
    i = NINT(r) ! Rounds to the nearest integer
    print *, 'Rounded value of r is: ', i ! Output: 9
end program conversion_pitfalls
```

It is often safer to use the NINT function for rounding real numbers to the nearest integer rather than truncating them with INT.

Understanding type conversion and type casting is essential for writing precise and efficient Fortran programs. By carefully managing type conversions, programmers can ensure data integrity and avoid common pitfalls associated with type mismatches.

2.9 Variable Scope and Lifetime

The scope and lifetime of variables in Fortran are fundamental concepts that determine the visibility and duration of a variable within a program. Understanding these concepts is crucial for writing efficient and error-free code. In Fortran, the scope of a variable refers to the regions of the program where the variable can be accessed, whereas the lifetime refers to the duration for which the variable retains its value during program execution.

In Fortran, variables can have different scopes:

- Local Scope
- Module Scope
- Global Scope

Local Scope: Local variables are declared within a subroutine, function, or block and are only accessible within that context. These variables exist only for the duration of the execution of the encapsulating procedure. Once the procedure completes, the memory allocated for these local variables is released.

```
PROGRAM ExampleLocalScope
  CALL SubroutineA()

CONTAINS
  SUBROUTINE SubroutineA()
    INTEGER :: varA
    varA = 10
    PRINT *, 'Value of varA in SubroutineA: ', varA
  END SUBROUTINE SubroutineA

  SUBROUTINE SubroutineB()
    INTEGER :: varA
    varA = 20
    PRINT *, 'Value of varA in SubroutineB: ', varA
  END SUBROUTINE SubroutineB

END PROGRAM ExampleLocalScope
```

```
Output:
Value of varA in SubroutineA: 10
Value of varA in SubroutineB: 20
```

In this example, varA is a local variable in both SubroutineA and SubroutineB. Despite having the same name, these variables are distinct and reside in separate memory locations.

Module Scope: Variables declared within a module are accessible to any procedure or function that uses the module. These variables can be thought of as having a shared scope across procedures that include the module. The lifetime of module variables starts when the program begins execution and ends when the program terminates.

```
MODULE ExampleModule
  INTEGER :: sharedVar
END MODULE ExampleModule

PROGRAM ExampleModuleScope
  USE ExampleModule
  CALL SubroutineA()
  CALL SubroutineB()
END PROGRAM ExampleModuleScope

SUBROUTINE SubroutineA()
```

```
  USE ExampleModule
  sharedVar = 10
  PRINT *, 'Value of sharedVar in SubroutineA: ', sharedVar
END SUBROUTINE SubroutineA

SUBROUTINE SubroutineB()
  USE ExampleModule
  PRINT *, 'Value of sharedVar in SubroutineB: ', sharedVar
END SUBROUTINE SubroutineB
```

```
Output:
Value of sharedVar in SubroutineA: 10
Value of sharedVar in SubroutineB: 10
```

Here, sharedVar is declared in the module ExampleModule and is accessible in both SubroutineA and SubroutineB due to the USE ExampleModule statement. Changes made to sharedVar in SubroutineA are reflected in SubroutineB.

Global Scope: Fortran does not directly support global variables in the traditional sense used in some other programming languages. Instead, global variable functionality is typically achieved using modules, as described above.

Scope of Derived Types and Structures: In addition to simple variables, Fortran allows the definition of complex data types using the TYPE keyword. The scope rules for these derived types are the same as for simple variables.

```
MODULE ExampleModule
  TYPE :: CustomType
    INTEGER :: componentA
    REAL :: componentB
  END TYPE CustomType

  TYPE(CustomType) :: varType
END MODULE ExampleModule

PROGRAM ExampleTypeScope
  USE ExampleModule

  varType%componentA = 5
  varType%componentB = 3.14
  PRINT *, 'componentA: ', varType%componentA
  PRINT *, 'componentB: ', varType%componentB
END PROGRAM ExampleTypeScope
```

```
Output:
componentA: 5
componentB: 3.1400001
```

Variable Lifetime: The lifetime of a variable can be automatic or static. Automatic variables are allocated when a procedure is called and deallocated when the procedure exits. Static variables, on the other hand, retain their value between calls to the procedure.

To declare a static variable in a subroutine or function, the SAVE attribute is used.

```
SUBROUTINE StaticVariableExample()
  INTEGER, SAVE :: staticVar
  staticVar = staticVar + 1
  PRINT *, 'Value of staticVar: ', staticVar
END SUBROUTINE StaticVariableExample
```

```
Output - First call:
Value of staticVar: 1
Output - Second call:
Value of staticVar: 2
Output - Third call:
Value of staticVar: 3
```

In this subroutine, the variable staticVar retains its value between calls due to the SAVE attribute. Each time the subroutine is called, staticVar increments its value by 1. Without the SAVE attribute, staticVar would be reinitialized to 0 on each call, resulting in the output always being 1.

Understanding these concepts ensures that variables and their respective data are correctly managed and accessed throughout the program's execution, enhancing both functionality and maintainability.

2.10 Constants and Parameters

In Fortran programming, constants and parameters play a crucial role in creating efficient, maintainable, and readable code. Constants represent fixed values that do not change during the execution of a program, while parameters are constants with a name, allowing for easier code modifications and improvements in code clarity.

Constants in Fortran can be classified broadly into two categories: literal constants and named constants. Literal constants are explicit values written in the code, such as 123, 3.14, or 'Hello'. Named constants, also referred to as parameters, are given a symbolic name using the parameter attribute, enhancing code readability and maintainability.

To declare named constants in Fortran, the parameter keyword is used. The syntax for declaring parameters is as follows:

```
[type] , parameter :: name = value
```

Here, type specifies the data type of the constant, name is the symbolic name of the constant, and value is the fixed value assigned to the constant.

Consider the example below, which demonstrates how to declare various types of constants in Fortran:

```
integer, parameter :: max_iter = 1000
real, parameter :: pi = 3.141592653589793
character(len=20), parameter :: welcome_message = 'Welcome to Fortran!'
```

In the above code:

- max_iter is an integer constant with a value of 1000.
- pi is a real constant representing the value of π.
- welcome_message is a character constant containing the string 'Welcome to Fortran!'.

Using named constants in Fortran offers several advantages:

- **Maintainability**: Constants are declared in a single place, making updates straightforward. For example, if the value of π needs to be altered for precision considerations, only the declaration line needs to be changed.
- **Readability**: Named constants improve the readability of code. Rather than having magic numbers scattered throughout the code base, a well-named constant like pi clearly conveys its purpose.
- **Avoiding Errors**: Using parameters reduces the likelihood of typographical errors that can occur with manually repeating constant values. It also mitigates the risk of accidental modifications since parameters are immutable after their definition.

Below is a practical example demonstrating the use of named constants in a simple Fortran program that calculates the circumference of a circle:

```
program calculate_circumference
    implicit none

    real, parameter :: pi = 3.141592653589793
    real :: radius, circumference

    write(*,*) 'Enter the radius of the circle:'
    read(*,*) radius

    circumference = 2.0 * pi * radius

    write(*,*) 'The circumference of the circle is:', circumference
end program calculate_circumference
```

When executed, the program will prompt the user to input the radius of the circle and then compute and display the circumference. Using the parameter pi ensures that the value of π is consistent and easily adjustable if needed.

```
Enter the radius of the circle:
5.0
The circumference of the circle is:   31.415928
```

Named constants can also be used in conjunction with derived data types and modules to structure complex programs more effectively. Consider the following example where constants are encapsulated in a module to calculate the gravitational force between two masses:

```
module constants
    implicit none
    real, parameter :: g = 6.67430e-11 ! Gravitational constant
end module constants

program gravitational_force
    use constants
    implicit none

    real :: mass1, mass2, distance, force

    write(*,*) 'Enter the mass of the first object (in kg):'
    read(*,*) mass1
    write(*,*) 'Enter the mass of the second object (in kg):'
    read(*,*) mass2
    write(*,*) 'Enter the distance between the objects (in m):'
    read(*,*) distance

    force = g * (mass1 * mass2) / (distance ** 2)

    write(*,*) 'The gravitational force between the objects is:', force
end program gravitational_force
```

In this example:

- The gravitational constant g is defined in a module named constants.
- The main program uses the constants module to access g, demonstrating modular programming and the reusability of constants.

```
Enter the mass of the first object (in kg):
1000
Enter the mass of the second object (in kg):
2000
Enter the distance between the objects (in m):
10
The gravitational force between the objects is: 1.33486e-05
```

Parameters can be defined with various data types, such as integer, real, complex, character, and logical, providing flexibility in representing constants in different forms. It is important to note that once a parameter is declared, its value cannot be altered during the program's execution. This immutability is enforced by the Fortran language, ensuring that parameters remain constant throughout the code.

```
logical, parameter :: is_valid = .true.
complex, parameter :: i_unit = (0.0, 1.0)
```

is_valid is a logical constant representing a boolean value of .true., and i_unit is a complex constant representing the imaginary unit.

Constants and parameters are indispensable tools in Fortran programming, providing reliability, clarity, and simplicity in coding practices. Their proper use enhances the overall quality and correctness of scientific and engineering computations carried out using Fortran.

2.11 Naming Conventions

In Fortran, naming conventions are crucial for writing clear, maintainable, and error-free code. A well-chosen variable name can make a program comprehensible, thereby reducing the risk of bugs and aiding in the debugging process. Fortran imposes specific rules and recommendations for naming variables, which encapsulate both syntactical obligations and best practices.

A variable name in Fortran must adhere to the following rules:

- Variable names must begin with a letter (A-Z or a-z).
- Subsequent characters can be letters (A-Z, a-z), digits (0-9), or underscores (_).
- Variable names are case-insensitive, thus Variable_1 and variable_1 would refer to the same entity.
- The length of variable names is compiler-dependent, but standards suggest a maximum length of 31 characters for backward compatibility.

Here's a valid example of variable naming in Fortran:

```
integer :: i, counter, sum_total, sum_Total
```

Despite both sum_total and sum_Total being technically correct and equivalent due to the language's case-insensitivity, it is advisable to maintain consistent capitalization throughout the code for better clarity and readability.

Following naming conventions not only enhances readability but also aids in avoiding conflicts and potential errors. Good practices for naming variables in Fortran include:

- Use descriptive names that convey the purpose of the variable. For instance, use total_sum rather than ts.
- Adopt a consistent naming style. Common styles include camelCase (e.g., totalSum) and snake_case (e.g., total_sum). Choose a style and apply it consistently throughout the codebase.
- Avoid single-letter names except in conventional loop indices or when the variable's purpose is exceedingly clear and limited in scope (e.g., i, j for loop counters).
- Prefix boolean variables with 'is', 'has', or 'can' to indicate their logical nature (e.g., is_valid, has_error, can_proceed).
- Avoid using Fortran's reserved keywords as variable names (e.g., integer, real, if, then).

The following example demonstrates these conventions in practice:

```
integer :: num_students, total_score
logical :: is_valid, has_passed
character(len=100) :: student_name
```

In the above code: - num_students and total_score are descriptive names indicating they store the number of students and total score, respectively. - is_valid and has_passed explicitly state their logical type through their prefixes. - student_name is self-explanatory, indicating it holds a student's name.

Furthermore, the use of constants and parameters in Fortran also benefits from adopting clear naming conventions. These elements should have easily identifiable names, often in uppercase letters to distinguish them from regular variables. Constants and parameters provide fixed values that do not change during program execution, enhancing code maintainability.

```
integer, parameter :: MAX_STUDENTS = 30
real, parameter :: PI = 3.14159
```

In the given example: - $MAX\_STUDENTS$ and PI use uppercase letters to indicate they are constants. - These identifiers are unambiguous, immediately informing the reader of their roles and immutability.

Adopting proper naming conventions thus not only fosters clear and organized code but also contributes to the functional and semantic integrity of the program, facilitating better collaboration and comprehension among developers.

Chapter 3

Control Structures

This chapter focuses on the essential control structures in Fortran that allow for decision-making and flow control within programs. It covers conditional statements such as IF-THEN-ELSE and SELECT CASE, as well as loop constructs like DO and DO WHILE. Readers will also learn about loop control statements, including EXIT and CYCLE, and how to construct complex conditions and nested control structures. Additionally, the chapter addresses error and exception handling, incorporating these elements into user-defined functions, alongside best practices for writing robust and maintainable code.

3.1 Introduction to Control Structures

Control structures form the backbone of programming in Fortran, facilitating logical flow and decision-making capabilities in code execution. Effective use of control structures allows for both straightforward and complex operations, ensuring programs are robust, efficient, and maintainable. This section introduces the primary control structures in Fortran, setting the stage for the more detailed exploration in subsequent sections.

Control structures in Fortran can be broadly classified into conditional statements and loops. Conditional statements enable decisions to be made in the code based on certain criteria, while loops allow repetitive execution of a block of code as long as specified conditions are met.

1. Conditional Statements

Conditional statements evaluate logical conditions and execute code blocks accordingly. Fortran provides several forms of conditional statements:

- **IF-THEN-ELSE**: This is the most basic form of conditional statement, allowing code to be executed if a certain condition is true, with an optional else block for alternative execution.
- **IF-THEN-ELSEIF-ELSE**: An extended version of the IF-THEN-ELSE statement, which allows multiple conditions to be checked sequentially.
- **SELECT CASE**: This statement provides a way to execute one of several possible blocks of code, based on the value of an expression.

```
! IF-THEN-ELSE example
IF (a > b) THEN
    PRINT*, 'a is greater than b'
ELSE
    PRINT*, 'a is not greater than b'
END IF

! SELECT CASE example
SELECT CASE (color)
    CASE ('red')
        PRINT*, 'Color is red'
    CASE ('blue')
        PRINT*, 'Color is blue'
    CASE DEFAULT
        PRINT*, 'Unknown color'
END SELECT
```

2. Loops

Loops are a fundamental part of control structures, enabling the execution of code blocks multiple times. Fortran offers several loop constructs:

- **DO Loop**: The simplest form of loop, iterating over a range of values.
- **DO WHILE Loop**: This loop continues as long as a specified condition is true.
- **Exit and Cycle Statements**: These are used to control loop execution, either to prematurely exit a loop or skip a loop iteration.

```
! DO loop example
DO i = 1, 10
   PRINT*, i
END DO

! DO WHILE example
DO WHILE (i <= 10)
   PRINT*, i
   i = i + 1
END DO

! EXIT and CYCLE example
DO i = 1, 10
   IF (i == 5) CYCLE
   IF (i == 8) EXIT
   PRINT*, i
END DO
```

3. Constructing Complex Conditions

Constructing complex conditions is vital for nuanced decision-making in programs. Fortran offers logical operators to compose more intricate conditional statements:

- **AND**: Combines conditions such that both must be true.
- **OR**: Combines conditions such that one or both must be true.
- **NOT**: Inverts the logical value of a condition.

```
IF (a > b .AND. a < c) THEN
   PRINT*, 'a is between b and c'
END IF

IF (x == y .OR. x == z) THEN
   PRINT*, 'x equals y or z'
END IF

IF (.NOT. condition) THEN
   PRINT*, 'condition is false'
END IF
```

4. Combining Control Structures

Combining control structures can address more sophisticated programming needs. For example, nested loops and conditional statements allow for multiple layers of decision making and iteration within programs.

```
DO i = 1, 3
   DO j = 1, 3
      IF (i == j) THEN
         PRINT*, 'i equals j at', i
```

```
        ELSE
            PRINT*, 'i:', i, 'j:', j
        END IF
    END DO
END DO
```

Understanding control structures is essential for writing efficient, readable, and maintainable Fortran code. Each control structure provides specific capabilities that, when used correctly, enable creating complex and effective computational solutions.

3.2 Conditional Statements: IF-THEN-ELSE

Conditional statements are fundamental in controlling the flow of a Fortran program. The primary conditional structure in Fortran is the IF-THEN-ELSE statement. This structure allows for executing different blocks of code based on the evaluation of logical conditions. It enables decision-making, which is crucial for developing robust and flexible programs.

The basic form of the IF-THEN-ELSE statement in Fortran is as follows:

```
IF (logical_expression) THEN
    ! statements
ELSE IF (another_logical_expression) THEN
    ! other statements
ELSE
    ! default statements
END IF
```

In detail, the logical_expression and another_logical_expression are expressions that evaluate to a logical value (.TRUE. or .FALSE.). Depending on the evaluation of these expressions, different blocks of code are executed.

Consider a practical example where a program needs to check if a number is positive, negative, or zero. The Fortran code implementing this logic is as follows:

```
PROGRAM CheckNumber
    IMPLICIT NONE
    INTEGER :: number

    ! Read a number from user
    PRINT *, "Enter a number:"
    READ *, number

    ! Check if the number is positive, negative, or zero
```

```
    IF (number > 0) THEN
        PRINT *, "The number is positive."
    ELSE IF (number < 0) THEN
        PRINT *, "The number is negative."
    ELSE
        PRINT *, "The number is zero."
    END IF
END PROGRAM CheckNumber
```

In this example:

- If number is greater than 0, the program prints "The number is positive."
- If number is less than 0, the program prints "The number is negative."
- If number is zero, the program prints "The number is zero."

Fortran provides a simplified form of the IF statement when only one condition and one corresponding action are needed. This is known as the one-line IF statement:

```
IF (logical_expression) statement
```

This form is useful for concise condition checking. For instance, suppose we want to print a message only if a given number is positive:

```
IF (number > 0) PRINT *, "The number is positive."
```

In scenarios requiring more complex conditionals, one can use nested IF-THEN-ELSE statements. These allow evaluating multiple layers of conditions, as shown in the following example:

```
PROGRAM NestedConditions
    IMPLICIT NONE
    REAL :: temperature

    ! Read the temperature from user
    PRINT *, "Enter the temperature in Celsius:"
    READ *, temperature

    ! Determine the weather condition
    IF (temperature > 30.0) THEN
        PRINT *, "It's hot."
    ELSE IF (temperature > 20.0) THEN
        PRINT *, "It's warm."
    ELSE
        IF (temperature > 10.0) THEN
            PRINT *, "It's cool."
        ELSE
            PRINT *, "It's cold."
        END IF
```

```
    END IF
END PROGRAM NestedConditions
```

In this code:

- If temperature is greater than 30.0, the program prints "It's hot."
- If temperature is between 20.0 and 30.0, the program prints "It's warm."
- If temperature is between 10.0 and 20.0, the program prints "It's cool."
- If temperature is less than or equal to 10.0, the program prints "It's cold."

Care must be exercised when nesting IF statements to maintain code readability and correctness. It's important to ensure that each END IF matches its corresponding IF statement. Also, for clarity, the code can be indented to reflect the nested structure accurately.

To summarize, the IF-THEN-ELSE control structure in Fortran is vital for making decisions within a program. By evaluating logical expressions, it directs the execution flow to appropriate code blocks, allowing for dynamic and responsive programs.

3.3 SELECT CASE Statements

The SELECT CASE statement in Fortran offers a structured method for handling multiple conditional branches. It is an alternative to using multiple IF-THEN-ELSE statements, often resulting in more readable and maintainable code when dealing with numerous conditions.

The SELECT CASE construct tests expressions against a series of values or value ranges, executing the associated block of code for the first matching condition. Here, we delve into the syntax, use cases, and best practices for utilizing SELECT CASE statements effectively.

Syntax and Structure

The SELECT CASE construct starts with the SELECT CASE statement, which evaluates a scalar expression. This is followed by one or more CASE blocks, each specifying conditions that are compared against the scalar value. The syntax is illustrated below:

```
SELECT CASE (scalar_expression)
    CASE (case_value_1)
        ! Block of code
    CASE (case_value_2)
        ! Block of code
    CASE (case_value_3)
        ! Block of code
    CASE DEFAULT
        ! Block of code
END SELECT
```

- scalar_expression: A scalar expression whose value is evaluated.
- case_value_n: One or more values or ranges of values that the scalar expression is compared against.
- CASE DEFAULT: An optional block that executes if no other CASE value matches.

Basic Example

Consider a scenario where you need to categorize numbers based on their value. Using SELECT CASE makes the categorization clear and concise.

```
PROGRAM categorize_numbers
    IMPLICIT NONE
    INTEGER :: number

    PRINT *, 'Enter an integer: '
    READ *, number

    SELECT CASE (number)
        CASE (1)
            PRINT *, 'Number is one.'
        CASE (2:5)
            PRINT *, 'Number is between two and five.'
        CASE (6, 7, 8)
            PRINT *, 'Number is six, seven, or eight.'
        CASE DEFAULT
            PRINT *, 'Number is outside the range of 1 to 8.'
    END SELECT
END PROGRAM categorize_numbers
```

This example allows for categorizing the input number into distinct groups. Note the compactness and clarity compared to a series of IF-THEN-ELSE statements.

Ranges and Multiple Values

The CASE statement supports specifying value ranges and multiple values, separated by commas. Ranges are specified using the format lower:upper. If the scalar_expression falls within this range, the corresponding code block executes.

```
SELECT CASE (number)
    CASE (10:20)
        PRINT *, 'Number is between 10 and 20.'
    CASE (25, 30, 35)
        PRINT *, 'Number is either 25, 30, or 35.'
    CASE (-5:-1)
        PRINT *, 'Number is a negative integer between -5 and -1.'
    CASE DEFAULT
        PRINT *, 'Number does not match any specified cases.'
END SELECT
```

This capability enables more versatile and extensive conditional checks.

Nested SELECT CASE Constructs

Nesting SELECT CASE constructs is permissible for more intricate decision-making processes. However, caution is advisable to maintain code readability.

```
PROGRAM nested_select_case
    IMPLICIT NONE
    CHARACTER(len=10) :: color
    INTEGER :: intensity

    PRINT *, 'Enter a color (red, green, blue): '
    READ *, color

    PRINT *, 'Enter intensity (1-10): '
    READ *, intensity

    SELECT CASE (color)
        CASE ('red')
            SELECT CASE (intensity)
                CASE (1:5)
                    PRINT *, 'Light red'
                CASE (6:10)
                    PRINT *, 'Dark red'
            END SELECT
        CASE ('green')
            SELECT CASE (intensity)
                CASE (1:5)
                    PRINT *, 'Light green'
                CASE (6:10)
                    PRINT *, 'Dark green'
            END SELECT
        CASE ('blue')
            SELECT CASE (intensity)
                CASE (1:5)
                    PRINT *, 'Light blue'
                CASE (6:10)
                    PRINT *, 'Dark blue'
            END SELECT
        CASE DEFAULT
            PRINT *, 'Unknown color'
    END SELECT
```

```
END PROGRAM nested_select_case
```

In this example, the color and its intensity are evaluated through nested SELECT CASE statements, demonstrating how nested constructs manage complex multi-dimensional conditional logic.

Error Handling

Incorporating a CASE DEFAULT clause is a recommended practice to handle unexpected or erroneous input gracefully. This default block executes when none of the specified CASE values match, thus serving as a catch-all.

```
PROGRAM handle_errors
    IMPLICIT NONE
    INTEGER :: option

    PRINT *, 'Select an option (1-3): '
    READ *, option

    SELECT CASE (option)
        CASE (1)
            PRINT *, 'Option 1 selected.'
        CASE (2)
            PRINT *, 'Option 2 selected.'
        CASE (3)
            PRINT *, 'Option 3 selected.'
        CASE DEFAULT
            PRINT *, 'Invalid option, please select 1, 2, or 3.'
    END SELECT
END PROGRAM handle_errors
```

Implementing the CASE DEFAULT clause ensures robustness, aiding in preventing the program from undefined behaviors due to unexpected inputs.

The SELECT CASE statement is essential for writing clean and efficient multi-branch conditional logic in Fortran. Proper understanding and implementation of this control structure contribute to the development of organized and maintainable code.

3.4 Loop Constructs: DO and DO WHILE

Loop constructs in Fortran are vital for repetitive execution of code blocks. Two primary loop constructs, DO and DO WHILE, facilitate iteration until specific conditions are met. Mastery of these constructs allows for the efficient handling of computations requiring repetition.

The DO loop is a counter-controlled loop, ideal for scenarios where the number of iterations is known before entering the loop. It consists of an initialization, a termination condition, and an increment or decrement step.

```
DO i = 1, 10, 2
    print *, "The value of i is ", i
END DO
```

In this example, i initializes at 1, increments by 2 per iteration, and stops at or before 10. The output generated displays as follows:

```
The value of i is 1
The value of i is 3
The value of i is 5
The value of i is 7
The value of i is 9
```

The DO loop can also manage decrements:

```
DO i = 10, 1, -3
    print *, "The value of i is ", i
END DO
```

Here, DO begins at 10, decreases by 3 per iteration, and terminates at or before 1, producing:

```
The value of i is 10
The value of i is 7
The value of i is 4
```

Nested DO loops are useful for multidimensional iterations:

```
DO i = 1, 3
    DO j = 1, 3
        print *, "i = ", i, " j = ", j
    END DO
END DO
```

This nested configuration results in:

```
i = 1 j = 1
i = 1 j = 2
i = 1 j = 3
i = 2 j = 1
i = 2 j = 2
i = 2 j = 3
i = 3 j = 1
i = 3 j = 2
i = 3 j = 3
```

The DO WHILE loop is condition-controlled and iterates as long as its condition remains true:

```
i = 1
DO WHILE (i <= 5)
    print *, "The value of i is ", i
    i = i + 1
END DO
```

The loop ceases when i exceeds 5, yielding:

```
The value of i is 1
The value of i is 2
The value of i is 3
The value of i is 4
The value of i is 5
```

For complex conditions:

```
i = 0
j = 5
DO WHILE (i < 4 .AND. j > 1)
    print *, "i = ", i, " j = ", j
    i = i + 1
    j = j - 1
END DO
```

This produces:

```
i = 0 j = 5
i = 1 j = 4
i = 2 j = 3
i = 3 j = 2
```

Combining DO and DO WHILE, intricate structures can be constructed. Consider a simulation where a temperature value must compute using nested DO and DO WHILE:

```
REAL :: temperature(10, 10)
INTEGER :: i, j
DO i = 1, 10
    j = 1
    DO WHILE (j <= 10)
        temperature(i, j) = i * j * 0.5
        print *, "temperature(", i, ",", j, ") = ", temperature(i, j)
        j = j + 1
    END DO
END DO
```

Output:

```
temperature( 1 , 1 ) = 0.50
temperature( 1 , 2 ) = 1.00
temperature( 1 , 3 ) = 1.50
temperature( 1 , 4 ) = 2.00
...
temperature( 10 , 8 ) = 40.00
temperature( 10 , 9 ) = 45.00
temperature( 10 , 10 ) = 50.00
```

In this detailed examination, DO manages the outer loop ranging from 1 to 10 and DO WHILE governs the inner loop. The interplay of these loops allows robust control over the iterations and computations necessary for advanced simulations.

3.5 Loop Control Statements: EXIT and CYCLE

In Fortran, loop control statements provide mechanisms to alter the flow of iteration within loops. Two primary statements, EXIT and CYCLE, are essential for controlling loop execution. Both are used within looping constructs like DO and DO WHILE to manage the flow of control precisely and efficiently.

The EXIT statement allows for premature termination of a loop. When an EXIT statement is encountered within a loop, the control immediately transfers to the statement following the end of the loop. This can be particularly useful when certain conditions render further iterations unnecessary. Consider the following example demonstrating the EXIT statement within a DO loop:

```
PROGRAM ExitExample
   IMPLICIT NONE
   INTEGER :: i

   DO i = 1, 10
      PRINT *, 'Iteration:', i
      IF (i == 5) EXIT
   END DO

   PRINT *, 'Loop exited at iteration 5'
END PROGRAM ExitExample
```

In this example, the loop iterates from 1 to 10. However, when i equals 5, the EXIT statement triggers, causing the loop to terminate early. The output would be:

```
Iteration: 1
Iteration: 2
Iteration: 3
Iteration: 4
Iteration: 5
Loop exited at iteration 5
```

The CYCLE statement serves a different purpose: it skips the rest of the current loop iteration and proceeds directly to the next iteration. This can be used when certain conditions necessitate bypassing specific computations within a loop. Here is an illustration:

```
PROGRAM CycleExample
   IMPLICIT NONE
   INTEGER :: i

   DO i = 1, 10
      IF (MOD(i, 2) == 0) CYCLE
      PRINT *, 'Odd iteration:', i
   END DO
```

```
    PRINT *, 'Loop completed'
END PROGRAM CycleExample
```

In this case, the loop iterates from 1 to 10. However, the CYCLE statement causes the loop to skip even iterations, leading to the following output:

```
Odd iteration: 1
Odd iteration: 3
Odd iteration: 5
Odd iteration: 7
Odd iteration: 9
Loop completed
```

Combining EXIT and CYCLE within nested loops can create complex control flows. In nested loops, these statements apply to the innermost loop unless labeled. Consider the following example:

```
PROGRAM NestedLoopControl
    IMPLICIT NONE
    INTEGER :: i, j

    DO i = 1, 3
        DO j = 1, 3
            IF (i == j) CYCLE
            IF (i + j == 4) EXIT
            PRINT *, 'i =', i, ', j =', j
        END DO
        PRINT *, 'Completed inner loop for i =', i
    END DO

    PRINT *, 'All loops completed'
END PROGRAM NestedLoopControl
```

This program demonstrates how CYCLE and EXIT interact within nested loops. The CYCLE statement skips iterations when i equals j. When the sum of i and j equals 4, the EXIT statement terminates the inner loop. The output is:

```
i = 1 , j = 2
Completed inner loop for i = 1
i = 2 , j = 1
Completed inner loop for i = 2
i = 3 , j = 1
Completed inner loop for i = 3
All loops completed
```

Labeling loops can target EXIT and CYCLE more precisely. Consider the following example with labeled loops:

```
PROGRAM LabeledLoopControl
    IMPLICIT NONE
    INTEGER :: i, j

    outer: DO i = 1, 3
        inner: DO j = 1, 3
```

```
        IF (i == j) CYCLE inner
        IF (i + j == 4) EXIT outer
        PRINT *, 'i =', i, ', j =', j
    END DO inner
    PRINT *, 'Completed inner loop for i =', i
  END DO outer

  PRINT *, 'All loops completed'
END PROGRAM LabeledLoopControl
```

Here, the labels outer and inner are used to indicate which loop the statements affect. The labeled CYCLE inner statement skips iterations when i equals j, while EXIT outer terminates the outer loop when the sum of i and j equals 4. The output is:

```
i = 1 , j = 2
i = 2 , j = 1
All loops completed
```

Understanding EXIT and CYCLE statements is crucial for efficiently controlling loop execution and improving the responsiveness and performance of Fortran programs.

3.6 Nested Control Structures

Nested control structures in Fortran enhance the ability to perform more complex and intricate decision-making and looping mechanisms by embedding one control structure within another. This section aims to elucidate the nested forms of IF-THEN-ELSE, SELECT CASE, and loop constructs, including the meticulous handling of nested layers.

One of the practical scenarios involves nesting IF-THEN-ELSE within a DO loop to conditionally execute a set of statements multiple times. Consider the following example, which demonstrates a nested IF-THEN-ELSE inside a DO loop:

```
PROGRAM Nested_IF_DO
  IMPLICIT NONE
  INTEGER :: i

  DO i = 1, 10
    IF (MOD(i, 2) == 0) THEN
      PRINT *, 'Number ', i, ' is even.'
    ELSE
      PRINT *, 'Number ', i, ' is odd.'
    END IF
  END DO

END PROGRAM Nested_IF_DO
```

```
Number      1 is odd.
Number      2 is even.
Number      3 is odd.
Number      4 is even.
Number      5 is odd.
Number      6 is even.
Number      7 is odd.
Number      8 is even.
Number      9 is odd.
Number     10 is even.
```

In this example, the DO loop iterates over a range of values from 1 to 10. For each iteration, the IF-THEN-ELSE structure checks the parity of the number and prints the appropriate message. The nested IF-THEN-ELSE within the DO loop allows for conditional branching during each iteration.

Similarly, nesting SELECT CASE statements within loops or other SELECT CASE statements facilitates multi-level decision-making. Consider the following example, where a SELECT CASE is nested inside another SELECT CASE to evaluate a variable's value more comprehensively:

```
PROGRAM Nested_SELECT_CASE
   IMPLICIT NONE
   INTEGER :: month

   PRINT *, 'Enter a month number (1-12):'
   READ *, month

   SELECT CASE (month)
      CASE (1, 2, 12)
         PRINT *, 'It is Winter'
         SELECT CASE (month)
            CASE (12)
               PRINT *, 'Month is December'
            CASE (1)
               PRINT *, 'Month is January'
            CASE (2)
               PRINT *, 'Month is February'
         END SELECT
      CASE (3:5)
         PRINT *, 'It is Spring'
      CASE (6:8)
         PRINT *, 'It is Summer'
      CASE (9:11)
         PRINT *, 'It is Autumn'
      CASE DEFAULT
         PRINT *, 'Invalid month'
   END SELECT

END PROGRAM Nested_SELECT_CASE
```

```
Enter a month number (1-12):
2
It is Winter
Month is February
```

In this example, the outer SELECT CASE determines the season based on the month number, while the nested SELECT CASE provides additional granularity by identifying the specific month within the winter season. Such nested structures significantly enhance the decision-making capabilities of the program.

Similarly, nesting DO loops can perform multi-dimensional iterations. For instance, iterating over a two-dimensional array requires two nested DO loops, as demonstrated below:

```
PROGRAM Nested_DO_Loops
    IMPLICIT NONE
    INTEGER, PARAMETER :: n = 3, m = 3
    INTEGER :: i, j
    INTEGER :: array(n, m)

    ! Initialize the array
    DO i = 1, n
        DO j = 1, m
            array(i, j) = (i - 1) * m + j
        END DO
    END DO

    ! Print the array
    PRINT *, '2D Array:'
    DO i = 1, n
        DO j = 1, m
            PRINT *, 'array(', i, ',', j, ') = ', array(i, j)
        END DO
    END DO

END PROGRAM Nested_DO_Loops
```

```
2D Array:
array(           1 ,           1 ) =            1
array(           1 ,           2 ) =            2
array(           1 ,           3 ) =            3
array(           2 ,           1 ) =            4
array(           2 ,           2 ) =            5
array(           2 ,           3 ) =            6
array(           3 ,           1 ) =            7
array(           3 ,           2 ) =            8
array(           3 ,           3 ) =            9
```

In this program, the nested DO loops first initialize and then print a 3x3 array. The outer loop iterates over the rows, while the inner loop iterates over the columns. Each element is accessed and modified using its respective coordinate indices.

For more complex control flows, the nesting can extend beyond two levels. For example, combining nested DO, IF-THEN-ELSE, and SELECT CASE within a single code segment further strengthens the decision and looping capabilities.

It is critical to properly indent nested control structures to ensure code readability and maintainability. Properly nested constructs can dramatically improve the clarity and efficiency of the code by enabling concise expression of multi-dimensional or multi-level logic conditions. Each structure should be aligned and indented consistently to avoid misinterpretation and errors during program execution.

3.7 Constructing Complex Conditions

In Fortran programming, constructing complex conditions is pivotal for developing robust and efficient programs. Complex conditions involve combining multiple logical expressions using logical operators to evaluate more intricate decision-making criteria. Fortran provides logical operators such as .AND., .OR., and .NOT. for this purpose.

Logical expressions are conditions that evaluate to either .TRUE. or .FALSE.. These expressions can be combined to form more complicated conditions essential for fine-tuned control flow within the program.

Logical Operators:

- .AND.: This operator returns .TRUE. if and only if both operands are .TRUE..
- .OR.: This operator returns .TRUE. if at least one of the operands is .TRUE..
- .NOT.: This operator returns the logical negation of the operand, transforming .TRUE. to .FALSE. and vice versa.

Consider the following Fortran code snippet that demonstrates combining logical conditions using these operators:

```
program complex_condition_example
   implicit none
   integer :: x, y
   logical :: condition1, condition2, final_condition

   ! Assigning values to variables
   x = 10
   y = 20

   ! Individual conditions
   condition1 = (x > 5)
   condition2 = (y < 25)

   ! Combining conditions using .AND. and .OR.
```

```
    final_condition = condition1 .AND. condition2

    ! Display result based on the combined condition
    if (final_condition) then
        print *, "Both conditions are true."
    else
        print *, "At least one of the conditions is false."
    end if

    ! Using .OR. operator
    final_condition = condition1 .OR. condition2

    if (final_condition) then
        print *, "At least one of the conditions is true."
    else
        print *, "Both conditions are false."
    end if

    ! Using .NOT. operator
    if (.NOT. condition1) then
        print *, "Condition1 is false."
    else
        print *, "Condition1 is true."
    end if
end program complex_condition_example
```

```
Both conditions are true.
At least one of the conditions is true.
Condition1 is true.
```

In the above example, condition1 is true because $(x > 5)$ evaluates to .TRUE., and condition2 is true because $(y < 25)$ evaluates to .TRUE.. The combination condition1 .AND. condition2 is true because both conditions are true. This results in the first print statement being executed. The second combination condition1 .OR. condition2 is also true since at least one of the conditions is true, leading to the second print statement. The .NOT. condition1 results in false since condition1 is true, causing the third print statement to be executed.

Constructing complex conditions often involves nesting logical operators. Nested conditions can efficiently handle multifaceted decision-making scenarios. For instance, let's consider a scenario where a decision is based not only on two conditions but on a more exhaustive logical expression.

```
program nested_conditions
    implicit none
    integer :: a, b, c
    logical :: result

    ! Assigning values to variables
    a = 15
    b = 10
    c = 5

    ! Complex nested condition
```

```
    result = ((a > b) .AND. (b > c)) .OR. ((a < b) .AND. (c < a))

    ! Display the result of the nested condition
    if (result) then
        print *, "The complex condition is true."
    else
        print *, "The complex condition is false."
    end if
end program nested_conditions
```

```
The complex condition is true.
```

Here, the variable result holds a logical expression involving nested conditions. The expression ((a > b) .AND. (b > c)) .OR. ((a < b) .AND. (c < a)) ensures that the final decision accounts for multiple possibilities. Specifically, it checks if both a is greater than b and b is greater than c, or alternatively, if a is less than b and c is less than a. Since the initial condition is true ($a > b$ and $b > c$), the complete logical expression evaluates to true.

In practice, it is critical to ensure that complex conditions are clear and maintainable. Overuse of nested and intricate logical expressions can lead to hard-to-read and error-prone code. Hence, adopting best practices, such as breaking down complex conditions into simpler, well-named logical variables, significantly enhances code readability and maintainability.

Fortran programmers must also be cautious about the operator precedence when combining logical expressions. Without proper use of parentheses, the intended logic might not be accurately captured, leading to unexpected behavior. Operator precedence rules determine how an expression involving multiple operators is evaluated. In Fortran, logical operators follow the precedence:

1. .NOT.
2. .AND.
3. .OR.

Understanding and correctly applying these precedence rules ensures that complex conditions are evaluated as intended. When in doubt, use parentheses to make the precedence explicit and avoid ambiguity in logical expressions. By carefully constructing complex conditions and prioritizing clarity, programmers can effectively manage control flow, ensuring that their code is both robust and easily comprehensible.

3.8 Error Handling and Exception Handling

Error handling in Fortran is a critical aspect for writing robust and maintainable code. This section delves deeply into techniques for identifying, managing, and rectifying errors and exceptions during the execution of Fortran programs.

A common approach to error handling in Fortran involves checking the status of operations that may fail, such as file I/O operations or numerical computations, and then taking appropriate measures based on the success or failure of these operations. Let's consider how to handle errors using intrinsic functions and specific control structures.

To illustrate this, let's start with an example demonstrating handling a common error scenario, such as attempting to open a non-existent file:

```
PROGRAM FileOpenErrorHandling
  IMPLICIT NONE
  INTEGER :: io_status
  CHARACTER(LEN=256) :: filename
  CHARACTER(LEN=512) :: errmsg

  ! Assign a non-existent filename
  filename = 'nonexistentfile.dat'

  ! Attempt to open the file for reading
  OPEN(UNIT=1, FILE=filename, STATUS='OLD', IOSTAT=io_status, IOMSG=
       errmsg)

  ! Check the status and handle the error
  IF (io_status /= 0) THEN
    PRINT*, 'Error opening file:', TRIM(errmsg)
  ELSE
    PRINT*, 'File opened successfully.'
    CLOSE(UNIT=1)
  END IF

END PROGRAM FileOpenErrorHandling
```

In this code, the OPEN statement tries to open a file and returns an I/O status in io_status. If io_status is not zero, an error occurred, and the program prints an error message using the IOMSG variable, which contains the error description.

Another critical aspect of error handling is managing numerical computation errors. Consider the following example, in which division by zero is safely managed:

```
PROGRAM DivisionErrorHandling
  IMPLICIT NONE
  REAL :: numerator, denominator, result

  numerator = 10.0
```

```
  denominator = 0.0

  ! Check if the denominator is zero before division
  IF (denominator == 0.0) THEN
    PRINT*, 'Error: Division by zero is not allowed.'
  ELSE
    result = numerator / denominator
    PRINT*, 'Result: ', result
  END IF

END PROGRAM DivisionErrorHandling
```

In this sketched example, the program checks whether the denominator is zero before performing the division to avoid runtime errors.

Fortran also offers the ability to handle errors through the use of exception handling mechanisms such as ERR= and IOSTAT= specifiers. Consider a more complex error handling scenario when reading from a file:

```
PROGRAM ReadFileErrorHandling
  IMPLICIT NONE
  INTEGER :: io_status
  CHARACTER(LEN=256) :: filename
  CHARACTER(LEN=512) :: errmsg
  INTEGER, PARAMETER :: max_len = 100
  CHARACTER(LEN=80) :: line
  INTEGER :: unit

  ! Initialize variables
  filename = 'data.txt'
  unit = 10

  ! Attempt to open the file
  OPEN(UNIT=unit, FILE=filename, STATUS='OLD', IOSTAT=io_status, IOMSG=
      errmsg)

  ! Check for errors in file opening
  IF (io_status /= 0) THEN
    PRINT*, 'Error opening file:', TRIM(errmsg)
    STOP
  END IF

  ! Read lines from the file and handle potential errors
  DO
    READ(unit, '(A)', IOSTAT=io_status) line

    IF (io_status < 0) THEN
      EXIT ! End of file
    ELSE IF (io_status > 0) THEN
      PRINT*, 'Error reading file:', TRIM(errmsg)
      EXIT
    ELSE
      PRINT*, 'Line read: ', TRIM(line)
    END IF
  END DO

  CLOSE(UNIT=unit)
END PROGRAM ReadFileErrorHandling
```

In this example, error handling is done both when opening the file and while reading from it. The READ statement checks the io_status to detect read errors, differentiate between end-of-file and other errors, and respond accordingly.

Beyond explicit checking of IOSTAT, Fortran also supports user-defined handling of floating-point errors through IEEE arithmetic modules. Here's an example of setting and checking for numerical errors using IEEE modules:

```
PROGRAM FloatingPointErrorHandling
  USE, INTRINSIC :: IEEE_EXCEPTIONS
  IMPLICIT NONE

  REAL :: x, y, result
  LOGICAL :: overflow, underflow, divide_by_zero

  ! Set up initial values
  x = 10.0
  y = 0.0

  ! Begin error checking block
  CALL IEEE_GET_FLAG(IEEE_OVERFLOW, overflow)
  CALL IEEE_GET_FLAG(IEEE_UNDERFLOW, underflow)
  CALL IEEE_GET_FLAG(IEEE_DIVIDE_BY_ZERO, divide_by_zero)

  PRINT*, 'Initial flags - Overflow:', overflow, ' Underflow:', underflow, &
          ' Divide by zero:', divide_by_zero

  ! Arithmetic operation that may cause a floating-point exception
  CALL IEEE_SET_FLAG(IEEE_OVERFLOW, .FALSE.)
  result = x / y

  ! Check for floating-point errors
  CALL IEEE_GET_FLAG(IEEE_OVERFLOW, overflow)
  CALL IEEE_GET_FLAG(IEEE_UNDERFLOW, underflow)
  CALL IEEE_GET_FLAG(IEEE_DIVIDE_BY_ZERO, divide_by_zero)

  PRINT*, 'After operation - Overflow:', overflow, ' Underflow:', underflow, &
          ' Divide by zero:', divide_by_zero

END PROGRAM FloatingPointErrorHandling
```

In this program, IEEE floating point error flags are used to detect exceptions such as overflow, underflow, and division by zero, ensuring that potential errors in arithmetic computations are captured and managed.

By utilizing these techniques, Fortran programmers can handle errors gracefully, allowing for more robust and maintainable code. Controlling how errors are processed not only helps in identifying issues promptly but also ensures that programs can recover or terminate gracefully, providing users with informative error messages and maintaining the integrity of data and operations.

3.9 Constructing User-Defined Functions with Control Structures

The ability to construct user-defined functions is a key feature in Fortran that allows for modular programming, increasing readability and reusability of code. Integrating control structures within user-defined functions provides sophisticated functionality by allowing the function to perform conditional operations and iterative processes.

A user-defined function in Fortran is declared using the FUNCTION keyword, and it typically includes control structures such as IF-THEN-ELSE, SELECT CASE, and loops like DO and DO WHILE. These control structures enable the function to make decisions, process data in loops, and handle errors effectively. Let us delve into the practical aspects of integrating these control structures into user-defined functions.

```
FUNCTION ComputeFactorial(n)
  INTEGER :: ComputeFactorial
  INTEGER, INTENT(IN) :: n
  INTEGER :: i

  ComputeFactorial = 1
  DO i = 1, n
    ComputeFactorial = ComputeFactorial * i
  END DO
END FUNCTION ComputeFactorial
```

In the above example, the function ComputeFactorial computes the factorial of an integer n using a DO loop. The DO loop iterates from 1 to n, multiplying the current value of the loop variable i each time to the function's result variable ComputeFactorial.

Control structures can also manage decision-making within functions. The IF-THEN-ELSE construct is particularly useful for adding conditions within a function, as illustrated below.

```
FUNCTION CalculateDiscount(price, category)
  REAL :: CalculateDiscount
  REAL, INTENT(IN) :: price
  CHARACTER(LEN=*), INTENT(IN) :: category

  IF (category == 'A') THEN
    CalculateDiscount = price * 0.95
  ELSE IF (category == 'B') THEN
    CalculateDiscount = price * 0.90
  ELSE
    CalculateDiscount = price * 0.85
  END IF
END FUNCTION CalculateDiscount
```

This example demonstrates a function CalculateDiscount, which calculates a discount based on the product category. It uses IF-THEN-ELSE statements to determine the discount rate for different product categories and applies the appropriate rate to the input price.

Nested control structures enable more complex logical operations within functions. The combination of loops and conditional statements within a function enhances its capability to handle complex tasks.

```
FUNCTION MatrixSum(matrix)
  INTEGER :: MatrixSum
  INTEGER, DIMENSION(:,:), INTENT(IN) :: matrix
  INTEGER :: i, j

  MatrixSum = 0
  DO i = 1, SIZE(matrix, 1)
    DO j = 1, SIZE(matrix, 2)
      IF (matrix(i, j) > 0) THEN
        MatrixSum = MatrixSum + matrix(i, j)
      END IF
    END DO
  END DO
END FUNCTION MatrixSum
```

Here, the function MatrixSum calculates the sum of all positive elements in a 2D array matrix. It employs nested DO loops to iterate through each element of the array, combined with an IF statement to only add positive numbers to the sum.

For more advanced decision-making, the SELECT CASE construct can replace multiple IF-THEN-ELSE statements, offering a clearer and potentially more efficient method of handling multiple conditions.

```
FUNCTION DetermineGrade(score)
  CHARACTER :: DetermineGrade
  REAL, INTENT(IN) :: score

  SELECT CASE (score)
    CASE (90.0:100.0)
      DetermineGrade = 'A'
    CASE (80.0:89.9)
      DetermineGrade = 'B'
    CASE (70.0:79.9)
      DetermineGrade = 'C'
    CASE (60.0:69.9)
      DetermineGrade = 'D'
    CASE DEFAULT
      DetermineGrade = 'F'
  END SELECT
END FUNCTION DetermineGrade
```

In this example, the function DetermineGrade assigns a letter grade to a numerical score using the SELECT CASE construct. This approach enhances readability and organization when handling multiple discrete ranges.

Integrating error handling into functions ensures robustness. Functions can handle unexpected or erroneous conditions gracefully using control structures.

```
FUNCTION SafeDivide(a, b)
  REAL :: SafeDivide
  REAL, INTENT(IN) :: a, b

  IF (b == 0.0) THEN
    PRINT *, "Error: Division by zero"
    STOP
  ELSE
    SafeDivide = a / b
  END IF
END FUNCTION SafeDivide
```

The SafeDivide function safely performs division, checking for division by zero with an IF statement. If the denominator b is zero, it prints an error message and halts the program using the STOP statement.

User-defined functions in Fortran can be designed to be modular and flexible by embedding appropriate control structures. This practice not only enhances functionality but also contributes to producing cleaner, more maintainable, and fault-tolerant code. By mastering these techniques, readers can construct sophisticated functions that leverage Fortran's full potential for complex computational tasks.

3.10 Best Practices for Control Structures in Fortran

In this section, we will explore best practices for using control structures in Fortran to ensure that your code is both robust and maintainable. Adhering to these practices will help in writing programs that are easier to understand, debug, and extend. These guidelines will cover naming conventions, code readability, logical structure, and optimization techniques.

Consistent Naming Conventions

Using descriptive and consistent naming conventions for variables, loops, and conditional constructs significantly improves the readability of your programs. Here are a few key points to remember:

- Use CamelCase or snake_case for variable names and ensure they are descriptive. For example, totalSum or total_sum is preferable over ts.
- For loop indices, use meaningful names if possible. Instead of using generic indices such as i, j, or k, prefer something more descriptive like rowIndex, colIndex, if it makes sense in the context.
- Functions and subroutine names should clearly convey their purpose, e.g., calculateMean or findMaxValue.

Indentation and Code Block Formatting

Proper indentation and formatting of control structures are paramount to the readability of your code. Always align the body of IF, DO, and SELECT CASE constructs to visually separate the conditional logic from the main code flow.

```
IF (condition) THEN
    ! Statements executed when condition is true
    CALL some_subroutine()
ELSE
    ! Statements executed when condition is false
    CALL alternative_subroutine()
END IF
```

- Maintain a consistent indentation level, usually 2 or 4 spaces.
- Use blank lines to separate logical sections of the code, improving readability.

Avoid Deep Nesting of Control Structures

Deeply nested control structures can make the code difficult to read and understand. Strive to minimize the levels of nesting within your control structures. If a function becomes too complex, consider breaking it into smaller subroutines.

```
! Example of minimizing nesting
IF (condition1) THEN
    CALL handleCondition1()
ELSE IF (condition2) THEN
    CALL handleCondition2()
ELSE
    CALL handleOtherConditions()
END IF
```

Use of Modular Code

Modular programming involves dividing a program into smaller subprograms or modules, each performing a specific task. This not only makes the code more manageable but also allows for reuse and easy maintenance.

```
! Example subroutine
SUBROUTINE processInput(data)
    IMPLICIT NONE
    INTEGER, INTENT(IN) :: data
    ! Processing logic here
END SUBROUTINE processInput
```

Error and Exception Handling

Robust error handling is crucial for creating reliable programs. Fortran offers various mechanisms to catch and handle errors. Ensure that your code gracefully handles unexpected conditions and provides useful error messages.

```
SUBROUTINE readInput(fileID, array)
    INTEGER, INTENT(IN) :: fileID
    REAL, INTENT(OUT) :: array(:)
    INTEGER :: ios
    READ (fileID, *, IOSTAT=ios) array
    IF (ios /= 0) THEN
        PRINT*, "Error reading input from file"
        STOP
    END IF
END SUBROUTINE readInput
```

Making Use of Loop Control Statements

Loop control statements like EXIT and CYCLE can improve the readability and efficiency of loops. Use these statements to manage loop iterations more effectively.

```
DO i = 1, n
    IF (array(i) < 0) CYCLE
    ! Process only positive values
    CALL processValue(array(i))
    IF (array(i) > threshold) EXIT
END DO
```

Compiling and Optimization

Make use of compiler options to optimize your code for performance. Most Fortran compilers provide flags to enhance execution speed and detect potential issues during compilation. For example:

```
gfortran -O2 program.f90 -o optimized_program
```

Use the appropriate level of optimization depending on your program's requirements. While -O2 provides a good balance between compilation time and performance, higher levels like -O3 might be necessary for computational-intensive tasks.

By adhering to these best practices, you can write Fortran code that is not only efficient but also easy to read, maintain, and debug. Implementing these guidelines consistently across your codebase will lead to higher quality and more reliable software projects.

Chapter 4

Functions and Subroutines

This chapter provides a comprehensive guide to functions and subroutines in Fortran, highlighting their importance for modular and reusable code. Readers will learn how to define and call both functions and subroutines, understand the difference between them, and explore argument passing mechanisms. The chapter also delves into recursion, internal procedures, and the use of modules and contain blocks. Further, it covers intrinsic functions and subroutines, best practices for writing efficient procedures, and techniques for debugging, ensuring that readers can create well-structured and maintainable Fortran programs.

4.1 Introduction to Functions and Subroutines

In Fortran, functions and subroutines are fundamental constructs that enable the creation of modular, reusable, and maintainable code. These constructs facilitate the decomposition of complex problems into smaller, manageable parts. Functions and subroutines in Fortran serve different roles in program execution yet share several similarities in their definitions and usages.

Functions are designed to perform specific computations and return a single value. They can be invoked in expressions just like intrinsic functions. A function in Fortran is defined using the FUNCTION keyword followed by the function name. The return type of the function is specified along with the function definition. Functions must use a RETURN statement to output their result, and this result is assigned to a variable with the same name as the function.

Subroutines, on the other hand, are used to perform a series of actions that do not inherently return a value. Instead, they can modify the values of arguments passed to them. Subroutines are defined using the SUBROUTINE keyword. Unlike functions, subroutines do not have a return type, and they use the CALL statement to execute.

The general structure for defining a Fortran function is as follows:

```
FUNCTION function_name(arg1, arg2, ...)
  result_variable = ...
  RETURN
END FUNCTION function_name
```

For subroutines, the structure is slightly different:

```
SUBROUTINE subroutine_name(arg1, arg2, ...)
  ...
  RETURN
END SUBROUTINE subroutine_name
```

In both constructs, the arguments arg1, arg2, ... can be variables, arrays, or more complex data structures. These arguments allow functions and subroutines to interact with other parts of the program, making them versatile tools for code organization.

When defining arguments, it is crucial to understand their passage mechanisms. Fortran primarily uses "pass-by-reference," meaning that the address of the argument is passed to the function or subroutine, allowing for direct modifications of the original data. This is particularly useful in subroutines where multiple data points may need to be modified. Functions and subroutines can also use "pass-by-value" semantics, which involve passing a copy of the data, ensuring that the original data remains unchanged.

To call a function within a Fortran program, you simply include the function's name and arguments within an expression:

```
result = function_name(arg1, arg2, ...)
```

Subroutines are called using the CALL statement:

```
CALL subroutine_name(arg1, arg2, ...)
```

Let us consider a practical example to illustrate the usage of functions and subroutines. Suppose we need to calculate the area of a circle and print the result. We can define a function to compute the area and a subroutine to print the result:

```
PROGRAM CircleArea
  REAL :: radius, area

  PRINT *, 'Enter the radius of the circle:'
  READ *, radius

  area = CircleArea(radius)
  CALL PrintResult(area)
END PROGRAM CircleArea

FUNCTION CircleArea(r)
  REAL :: CircleArea
  REAL, INTENT(IN) :: r
  REAL, PARAMETER :: pi = 3.14159

  CircleArea = pi * r * r
END FUNCTION CircleArea

SUBROUTINE PrintResult(a)
  REAL, INTENT(IN) :: a

  PRINT *, 'The area of the circle is: ', a
END SUBROUTINE PrintResult
```

Executing this program will prompt the user for the radius, compute the area using the CircleArea function, and print the result using the PrintResult subroutine.

```
Enter the radius of the circle:
5.0
The area of the circle is: 78.53975
```

This example highlights the modularity and reusability that functions and subroutines bring to Fortran programming. Functions encapsulate specific computations, making the code more readable and maintainable, while subroutines encapsulate actions or operations, facilitating better code organization and reuse.

4.2 Defining and Calling Functions

In Fortran, functions are a core construct that encapsulates computational logic, allowing for code modularity and reuse. A function in Fortran can perform computations and return a single value. To define a function, you need to specify its name, input arguments, and the type of the value it returns. This section elaborates on the syntax and conventions for defining and calling functions in Fortran, along with examples to illustrate their use.

Defining a Function

A function in Fortran is defined using the function keyword, followed by an identifier that serves as the function's name. The general form of a function definition in Fortran is as follows:

```
function function_name(argument_list) result(result_name)
    implicit none
    ! Declarations
    <declaration and initialization of arguments and local variables>
    <actual computational statements>

    ! Set the result of the function
    result_name = <result_value>

end function function_name
```

The implicit none statement is used to enforce explicit declaration of all variables, which reduces errors due to undeclared or misdeclared variables.

Here is a simple example of a Fortran function that calculates the square of an integer:

```
function square(x) result(y)
    implicit none
    integer, intent(in) :: x
    integer :: y

    y = x * x

end function square
```

In this example:

- square is the function name.
- x is the input argument of type integer.
- y is the result of the function, also of type integer.
- y = x * x is the computational statement that assigns the square of x to y.

Calling a Function

To call a function, you use its name followed by a parenthesis-enclosed argument list. The function call can be used in expressions, assignments, or as part of more complex statements.

Consider the following example which calls the previously defined square function:

```
program example
    implicit none
    integer :: num, result

    num = 5
    result = square(num)
    print *, "The square of ", num, " is ", result
end program example
```

The output of the above code would be:

```
The square of  5 is 25
```

Argument Type and Intent

In Fortran functions, you need to declare the type and intent of each argument. The intent attribute specifies the intended use of an argument:

- intent(in): The argument is passed to the function, and its value cannot be modified within the function.
- intent(out): The argument is used to return a value from the function to the caller.
- intent(inout): The argument is passed to the function, may be modified within the function, and the modified value is returned to the caller.

Consider a function that computes the hypotenuse of a right-angle triangle given the lengths of the other two sides:

```
function hypotenuse(a, b) result(c)
    implicit none
    real, intent(in) :: a, b
    real :: c

    c = sqrt(a**2 + b**2)
end function hypotenuse
```

Returning Arrays from Functions

Fortran functions can also return arrays. However, you must properly declare the array dimensions. Here is an example of a function that generates an identity matrix of given size:

```
function identity_matrix(n) result(matrix)
    implicit none
    integer, intent(in) :: n
    real :: matrix(n, n)
    integer :: i
```

```
    matrix = 0.0
    do i = 1, n
        matrix(i, i) = 1.0
    end do
end function identity_matrix
```

Calling Functions in Expressions

In Fortran, functions can be used within expressions, much like intrinsic functions. Here is an example that demonstrates calling user-defined functions within complex expressions:

```
program func_in_expression
    implicit none
    real :: a, b, h

    a = 3.0
    b = 4.0
    h = 2.0 * hypotenuse(a, b)
    print *, "The doubled hypotenuse is ", h
end program func_in_expression
```

The output of this code would be:

```
The doubled hypotenuse is 10.0
```

Understanding how to define and call functions is vital for creating modular, readable, and efficient Fortran programs. By encapsulating computational logic within functions, you promote code reuse and maintainability, key principles in software engineering.

4.3 Defining and Calling Subroutines

Subroutines in Fortran serve as a critical component for writing modular, reusable, and organized code. Unlike functions, subroutines do not return a value directly. Instead, they may modify the values of their arguments or carry out procedures like input/output operations. Understanding how to define and call subroutines correctly is essential for efficient Fortran programming. This section details the syntax, principles, and best practices for working with subroutines.

To define a subroutine in Fortran, we use the subroutine keyword followed by the subroutine name and an optional list of arguments. The subroutine definition is encapsulated between the subroutine and end subroutine statements. Each argument in the optional argument list can have attributes defined within the subroutine.

```
subroutine sub_name(arg1, arg2, ...)
```

```
    ! Declarations
    ! Execution statements
end subroutine sub_name
```

Here's an example of a simple subroutine that swaps the values of two integer variables:

```
subroutine swap(x, y)
    integer, intent(inout) :: x, y
    integer :: temp

    temp = x
    x = y
    y = temp
end subroutine swap
```

In this example, the subroutine swap receives two integer arguments x and y. The intent(inout) attribute indicates that these arguments can be modified by the subroutine. The variable temp serves as a temporary storage to facilitate the swapping process.

To call a subroutine, use the call statement followed by the subroutine name and actual arguments, if any.

```
call sub_name(arg1, arg2, ...)
```

Continuing with the previous example, here's how to call the swap subroutine within a program:

```
program test_swap
    integer :: a, b
    a = 5
    b = 10

    print *, 'Before swap: ', a, b
    call swap(a, b)
    print *, 'After swap: ', a, b
end program test_swap
```

Upon executing this program, the output would be:

```
Before swap: 5 10
After swap: 10 5
```

It is evident from the example that the values of a and b are swapped after calling the swap subroutine.

Subroutines can also have local variables, which are defined within the subroutine itself. These variables are distinct from the main program and other subroutines, having their scope limited to the subroutine in which they are declared.

Additionally, Fortran supports passing arguments by reference and by value, though it predominantly uses pass-by-reference. The use of the intent attribute clarifies the intended use of each argument, improving readability and aiding in preventing unintended side effects.

Pass-by-Reference Example:

```
subroutine modify_array(arr, n)
    integer, intent(inout) :: arr(:)
    integer, intent(in) :: n
    integer :: i

    do i = 1, n
        arr(i) = arr(i) * 2
    end do
end subroutine modify_array
```

In this example, the array arr is modified directly within the subroutine as it is passed by reference, and the scalar n is passed by value, ensuring its original value remains unaltered.

Passing Constants and Expressions: Arguments can be constants or expressions, but one must ensure they conform to the subroutine's intent specifications to avoid errors. For instance, passing a constant to an intent(inout) argument would result in a compilation error.

Error checking and handling in subroutines can be performed using conditional statements to ensure robustness and reliability. This approach enables handling of invalid inputs and edge cases gracefully without causing runtime failures.

Best practices for writing subroutines include:

- Use descriptive names for subroutines and arguments for clarity.
- Document subroutines with comments that describe their purpose and usage.
- Minimize the number of arguments to avoid complexity.
- Use intent attributes to specify how each argument is to be used.
- Ensure subroutines perform a single, well-defined task.

By adhering to these principles, Fortran programmers can write subroutines that enhance code readability, reusability, and maintainability, facilitating the development of large and complex applications. The next sections will delve into more advanced features and uses of Fortran subroutines.

4.4 Difference Between Functions and Subroutines

In Fortran, both functions and subroutines are constructs that enable the reuse of code by encapsulating a sequence of instructions into a callable unit. However, they serve different purposes and have distinct characteristics. Understanding these differences is crucial for writing efficient and maintainable code.

Functions are designed to perform specific computations and return a single value. The syntax for defining a function in Fortran includes specifying the return type. For instance:

```
FUNCTION add(a, b)
  INTEGER :: a, b, add
  add = a + b
END FUNCTION add
```

In the example above, the function add takes two integer arguments, sums them, and returns the result. The returned value can be used directly in expressions, making functions ideal for mathematical computations and where a single result is needed.

Subroutines, on the other hand, do not return a value directly. Instead, they perform operations that may modify their arguments or produce side effects. Subroutines are defined using the SUBROUTINE keyword:

```
SUBROUTINE swap(x, y)
  INTEGER :: x, y, temp
  temp = x
  x = y
  y = temp
END SUBROUTINE swap
```

In this example, the subroutine swap exchanges the values of its integer arguments x and y. Since subroutines do not produce return values, their usefulness lies in their ability to operate on multiple variables or perform procedures that do not require returning a single result.

To illustrate the differences more clearly, consider the way functions and subroutines are invoked. Functions are called within expressions and the return value is used for further computation:

```
INTEGER :: result
result = add(3, 5)
PRINT *, result ! Outputs 8
```

Subroutines are invoked as standalone statements, and any changes to the arguments are realized after the subroutine executes:

```
INTEGER :: num1, num2
num1 = 10
num2 = 20
CALL swap(num1, num2)
PRINT *, num1, num2 ! Outputs 20 10
```

An additional consideration is the way arguments are passed to functions and subroutines. By default, Fortran uses call-by-reference, meaning that the subroutine or function operates on the original data. However, call-by-value can be simulated using INTENT attributes or by passing constants or expressions. This distinction is particularly important in subroutines where intention to modify arguments must be explicitly managed.

Functions enforce a strict return type and can only return values of this type. This constraint ensures that functions are predictable in terms of their output. Conversely, subroutines offer greater flexibility since they can modify multiple arguments of different types, making them suitable for tasks involving extensive data manipulation.

To emphasize the practical applications, consider situations where each construct might be preferred. Functions are used when:

- A single resultant value is needed from a computation.
- The result will be used in conditional checks or expressions.
- The operation has a clear input-output relationship.

Subroutines are used when:

- Multiple values need to be processed or modified.
- Operations include significant side effects, such as I/O or state changes.
- Organizing complex procedures that do not fit the single-output constraint of functions.

The choice between functions and subroutines directly influences code readability and maintenance. Using functions for simple computations enhances clarity, as the return value can be directly embedded in expressions. Subroutines, with their capability to handle complex operations, aid in breaking down large tasks into manageable pieces.

When designing Fortran programs, leveraging both functions and subroutines appropriately enables the creation of modular, clean, and efficient code. Balancing the computational precision of functions with the procedural capabilities of subroutines ensures that different aspects of the program are handled by the most suitable construct.

4.5 Passing Arguments: By Value and By Reference

Fortran, like many other programming languages, supports multiple methods for passing arguments to functions and subroutines. Understanding these methods is crucial for writing efficient and predictable code. The two primary mechanisms for passing arguments are by value and by reference.

When arguments are passed by value, the function or subroutine receives a copy of the argument's value. Any modifications made to the argument within the function do not affect the original variable. On the other hand, passing by reference means the function or subroutine receives a reference (or address) to the original variable, so modifications within the procedure affect the original variable.

By default, Fortran uses pass-by-reference for most arguments. This behavior is efficient because it avoids the overhead of copying large amounts of data. However, it requires careful handling to avoid unintended side effects.

```
program main
   implicit none
   integer:: x = 10, y = 20

   print *, 'Before calling subroutine: x =', x, ' y =', y
   call swap(x, y)
   print *, 'After calling subroutine: x =', x, ' y =', y

contains
   subroutine swap(a, b)
      integer, intent(inout):: a, b
      integer:: temp

      temp = a
      a = b
      b = temp
   end subroutine swap
end program main
```

In the swap subroutine, the intent(inout) attribute specifies that the arguments a and b are intended for both input and output; they can be modified within the subroutine. The changes made to a and b directly alter the values of x and y in the calling program.

One potential downside of passing arguments by reference is that it can lead to unintended aliasing, where two different argument names refer to the same memory location. This can cause subtle bugs that are difficult to trace. To mitigate this, Fortran provides the intent attribute to clarify how arguments are used within procedures.

```
subroutine compute_sum(arr, n, sum)
    real, intent(in):: arr(:)
    integer, intent(in):: n
    real, intent(out):: sum
    integer:: i

    sum = 0.0
    do i = 1, n
        sum = sum + arr(i)
    end do
end subroutine compute_sum
```

In this subroutine, arr and n are input arguments (intent(in)), which means they are read-only within the subroutine. The argument sum is an output argument (intent(out)), which guarantees that its value is set by the subroutine. By specifying the intents, the risk of unintended side effects is reduced, and the subroutine's purpose is clearer.

Alternatively, passing by value in Fortran can be achieved using the value attribute, introduced in the Fortran 2003 standard. When an argument is passed by value, the procedure receives its own copy of the argument, and changes to the argument do not affect the original variable in the calling procedure.

```
subroutine increment_value(val), bind(C)
    integer, value:: val
    val = val + 1
end subroutine increment_value
```

In the above example, the value attribute indicates that val should be passed by value. This is particularly useful when interfacing with C code using Fortran's interoperability features (bind(C)). Note that any modification to val within the subroutine does not affect the variable in the calling code.

Understanding the distinction between pass-by-value and pass-by-reference is fundamental for effective programming in Fortran. The choice between these methods impacts performance, safety, and the predictability of code behavior. By employing attributes like intent and value, programmers can write clear, efficient, and maintainable Fortran procedures.

4.6 Return Values in Functions

In Fortran, functions are used to perform tasks and return a value that can be utilized within an expression or assigned to a variable. Understanding how return values work is crucial for writing effective and modular code. This section will cover the definition of return values in Fortran functions, various methods to retrieve these values, and best practices for handling return values.

Functions in Fortran are defined using the FUNCTION keyword, followed by the function name and an optional argument list. The return type of the function is specified before the FUNCTION keyword, or using the RESULT keyword inside the function definition. The function computes a value and then returns it to the calling environment. The general structure of a Fortran function is as follows:

```
type FUNCTION function_name(arguments)
    ! local variable declarations
    type :: result_var
    ! executable statements
    result_var = computed_value
    function_name = result_var
END FUNCTION function_name
```

Where type represents the data type of the function's return value, function_name is the identifier for the function, arguments represents the input parameters, and result_var is an optional variable used to store the value to be returned.

Basic Return Mechanism

Let's consider a simple function that calculates the square of an integer. Below is the function definition and its usage:

```
INTEGER FUNCTION square(x)
    INTEGER :: x
    square = x * x
END FUNCTION square
```

When this function is called, it receives an integer x as an argument, computes the square of x, and returns the result. The function call and usage can be demonstrated as follows:

```
PROGRAM main
    INTEGER :: num, result
```

```
    num = 5
    result = square(num)
    PRINT *, "The square of ", num, " is ", result
END PROGRAM main
```

Executing the program will display:

```
The square of 5 is 25
```

Using the RESULT Clause

Fortran provides a mechanism to specify an explicit name for the result of a function using the RESULT keyword. This can improve code readability and avoid potential naming conflicts. Below is the same square function, rewritten to utilize the RESULT clause:

```
INTEGER FUNCTION square(x) RESULT(res)
    INTEGER :: x
    INTEGER :: res
    res = x * x
END FUNCTION square
```

The main advantage of using the RESULT clause is that it clearly distinguishes the return value from the function name. This approach can be particularly beneficial in more complex functions.

Handling Different Data Types

Fortran functions can return values of various data types, including INTEGER, REAL, COMPLEX, and user-defined types. Each function must declare the return type accordingly. Consider a function that returns the hypotenuse of a right triangle given the lengths of its two legs:

```
REAL FUNCTION hypotenuse(a, b)
    REAL :: a, b
    hypotenuse = SQRT(a*a + b*b)
END FUNCTION hypotenuse
```

Calling this function in a program:

```
PROGRAM main
    REAL :: side1, side2, hyp
    side1 = 3.0
    side2 = 4.0
    hyp = hypotenuse(side1, side2)
    PRINT *, "The hypotenuse is ", hyp
END PROGRAM main
```

The output produced is:

```
The hypotenuse is 5.0
```

Best Practices for Return Values

Adhering to best practices for defining and handling return values in functions ensures that the code remains clean, maintainable, and free of bugs. Some guidelines to follow include:

- Always specify the type for the result variable to avoid any ambiguity.
- Use the RESULT clause for clarity, especially in functions with multiple statements.
- Ensure that the function returns a value for all possible execution paths to avoid undefined behavior.
- Write comprehensive test cases to verify that the function returns correct values for a range of input scenarios.

Correctly implementing and handling return values in Fortran functions enhances code modularity and reusability, which are key aspects of efficient programming.

4.7 Recursion in Functions and Subroutines

Recursion is a powerful concept in programming, where a function or subroutine calls itself to solve a problem. In Fortran, recursion can be implemented for both functions and subroutines, allowing complex problems to be broken down into simpler, more manageable tasks. This process typically involves a base case, which terminates the recursive calls, and a recursive case, which breaks down the problem and leads to the base case.

To enable recursion in Fortran, one must use the RECURSIVE keyword in the function or subroutine declaration. Let's discuss the application of recursion through examples.

Example: Factorial Calculation Using a Recursive Function

The factorial of a non-negative integer n is the product of all positive integers less than or equal to n. The factorial function, denoted as $n!$, can be defined recursively as:

$$n! = \begin{cases} 1 & \text{if } n = 0 \\ n \cdot (n-1)! & \text{if } n > 0 \end{cases}$$

Here is the Fortran implementation of the factorial function using recursion:

```
RECURSIVE FUNCTION factorial(n) RESULT(res)
  IMPLICIT NONE
  INTEGER, INTENT(IN) :: n
  INTEGER :: res

  IF (n == 0) THEN
    res = 1
  ELSE
    res = n * factorial(n - 1)
  END IF
END FUNCTION factorial
```

To call this function, you can write:

```
PROGRAM test_factorial
  IMPLICIT NONE
  INTEGER :: result

  result = factorial(5)
  PRINT *, 'Factorial of 5 is: ', result
END PROGRAM test_factorial
```

The output of the program should be:

```
Factorial of 5 is:        120
```

Example: Fibonacci Series Using a Recursive Function

The Fibonacci sequence is another classical example where recursion is commonly applied. The sequence is defined as:

$$F(n) = \begin{cases} 0 & \text{if } n = 0 \\ 1 & \text{if } n = 1 \\ F(n-1) + F(n-2) & \text{if } n > 1 \end{cases}$$

The recursive function in Fortran for calculating the n-th Fibonacci number is:

```
RECURSIVE FUNCTION fibonacci(n) RESULT(res)
  IMPLICIT NONE
  INTEGER, INTENT(IN) :: n
  INTEGER :: res

  IF (n == 0) THEN
    res = 0
  ELSE IF (n == 1) THEN
    res = 1
  ELSE
    res = fibonacci(n - 1) + fibonacci(n - 2)
  END IF
END FUNCTION fibonacci
```

To call this function, you can write:

```
PROGRAM test_fibonacci
  IMPLICIT NONE
  INTEGER :: result

  result = fibonacci(10)
  PRINT *, 'The 10th Fibonacci number is: ', result
END PROGRAM test_fibonacci
```

The output of the program should be:

```
The 10th Fibonacci number is:          55
```

Recursive Subroutines

While recursion is often implemented in functions, it can also be applied in subroutines. Subroutines differ from functions primarily in that they do not return a value directly but instead modify their arguments or change program state.

Consider a recursive subroutine that prints numbers from n down to 1:

```
RECURSIVE SUBROUTINE print_numbers(n)
  IMPLICIT NONE
  INTEGER, INTENT(IN) :: n

  IF (n > 0) THEN
    PRINT *, n
    CALL print_numbers(n - 1)
  END IF
END SUBROUTINE print_numbers
```

To call this subroutine, you can write:

```
PROGRAM test_print_numbers
  IMPLICIT NONE

  CALL print_numbers(5)
END PROGRAM test_print_numbers
```

The output of the program should be:

```
          5
          4
          3
          2
          1
```

Considerations for Using Recursion

While recursion can simplify the implementation of certain algorithms, it is important to consider its limitations and potential drawbacks:

- **Performance Overhead:** Recursive calls can introduce additional overhead due to repeated function calls and memory usage for maintaining call stacks. In performance-critical applications, an iterative solution may be more efficient.

- **Stack Overflow:** Deep recursion can lead to stack overflow if the base case is not reachable within a reasonable number of recursive calls. Ensure that base cases are well-defined to avoid infinite recursion.
- **Readability and Maintainability:** While recursion can make code more readable for certain problems, excessive use of recursion may reduce code clarity. It's vital to strike a balance between simplicity and comprehensibility.

Understanding and applying recursion in Fortran enables the development of elegant solutions for problems traditionally suited for recursive approaches. Properly implemented, recursion can be a powerful tool in a programmer's arsenal.

4.8 Internal Procedures

Internal procedures in Fortran are nested procedures that reside within the scope of another program unit, typically a program, function, or subroutine. These procedures enhance modular design and structure, offering encapsulation and scoping advantages. The defining characteristic of internal procedures is their operational dependency on the host program unit's environment, able to access its variables and parameters directly.

Internal procedures are declared with the contains statement, indicating the beginning of the internal procedure section. When using internal procedures, the host unit contains a main block, followed by the contains keyword, followed by the internal procedure definitions.

For illustration, consider a scenario where an internal procedure is used within a program unit.

```
program main
    implicit none
    integer :: n

    ! Assign a value to n
    n = 10

    ! Call the internal procedure
    call square_root(n)
```

```
contains

    subroutine square_root(num)
        integer, intent(in) :: num
        real :: result
        result = sqrt(real(num))
        print*, 'The square root of ', num, ' is ', result
    end subroutine square_root

end program main
```

Here, square_root is an internal subroutine within the main program. Note how square_root can directly access the variable n, taking it as an argument and computing its square root. The contains keyword demarcates the start of the internal procedure section.

Scope and Accessibility

Internal procedures exhibit unique scoping rules. Variables and parameters declared in the host program unit can be accessed by the internal procedure unless they possess the private attribute. Conversely, any variables declared within the internal procedure are local to that procedure and do not interfere with those in the host.

```
program scope_example
    implicit none
    integer :: value
    value = 5

    call inner_procedure()

    print*, 'Value in main program: ', value

contains

    subroutine inner_procedure()
        integer :: value
        value = 10
        print*, 'Value in subroutine: ', value
    end subroutine inner_procedure

end program scope_example
```

Output:

```
Value in subroutine:          10
Value in main program:          5
```

In this example, the value variable in the subroutine inner_procedure is local and shadows the value variable in the main program. Changes within inner_procedure do not affect the value variable in the main program.

Use in Functions

Internal procedures can also be used within functions, facilitating intricate calculations and operations encapsulated within a single function. Consider the following function example:

```
function compute_area(radius) result(area)
    implicit none
    real, intent(in) :: radius
    real :: area

    ! Ensure the radius is positive
    call verify_positive(radius)

    area = pi() * radius**2
contains

    subroutine verify_positive(r)
        real, intent(in) :: r
        if (r <= 0) then
            print*, 'Error: Radius must be positive.'
            stop
        end if
    end subroutine verify_positive

    real function pi()
        pi = 3.141592653589793
    end function pi

end function compute_area
```

In this case, both the verify_positive subroutine and the pi function are internal procedures within the compute_area function. They assist compute_area by verifying input and providing a mathematical constant, respectively.

Advantages and Best Practices

Internal procedures offer several compelling advantages:

- **Encapsulation:** They keep related procedures close to their point of use, improving readability and maintainability.
- **Locality:** Local treatment and modification of variables within the host unit make the code more structured.
- **Reusability within Scope:** Procedures can be reused within the same host unit without polluting the global namespace.

When employing internal procedures, consider the following best practices:

- Use descriptive names for both host units and internal procedures to ensure code clarity.

- Document the purpose and expected behavior of internal procedures thoroughly.
- Minimize dependencies by limiting the scope of variables used within internal procedures.

Through mindful application of internal procedures, Fortran programmers can write more organized, readable, and maintainable code, facilitating error reduction and code reusability in the host program context.

4.9 Modules and Contain Blocks

Modules and CONTAINS blocks are powerful features in Fortran that facilitate the organization and reuse of code. They allow for the encapsulation of related procedures and data definitions, which improves the maintainability and readability of the code.

Modules are collection units used to group related procedures and data. They help in encapsulating data and procedures, provide namespaces to avoid name conflicts, and enable the sharing of data among different program units. Here's a basic structure of a Fortran module:

```
MODULE module_name
  ! Module declarations
CONTAINS
  ! Module procedures
END MODULE module_name
```

In this structure, the MODULE statement begins the module definition and END MODULE concludes it. Between these statements, declarations for variables, constants, and other entities are placed, while the CONTAINS keyword indicates the start of the contained procedures.

CONTAINS **Blocks** are sections within program units like modules or main programs that allow the definition of internal procedures. These procedures are local to the module or program and cannot be accessed directly from outside. Below is an example illustrating the use of a CONTAINS block within a module.

```
MODULE MathOperations
  IMPLICIT NONE
  REAL :: PI = 3.141592653589793
CONTAINS
  REAL FUNCTION CircleArea(radius)
    REAL, INTENT(IN) :: radius
    CircleArea = PI * radius * radius
  END FUNCTION CircleArea
```

```
  REAL FUNCTION CircleCircumference(radius)
    REAL, INTENT(IN) :: radius
    CircleCircumference = 2 * PI * radius
  END FUNCTION CircleCircumference
END MODULE MathOperations
```

Here, the MathOperations module contains the declaration of the constant PI and two internal functions: CircleArea and CircleCircumference. The CONTAINS block encapsulates these functions, making them part of the module.

To use a module in another program or module, the USE statement is employed. This statement imports all public entities from a module into the scope of the program unit.

```
PROGRAM TestMathOperations
  USE MathOperations
  IMPLICIT NONE
  REAL :: radius, area, circumference

  radius = 5.0
  area = CircleArea(radius)
  circumference = CircleCircumference(radius)

  PRINT *, 'Radius:', radius
  PRINT *, 'Area:', area
  PRINT *, 'Circumference:', circumference
END PROGRAM TestMathOperations
```

In this example, the TestMathOperations program utilizes the MathOperations module. The USE statement imports the module's public entities, allowing the program to call the CircleArea and CircleCircumference functions.

Modules enhance code maintainability by centralizing the definition of procedures and data. They also facilitate the management of large Fortran programs by reducing code duplication and providing a clear structure. Moreover, they promote information hiding, which is crucial for the encapsulation principle in modular programming. By restricting the access to certain data or procedures, modules prevent unintended interference and misuse of internal components, thus ensuring the integrity of the program.

In the next example, a more complex module structure is shown, including the definition of private and public entities:

```
MODULE AdvancedMath
  IMPLICIT NONE
  PRIVATE
  PUBLIC :: CubeVolume, SphereVolume
```

```
  REAL, PARAMETER :: PI = 3.141592653589793
CONTAINS
  REAL FUNCTION CubeVolume(side)
    REAL, INTENT(IN) :: side
    CubeVolume = side**3
  END FUNCTION CubeVolume

  REAL FUNCTION SphereVolume(radius)
    REAL, INTENT(IN) :: radius
    SphereVolume = (4.0/3.0) * PI * radius**3
  END FUNCTION SphereVolume

  REAL FUNCTION CylinderVolume(radius, height)
    REAL, INTENT(IN) :: radius, height
    CylinderVolume = PI * radius**2 * height
  END FUNCTION CylinderVolume
END MODULE AdvancedMath
```

In this module, CubeVolume and SphereVolume functions are declared as public, allowing other program units to access them. Conversely, the CylinderVolume function is private and thus cannot be accessed from outside the module. This example illustrates how modules control the scope and access of contained entities, reinforcing encapsulation.

Lastly, it is important to highlight that when changes are made to a module's internal implementation, programs that use the module do not need to be altered unless the interface (e.g., the arguments list of public functions) changes. This feature reduces the effort required to maintain and update Fortran programs.

4.10 Intrinsic Functions and Subroutines

Intrinsic functions and subroutines are built-in capabilities provided by Fortran, enabling the programmer to perform common operations without the need to write these procedures from scratch. These intrinsically available functions and subroutines enhance productivity and ensure optimized performance for frequently used operations.

Intrinsic functions in Fortran span a wide range of operations, including arithmetic, mathematical, numeric, character manipulation, type conversion, and more. The intrinsic subroutines typically perform standard tasks that might be related to I/O operations and system-specific functionalities.

To effectively use intrinsic functions and subroutines, it is essential to be familiar with their syntax, properties, and limitations. This section will cover key intrinsic functions and subroutines, demonstrating their usage with examples.

Arithmetic and Mathematical Functions: Fortran provides a variety of intrinsic functions to perform arithmetic and mathematical operations. Commonly used functions include:

- real, dim, mod, abs, exp, log, sqrt, and trigonomteric functions such as sin, cos, tan, asin, acos, atan.

```
program math_intrinsics
  implicit none
  real :: x, result

  x = 16.0

  ! Square root
  result = sqrt(x) ! result is 4.0

  ! Natural logarithm
  result = log(x) ! result is approximately 2.7726

  ! Exponential function
  result = exp(1.0) ! result is approximately 2.7183

  ! Trigonometric functions
  result = sin(x) ! result of sin(16.0 radians)
  result = cos(x) ! result of cos(16.0 radians)

  print*, "Square root of ", x, " is ", sqrt(x)
  print*, "Natural log of ", x, " is ", log(x)
  print*, "Exponential of 1 is ", exp(1.0)
  print*, "Sine of ", x, " is ", sin(x)
  print*, "Cosine of ", x, " is ", cos(x)

end program math_intrinsics
```

In the example, intrinsic functions like sqrt, log, exp, sin, and cos are used to perform square root, natural logarithm, exponential, sine, and cosine operations respectively. The usage of these built-in functions simplifies numerical computations.

Character Manipulation Functions: Manipulating strings and characters is a common requirement in many programs. Fortran provides several intrinsic functions to process character data, such as len, trim, index, achar, and iachar.

```
program char_intrinsics
  implicit none
  character(20) :: str1, str2
  integer :: length, position

  str1 = "Hello, Fortran! "
  str2 = "Fortran"

  ! Length of string
```

```
  length = len(str1) ! length is 16

  ! Trim spaces
  print*, "Trimmed string is ->", trim(str1), "<-"

  ! Finding substring
  position = index(str1, str2) ! position is 8

  print*, "Length of string '", str1, "' is ", length
  print*, "Position of 'Fortran' in '", str1, "' is ", position

end program char_intrinsics
```

This illustration shows the utilization of len, trim, and index. The len function returns the length of the string including trailing spaces, trim removes trailing spaces, and index finds the starting index of a substring within a string.

Type Conversion Functions: Conversion between data types is often necessary in procedures. Fortran includes intrinsic functions such as int, real, nint, ceiling, and floor to facilitate this.

```
program type_conversion
  implicit none
  real :: x
  integer :: y
  x = 3.7

  ! Converting to integer
  y = int(x) ! y is 3

  ! Nearest integer
  y = nint(x) ! y is 4

  ! Ceiling and floor functions
  y = ceiling(x) ! y is 4
  y = floor(x) ! y is 3

  print*, "int(", x, ") = ", int(x)
  print*, "nint(", x, ") = ", nint(x)
  print*, "ceiling(", x, ") = ", ceiling(x)
  print*, "floor(", x, ") = ", floor(x)

end program type_conversion
```

Here, the int function casts the real number to an integer by truncating it, nint rounds to the nearest integer, while ceiling and floor compute the smallest integer greater than or equal to, and the largest integer less than or equal to the given number, respectively.

System and I/O Intrinsic Subroutines: Intrinsic subroutines perform operations such as array copying, memory allocation, and I/O operations. Commonly used ones include random_seed, random_number, date_and_time, and system_clock.

```
program io_intrinsics
  implicit none
  real :: rand_num
  integer :: hours, minutes, seconds, clock

  ! Initialize random seed
  call random_seed()

  ! Generate random number
  call random_number(rand_num)

  print*, "Generated random number: ", rand_num

  ! Get date and time
  call date_and_time(values=(/hours, minutes, seconds/))

  print*, "Current time: ", hours, ":", minutes, ":", seconds

  ! Get system clock
  call system_clock(count=clock)

  print*, "System clock count: ", clock

end program io_intrinsics
```

In this example, random_seed initializes the random number generator, and random_number produces a random number. The date_and_time subroutine retrieves the current time, and system_clock provides the system clock counter value.

To sum up, intrinsic functions and subroutines in Fortran are indispensable for efficient and precise programming. They eliminate the need for custom implementations for common operations, ensuring code is both optimized and easier to read.

4.11 Best Practices for Writing Functions and Subroutines

When writing functions and subroutines in Fortran, adhering to best practices can significantly enhance code readability, maintainability, and performance. This section outlines several key practices that facilitate the development of effective and reliable Fortran programs.

1. Clear and Descriptive Naming Conventions: Functions and subroutines should have clear, descriptive names that convey their purpose. The name should reflect the action performed or the result produced. For example, CalculateAverage is preferable to CalcAvg.

2. Use Explicit Interfaces: Always use explicit interfaces to ensure that the compiler can check the argument types and the return type against what the function or subroutine expects. This minimizes risks of type mismatches and enhances code reliability. Explicit interfaces can be provided by using modules or interface blocks.

```
module MathOperations
  implicit none
  contains
    real function CalculateAverage(values)
      real, intent(in) :: values(:)
      CalculateAverage = sum(values) / size(values)
    end function CalculateAverage
end module MathOperations
```

3. Specify Intent of Arguments: Use the intent attribute to specify whether arguments are in, out, or inout. This not only documents how the arguments are used but also allows the compiler to enforce proper usage.

```
subroutine UpdateArray(arr, multiplier)
  real, intent(inout) :: arr(:)
  real, intent(in) :: multiplier
  arr = arr * multiplier
end subroutine UpdateArray
```

4. Limit the Use of Global Variables: Minimize the use of global variables in your functions and subroutines. Global variables can lead to unintended side effects, making the program harder to debug. Prefer passing variables as arguments where possible.

5. Modularity: Functions and subroutines should perform a single task or a closely related group of tasks. Avoid writing large, monolithic functions/subroutines. Instead, break them down into smaller, well-defined units of work.

6. Use Proper Documentation: Commenting the purpose, input, output, and side effects of your functions and subroutines is crucial. Proper documentation helps other developers (and your future self) understand the code. Include a header comment block explaining the function's/subroutine's behavior.

```
!> @brief Calculates the factorial of a number.
!! @param n - The number for which the factorial is calculated
!! @return fact - The factorial of the number
integer function Factorial(n)
  integer, intent(in) :: n
  integer :: i
  fact = 1
  do i = 1, n
    fact = fact * i
  end do
end function Factorial
```

7. Consistency in Coding Style: Maintain a consistent coding style, such as indentation, naming conventions, and alignment of code. Consistency improves readability and maintainability. For example, always indent code within if statements and loops.

8. Error Handling: Implement proper error handling to manage exceptional situations gracefully, such as invalid input arguments. This can be done using error codes or specific handling routines to report issues without crashing the program.

```
subroutine SafeDivide(a, b, result, status)
  real, intent(in) :: a, b
  real, intent(out) :: result
  integer, intent(out) :: status
  if (b == 0.0) then
    status = -1
    result = 0.0
  else
    status = 0
    result = a / b
  end if
end subroutine SafeDivide
```

9. Performance Considerations: Be aware of the performance impact of your functions and subroutines. Optimize critical sections of code, use efficient algorithms, and minimize redundant computations. Use built-in functions when possible, as they are usually optimized.

10. Testing and Debugging: Write test cases to validate the functionality of your functions and subroutines. Utilize debugging tools and practices to identify and resolve issues early in the development process. Good testing ensures that the code behaves as expected under various conditions.

In summary, adhering to these best practices when writing functions and subroutines in Fortran will lead to more readable, maintainable, and efficient code. By focusing on clear naming, explicit interfaces, proper argument specification, modularity, documentation, consistency, error handling, performance, and thorough testing, developers can create robust and reliable programs.

4.12 Debugging Functions and Subroutines

Debugging is an essential aspect of developing robust and efficient Fortran programs, particularly when working with functions and subroutines. Understanding various debugging strategies and tools can significantly enhance the process of identifying and resolving issues within your code. In this section, we will explore techniques for debugging functions and subroutines and best practices to minimize and resolve errors effectively.

1. Using 'print' Statements

A straightforward method for debugging functions and subroutines is to insert 'print' statements at critical points within the code. This technique allows developers to monitor the values of variables and the flow of execution:

```
PROGRAM DebugExample
  IMPLICIT NONE

  INTEGER :: a
  a = 5
  CALL DebugSub(a)

END PROGRAM DebugExample

SUBROUTINE DebugSub(x)
  IMPLICIT NONE
  INTEGER, INTENT(IN) :: x

  PRINT *, 'Debug: Value of x is ', x

END SUBROUTINE DebugSub
```

Executing the above program would produce the output:

```
Debug: Value of x is 5
```

2. Compiler Flags

Modern Fortran compilers provide several flags to aid in debugging. Common flags include -g, which includes debugging information, and -fcheck=all (for gfortran), which enables runtime checks for various kinds of errors:

```
gfortran -g -fcheck=all debug_example.f90 -o debug_example
```

Compiling with these flags can help catch errors such as array bounds violations, uninitialized variables, or incorrect argument types.

3. Debugging Tools

Leveraging debugging tools such as the GNU Debugger (GDB) can be highly beneficial. GDB allows developers to step through code, set breakpoints, and inspect variable values:

```
gdb ./debug_example
(gdb) break DebugSub
(gdb) run
(gdb) print x
```

Using these commands, the program execution halts at the beginning of DebugSub, enabling you to inspect the value of x.

4. Tracking Variable Changes

Tracking the changes in variables over time is another critical debugging strategy. Consider the following example illustrating how to monitor variable changes within a function:

```
PROGRAM TrackVariableChanges
  IMPLICIT NONE

  INTEGER :: a, result
  a = 10
  result = ComputeSquare(a)
  PRINT *, 'Result is', result

END PROGRAM TrackVariableChanges

FUNCTION ComputeSquare(n) RESULT(square)
  IMPLICIT NONE
  INTEGER, INTENT(IN) :: n
  INTEGER :: square

  PRINT *, 'Debug: n=', n
  square = n * n
  PRINT *, 'Debug: square=', square

END FUNCTION ComputeSquare
```

Running this program will output debug messages that provide insights into the intermediate values:

```
Debug: n= 10
Debug: square= 100
Result is 100
```

5. Analyzing Stack Traces

When programs crash, understanding the stack trace can be pivotal. Stack traces point to the exact locations where issues occur, highlighting the call sequence that led to the error. Fortran's integration with GDB or other debuggers can help you extract valuable stack trace information.

6. Assertions

Employing assertions within functions and subroutines can act as sanity checks to ensure that program invariants hold as expected. Assertions can be implemented using the Fortran 2003 error stop feature:

```
PROGRAM AssertionExample
```

```
  IMPLICIT NONE

  INTEGER :: b
  b = -5
  CALL CheckPositive(b)

END PROGRAM AssertionExample

SUBROUTINE CheckPositive(y)
  IMPLICIT NONE
  INTEGER, INTENT(IN) :: y

  IF (y < 0) THEN
    PRINT *, 'Assertion failed: y should be non-negative'
    ERROR STOP
  END IF

END SUBROUTINE CheckPositive
```

Executing this program would terminate with an assertion message if y is negative.

7. Logging

For more extensive programs, integrating logging mechanisms allows for more structured and informative debug information. A logging framework can be created to log different levels of messages (e.g., INFO, WARN, ERROR):

```
PROGRAM LoggingExample
  IMPLICIT NONE
  CALL LogMessage('INFO', 'Program started')
  CALL PerformCalculation(7)

END PROGRAM LoggingExample

SUBROUTINE LogMessage(level, message)
  IMPLICIT NONE
  CHARACTER(LEN=*), INTENT(IN) :: level
  CHARACTER(LEN=*), INTENT(IN) :: message

  PRINT *, '[', level, ']', message

END SUBROUTINE LogMessage

SUBROUTINE PerformCalculation(n)
  IMPLICIT NONE
  INTEGER, INTENT(IN) :: n

  CALL LogMessage('INFO', 'Performing calculation')
  PRINT *, 'Result = ', n*n

END SUBROUTINE PerformCalculation
```

This structured approach provides clear insights into program behavior, making it easier to locate and fix issues.

Implementing effective debugging techniques within functions and subroutines enables developers to write reliable and maintainable Fortran code, significantly reducing the incidence of errors.

Chapter 5

Arrays and Array Operations

This chapter is dedicated to the use of arrays in Fortran, a crucial feature for scientific and numerical computing. Readers will learn how to declare, initialize, and access array elements, as well as perform common array operations such as addition, subtraction, multiplication, and division. The chapter covers single and multi-dimensional arrays, dynamic allocation, array slicing, and subarrays. Additionally, it discusses the use of array intrinsic functions, passing arrays to functions and subroutines, and common errors and debugging techniques, providing a solid foundation for efficient array manipulation in Fortran.

5.1 Introduction to Arrays in Fortran

Arrays are fundamental structures in Fortran, particularly suited for scientific and numerical computations. They enable the storage and manipulation of collections of data, organized in a structured manner. Understanding and effectively utilizing arrays in Fortran is essential for developing efficient, high-performance computational programs.

In Fortran, arrays are multi-dimensional, homogeneous data structures, meaning they consist of elements of the same data type organized in one or more dimensions. This allows for the representation of complex data models, such as matrices, tensors, and tabular data.

To effectively introduce arrays in Fortran, it is crucial to cover several key concepts and conventions. These include array declaration, initialization, and the rules governing array indexing and bounds. Analyzing these aspects will provide a strong foundation for more advanced topics such as array operations and dynamic allocation.

Array Declaration

Arrays in Fortran can be declared using the DIMENSION attribute or directly in the type declaration. The syntax for array declaration includes specifying the type of elements and the extents (sizes) of each dimension.

To declare a one-dimensional array of integers with 10 elements:

```
INTEGER, DIMENSION(10) :: array1d
```

Alternatively, the following syntax is also valid:

```
INTEGER :: array1d(10)
```

For multi-dimensional arrays, the extents of all dimensions must be specified. For example, to declare a two-dimensional array (matrix) of real numbers with 3 rows and 4 columns:

```
REAL :: matrix(3, 4)
```

It is crucial to observe that the dimensions are specified by the extents, indicating the number of elements along each dimension.

Array Initialization

Arrays in Fortran can be initialized at the time of declaration or during execution. Initialization at declaration time uses array constructors or implied DO loops.

To initialize a single-dimensional array with increasing integer values:

```
INTEGER, DIMENSION(5) :: array1d = (/ 1, 2, 3, 4, 5 /)
```

For initializing a two-dimensional array, explicit nestings of /, DO loops, or constructors can be used. For example:

```
REAL :: matrix(2, 2) = RESHAPE((/ 1.0, 2.0, 3.0, 4.0 /), (/ 2, 2 /))
```

The RESHAPE function is particularly useful for converting a one-dimensional array constructor into a multi-dimensional array of desired dimensions.

Array Indexing and Bounds

Fortran arrays are traditionally 1-based indexed, meaning the lower bound of an array index is 1 by default. This is a distinctive feature, contrasting with languages like C or Python which are 0-based indexed.

Accessing elements requires specifying their indices within the declared bounds. For a one-dimensional array:

```
array1d(3) = 10
```

The above assigns the value 10 to the third element of array1d.

In a two-dimensional array, both row and column indices must be provided:

```
matrix(2, 1) = 5.0
```

This sets the element in the second row and first column of matrix to 5.0.

It is important to note the handling of out-of-bounds errors. Attempting to access elements outside the declared extents results in runtime errors, necessitating careful attention to index bounds during array operations.

Array Attributes

Arrays in Fortran can have several attributes, such as ALLOCATABLE, POINTER, and TARGET. These attributes enable dynamic memory management and more sophisticated data structures.

An ALLOCATABLE array allows dynamic allocation and deallocation:

```
INTEGER, ALLOCATABLE :: dynamic_array(:)
```

Before usage, ALLOCATE and DEALLOCATE statements manage the memory:

```
ALLOCATE(dynamic_array(10))
! Use dynamic_array
DEALLOCATE(dynamic_array)
```

Pointers in Fortran provide a mechanism for referencing array elements indirectly:

```
INTEGER, POINTER :: ptr(:)
INTEGER, TARGET :: target_array(10)
ptr => target_array
```

The TARGET attribute permits the creation of variables that pointers can reference, a key aspect of dynamic data structures.

Accurately managing array memory using these attributes is central to efficient and reliable Fortran programming, ensuring optimal resource utilization and program stability.

5.2 Declaring and Initializing Arrays

In Fortran, declaring and initializing arrays is fundamental to effective array manipulations in scientific and numerical computing. Understanding the syntax and structure for arrays enables developers to harness the power of Fortran for extensive data handling.

Fortran arrays are used to store multiple values of the same type, which can be accessed via indices. The flexibility to handle single and multi-dimensional arrays caters to a wide range of computational requirements.

Array declaration begins with specifying the type and dimensions of the array. The DIMENSION attribute or the double colons (::) can be used for this purpose. Here are the syntactic details for declaring arrays in Fortran.

```
REAL, DIMENSION(10) :: array1
INTEGER :: array2(5)
COMPLEX, DIMENSION(2, 3) :: array3
```

In the above example: - array1 is a single-dimensional array containing 10 elements of type REAL. - array2 is a single-dimensional array of 5 INTEGER elements. - array3 is a two-dimensional array with dimensions 2x3, storing COMPLEX numbers.

Initializing arrays at the point of declaration can simplify the process of setting initial values. Fortran allows initialization using the data statement, array constructors, or directly in the declaration.

Initialization Using Data Statements The DATA statement can be used to initialize arrays. This method explicitly lists the values of the

array elements.

```
DATA array1 /1.0, 2.0, 3.0, 4.0, 5.0, 6.0, 7.0, 8.0, 9.0, 10.0/
DATA array2 /1, 2, 3, 4, 5/
```

This statement initializes array1 with ten real numbers, and array2 with five integers.

Initialization in Declaration

Fortran 90 and later versions allow array initialization directly within the declaration, using the = sign.

```
REAL, DIMENSION(10) :: array1 = (/1.0, 2.0, 3.0, 4.0, 5.0, 6.0, 7.0, 8.0, 9.0, 10.0/)
INTEGER, DIMENSION(5) :: array2 = (/1, 2, 3, 4, 5/)
```

This form provides a more concise way to initialize arrays, directly associating the array declaration with its initial values.

Array Constructors

Fortran provides robust mechanisms for array construction via array constructors. These constructors initiate arrays within a (/ ... /) structure.

```
INTEGER, DIMENSION(5) :: array2
array2 = (/1, 2, 3, 4, 5/)
```

Arrays constructed this way can be particularly useful in assignment statements or where arrays might need to be re-initialized throughout the code.

Examples of Multi-dimensional Array Initialization For multi-dimensional arrays, initialization follows a row-wise storage pattern. The initialization values are spread out across rows and columns in the sequence they are provided.

```
COMPLEX, DIMENSION(2, 3) :: array3
array3 = (/ (1.0,1.0), (2.0,2.0), (3.0,3.0), (4.0,4.0), (5.0,5.0), (6.0,6.0) /)
```

In this example, array3 will have the following structure:

```
(1.0,1.0) (2.0,2.0) (3.0,3.0)
(4.0,4.0) (5.0,5.0) (6.0,6.0)
```

Initialization Loops

Fortran also allows arrays to be initialized or updated within loops, offering programmatic control over array element values.

```
INTEGER :: i
REAL, DIMENSION(10) :: array1
```

```
DO i = 1, 10
   array1(i) = i * 1.1
END DO
```

This loop initializes each element of array1 to i * 1.1, where i varies from 1 to 10.

Implicit Initialization

While the explicit initialization techniques are generally preferred for clarity and control, Fortran also supports implicit initialization using default values. By initializing arrays with a single value, each element in the array is set to that value.

```
REAL, DIMENSION(10) :: array1 = 0.0
```

Every element in array1 gets the value 0.0. This can be especially useful for initializing arrays that need to be reset to a common baseline before a computation.

Understanding these techniques is crucial for efficient and error-free array manipulations in Fortran, directly affecting the performance and readability of the code. Each method serves different purposes and scenarios in array handling, offering a range of options to suit the needs of different computational tasks.

5.3 Accessing Array Elements

In Fortran, accessing elements within an array is a straightforward yet crucial operation, allowing for versatile manipulation and computational processes. An array reference specifies a particular element by providing its position within the array. This position is determined by subscripts or indices, each associated with one dimension of the array.

To access an array element, we use the variable name representing the array, followed by the subscript(s) enclosed in parentheses. For example, given a one-dimensional array, A, its first element is accessed as A(1). The specific index values needed for referencing follow the sequence and range defined at the time of the array's declaration.

```
PROGRAM AccessArrayElements
  IMPLICIT NONE
  INTEGER :: A(5)
  INTEGER :: i

  ! Initializing the array
  DO i = 1, 5
```

```
    A(i) = i * 10
  END DO

  ! Accessing and printing the elements
  DO i = 1, 5
    PRINT*, "Element ", i, " of array A: ", A(i)
  END DO

END PROGRAM AccessArrayElements
```

```
Element 1 of array A: 10
Element 2 of array A: 20
Element 3 of array A: 30
Element 4 of array A: 40
Element 5 of array A: 50
```

For multidimensional arrays, each dimension needs a corresponding index. Suppose we have a two-dimensional array B, declared as INTEGER :: B(3,4). The element in the first row and second column is accessed with B(1,2).

```
PROGRAM MultiDimensionalAccess
  IMPLICIT NONE
  INTEGER :: B(3,4)
  INTEGER :: i, j

  ! Initializing the array
  DO i = 1, 3
    DO j = 1, 4
      B(i,j) = i * j
    END DO
  END DO

  ! Accessing and printing the elements
  DO i = 1, 3
    DO j = 1, 4
      PRINT*, "Element (", i, ",", j, ") of array B: ", B(i,j)
    END DO
  END DO

END PROGRAM MultiDimensionalAccess
```

```
Element ( 1 , 1 ) of array B: 1
Element ( 1 , 2 ) of array B: 2
Element ( 1 , 3 ) of array B: 3
Element ( 1 , 4 ) of array B: 4
Element ( 2 , 1 ) of array B: 2
Element ( 2 , 2 ) of array B: 4
Element ( 2 , 3 ) of array B: 6
Element ( 2 , 4 ) of array B: 8
Element ( 3 , 1 ) of array B: 3
Element ( 3 , 2 ) of array B: 6
Element ( 3 , 3 ) of array B: 9
Element ( 3 , 4 ) of array B: 12
```

Fortran array indices usually start from 1 by default, but this can be changed by declaring the array with specific bounds. For example, if an array C is declared with bounds -2:2, the indices range from -2 to 2.

```
PROGRAM CustomBounds
  IMPLICIT NONE
  INTEGER :: C(-2:2)
  INTEGER :: i

  ! Initializing the array
  DO i = -2, 2
     C(i) = i * 10
  END DO

  ! Accessing and printing the elements
  DO i = -2, 2
     PRINT*, "Element ", i, " of array C: ", C(i)
  END DO

END PROGRAM CustomBounds
```

```
Element -2 of array C: -20
Element -1 of array C: -10
Element  0 of array C:   0
Element  1 of array C:  10
Element  2 of array C:  20
```

Array boundaries are essential to check while accessing elements to avoid out-of-bound errors, which lead to unpredictable behavior or system crashes. Fortran compilers can often catch such errors during array-bound checking in debug modes.

```
PROGRAM CheckBounds
  IMPLICIT NONE
  INTEGER :: D(4)

  ! Initialize array
  D = (/1, 2, 3, 4/)

  PRINT*, "Attempting to access an out-of-bounds element:"
  PRINT*, D(6) ! This will cause a runtime error

END PROGRAM CheckBounds
```

Ensuring array indices remain within defined ranges during array operations reduces the potential for such runtime errors. Fortran provides intrinsic functions like LBOUND and UBOUND to determine the lower and upper bounds of an array, aiding programmers in writing safer and more reliable code.

```
PROGRAM BoundsCheck
  IMPLICIT NONE
  INTEGER :: E(3)
  INTEGER :: lower, upper

  ! Initialize array
  E = (/5, 10, 15/)

  ! Get the array bounds
  lower = LBOUND(E, 1)
  upper = UBOUND(E, 1)
```

```
PRINT*, "Array E bounds: LBOUND =", lower, ", UBOUND =", upper
END PROGRAM BoundsCheck
```

```
Array E bounds: LBOUND = 1 , UBOUND = 3
```

Understanding these concepts enables effective utilization of arrays, leading towards proficient management of more complex data structures and algorithms.

5.4 Array Bounds and Dimensions

In Fortran, understanding array bounds and dimensions is imperative for efficient memory management and optimizing computational performance. This section will elucidate the mechanisms of defining both the lower and upper bounds of arrays, as well as establishing their dimensional characteristics.

Fortran arrays can have more flexible bounds compared to many other programming languages. The syntax for declaring the bounds and dimensions of arrays is straightforward. When declaring arrays, the bounds are specified in the dimension attribute.

Correctly setting the array bounds ensures that all elements are properly indexed and that the array occupies the designated memory space. Fortran arrays can range from zero-based to any user-defined bounds, enabling precise control over array indexing.

To declare a one-dimensional array with specific bounds in Fortran, consider the general form:

```
REAL, DIMENSION(LB:UB) :: array_name
```

Where LB is the lower bound and UB is the upper bound. For example:

```
REAL, DIMENSION(1:10) :: a
```

This declaration sets up an array a with bounds from 1 to 10, inclusive. These bounds can also be dynamically determined at runtime.

Arrays are not limited to one dimension. Fortran supports multi-dimensional arrays, which are declared similarly but accommodate additional indices. For a two-dimensional array:

```
REAL, DIMENSION(1:10, 1:5) :: b
```

This snippet creates a two-dimensional array b with bounds from 1 to 10 for the first dimension and 1 to 5 for the second dimension.

Fortran also allows arrays with arbitrary lower bounds, enhancing flexibility:

```
INTEGER, DIMENSION(-5:5) :: c
```

This declares an array c with bounds from -5 to 5.

When working with multi-dimensional arrays, each dimension can have different bounds:

```
REAL, DIMENSION(-3:3, 0:4, 1:6) :: d
```

Three-dimensional array d has bounds from -3 to 3 on the first dimension, 0 to 4 on the second, and 1 to 6 on the third.

Array Bounds Inquiry

Fortran provides intrinsic functions to inquire about array bounds, enhancing array manipulation and validation. Two key functions are: * LBOUND(array, dim): returns the lower bound of dimension dim of array. * UBOUND(array, dim): returns the upper bound of dimension dim of array.

Consider the following example to query bounds:

```
REAL, DIMENSION(-2:3, 1:4) :: e
PRINT *, LBOUND(e, 1) ! Prints -2
PRINT *, UBOUND(e, 1) ! Prints 3
PRINT *, LBOUND(e, 2) ! Prints 1
PRINT *, UBOUND(e, 2) ! Prints 4
```

These functions are particularly useful when performing array operations where bounds may vary or need confirmation.

Handling Arrays with Variable Bounds

Fortran allows declaration and allocation of arrays with variable bounds via the ALLOCATABLE attribute, providing dynamic flexibility:

```
REAL, ALLOCATABLE, DIMENSION(:) :: f
INTEGER :: lb, ub
lb = -3
ub = 5
ALLOCATE(f(lb:ub))
```

Here, f is an allocatable array, dynamically allocated with bounds from -3 to 5. The ability to dynamically allocate arrays significantly reduces memory wastage.

Retrieving Array Dimensions

Intrinsic functions also allow for determination of the number of dimensions of an array:

```
INTEGER :: num_dims
REAL, DIMENSION(1:4, 2:5, -1:2) :: g

num_dims = SIZE(SHAPE(g)) ! Returns 3, the number of dimensions
PRINT *, num_dims
```

The SHAPE function returns an array containing the extent (size) of each dimension, and the SIZE function determines the number of elements in that array, effectively yielding the total dimensions.

This section provides a structured approach to understanding and employing array bounds and dimensions in Fortran, ensuring correct array usage, memory allocation, and efficient computational processes.

5.5 Array Operations: Addition, Subtraction, Multiplication, Division

Array operations are fundamental in Fortran for mathematical computing. This section will delve into the specifics of performing addition, subtraction, multiplication, and division on arrays. These operations are essential for various algorithms and applications in scientific computing.

In Fortran, array operations are performed element-wise by default, allowing concise and readable code. Understanding these operations ensures efficient data manipulation and computational routines.

Array Addition

Array addition in Fortran involves the element-wise summation of two arrays of the same shape. The syntax for adding two arrays is straightforward:

```
real :: array1(3), array2(3), result(3)
array1 = (/1.0, 2.0, 3.0/)
array2 = (/4.0, 5.0, 6.0/)
result = array1 + array2
```

The result array will hold the summed values from array1 and array2. In this example, result will be (/5.0, 7.0, 9.0/). It is crucial to ensure that the arrays being added are conformable, meaning they must have the same dimensions. For instance, adding a 2x2 array to a 2x3 array will result in an error.

```
real :: array1(2,2), array2(2,2), result(2,2)
array1 = reshape((/1.0, 2.0, 3.0, 4.0/), (/2, 2/))
array2 = reshape((/ 5.0, 6.0, 7.0, 8.0/), (/2, 2/))
result = array1 + array2
! result will be (/ (/6.0, 8.0/), (/10.0, 12.0/) /)
```

Array Subtraction

Subtraction of arrays is performed similarly to addition. The operation is element-wise, and the arrays involved must be of the same shape:

```
real :: array1(3), array2(3), result(3)
array1 = (/5.0, 7.0, 9.0/)
array2 = (/1.0, 2.0, 3.0/)
result = array1 - array2
```

In this example, result will be (/4.0, 5.0, 6.0/). Again, it is critical to ensure the arrays being subtracted are conformable to avoid runtime errors.

Array Multiplication

Array multiplication in Fortran, when done by using the '*' operator, is an element-wise operation similar to addition and subtraction:

```
real :: array1(3), array2(3), result(3)
array1 = (/1.0, 2.0, 3.0/)
array2 = (/4.0, 5.0, 6.0/)
result = array1 * array2
```

In this case, result will be (/4.0, 10.0, 18.0/). Note that element-wise multiplication is different from matrix multiplication. For matrix multiplication, Fortran provides intrinsic functions such as MATMUL.

To perform matrix multiplication, the MATMUL intrinsic function should be used:

```
real :: matrix1(2,2), matrix2(2,2), result(2,2)
matrix1 = reshape((/1.0, 2.0, 3.0, 4.0/), (/2, 2/))
matrix2 = reshape((/5.0, 6.0, 7.0, 8.0/), (/2, 2/))
result = matmul(matrix1, matrix2)
! result will be (/ (/19.0, 22.0/), (/43.0, 50.0/) /)
```

Array Division

Division of arrays in Fortran operates similar to other arithmetic operations. It is performed element-wise and requires conformable arrays:

```
real :: array1(3), array2(3), result(3)
array1 = (/8.0, 9.0, 10.0/)
array2 = (/2.0, 3.0, 5.0/)
result = array1 / array2
```

This will result in result being (/4.0, 3.0, 2.0/). Division by zero should be handled carefully to prevent runtime errors or undefined behavior.

Handling Conformability and Broadcasting

While Fortran automatically handles element-wise operations, ensuring the arrays are of the same dimensions is imperative. Fortran does not support broadcasting inherently (automatically expanding smaller arrays to match dimensions of larger arrays as seen in some other languages like Python's NumPy). All arrays involved in arithmetic operations must be explicitly conformable.

Conformability can be managed using intrinsic functions or by manually adjusting array sizes through slicing and reshaping. Below is an example illustrating correct array reshaping:

```
real :: array1(6), matrix(2,3), result(2,3)
array1 = (/1.0, 2.0, 3.0, 4.0, 5.0, 6.0/)
matrix = reshape(array1, (/2, 3/))
result = matrix + 10.0
```

In this example, the matrix is reshaped to a 2x3 array and then added to a scalar value 10.0 for each element, demonstrating broadcasting-like behavior via scalar addition.

Expertise in handling array operations in Fortran not only simplifies code but also enhances performance by leveraging efficient underlying array manipulation techniques. Understanding the element-wise nature of these operations and ensuring the conformability of arrays is essential for error-free and optimal Fortran programming.

5.6 Multi-dimensional Arrays

Multi-dimensional arrays in Fortran are essential for representing structured data, frequently encountered in scientific and engineering computations. These arrays extend the concept of single-dimensional arrays to multiple dimensions, allowing storage and manipulation of data in a more natural format. This section details the declaration, initialization, access, and operations on multi-dimensional arrays.

To declare a multi-dimensional array, you specify the number of dimensions in the dimension attribute. Fortran arrays are indexed starting from 1 by default, though you can explicitly set the bounds.

```
! Declaration of a 2-dimensional array
real, dimension(3, 4) :: matrix

! Declaration of a 3-dimensional array
real, dimension(3, 4, 5) :: tensor
```

In this example, matrix is a 2-dimensional array with 3 rows and 4 columns, while tensor is a 3-dimensional array with dimensions 3x4x5.

Initializing multi-dimensional arrays can be performed at the time of declaration or through assignment statements. When initializing at the time of declaration, the values are specified in a way that aligns with the array's structure.

```
! Initialization of a 2-dimensional array at declaration
real, dimension(2, 2) :: mat = reshape([1.0, 2.0, 3.0, 4.0], shape=[2, 2])
```

The reshape function rearranges the one-dimensional array [1.0, 2.0, 3.0, 4.0] into a 2x2 matrix. Individual elements within multi-dimensional arrays are accessed using parentheses and indices corresponding to each dimension.

```
! Accessing elements in a 2-dimensional array
print*, mat(1, 1) ! Output: 1.0
print*, mat(2, 2) ! Output: 4.0

! Assigning values to specific elements
mat(1, 2) = 5.0
```

Operations on multi-dimensional arrays follow similar syntax to operations on single-dimensional arrays. Applying mathematical operations to entire arrays or their specific indices is central to efficient data manipulation.

```
! Declaring two 2-dimensional arrays
real, dimension(2, 2) :: array1 = reshape([1, 2, 3, 4], shape=[2, 2])
```

```
real, dimension(2, 2) :: array2 = reshape([5, 6, 7, 8], shape=[2, 2])

! Adding two arrays
real, dimension(2, 2) :: result
result = array1 + array2

! Printing the result
print*, result
```

```
! Output:
  6.0   8.0
 10.0  12.0
```

Fortran supports powerful intrinsic functions that operate on multi-dimensional arrays. For instance, the matmul function allows matrix multiplication.

```
! Declaring two compatible matrices for multiplication
real, dimension(2, 3) :: matA = reshape([1, 2, 3, 4, 5, 6], shape=[2, 3])
real, dimension(3, 2) :: matB = reshape([7, 8, 9, 10, 11, 12], shape=[3, 2])

! Resultant matrix of size 2x2
real, dimension(2, 2) :: matC

! Matrix multiplication using matmul
matC = matmul(matA, matB)

! Printing the result
print*, matC
```

```
! Output:
  58.0   64.0
 139.0  154.0
```

Dynamic allocation of multi-dimensional arrays provides flexibility, especially when array sizes are not known at compile time. This is accomplished using the allocate and deallocate statements.

```
! Declaration of a dynamic 2-dimensional array
real, allocatable, dimension(:, :) :: dynMatrix

! Allocating a 3x3 matrix
allocate(dynMatrix(3, 3))

! Assigning values to the dynamic matrix
dynMatrix = reshape([1, 2, 3, 4, 5, 6, 7, 8, 9], shape=[3, 3])

! Deallocating the dynamic matrix
deallocate(dynMatrix)
```

Efficient manipulation of multi-dimensional arrays is pivotal in Fortran programming, enabling complex computational solutions. Understanding the declaration, initialization, access methods, and intrinsic functions associated with multi-dimensional arrays empowers developers to utilize Fortran's strengths in handling large, structured datasets.

5.7 Dynamic Arrays and Allocation

Dynamic arrays in Fortran offer the flexibility to allocate and deallocate memory at runtime based on the requirements of the program. This feature is paramount in scientific computing where the problem size may not be known until execution time. In this section, we will explore the syntax and operations related to allocating and managing dynamic arrays in Fortran, ensuring efficient memory utilization.

To define a dynamic array in Fortran, the allocatable attribute is used. An allocatable array does not have fixed dimensions at declaration. Instead, its dimensions are specified during runtime using the allocate statement.

```
program dynamic_array_example
    integer, allocatable :: array(:)

    ! Allocate the array with 10 elements
    allocate(array(10))

    ! Initialize the array elements
    array = (/ (i, i=1,10) /)

    ! Print the array elements
    print *, array

    ! Deallocate the array to free memory
    deallocate(array)
end program dynamic_array_example
```

In this example, array is declared with the allocatable attribute. Memory for 10 elements is allocated at runtime using the allocate statement, and the array is subsequently initialized and printed. Finally, the deallocate statement is used to free the allocated memory.

For multi-dimensional dynamic arrays, the same principles apply, but the array is declared with multiple colons to denote its dimensions.

```
program dynamic_multi_array
    real, allocatable :: matrix(:,:)
    integer :: i, j

    ! Allocate the 2D array with dimensions 3x3
    allocate(matrix(3,3))

    ! Initialize the array elements
    do i = 1, 3
        do j = 1, 3
            matrix(i,j) = real(i+j)
        end do
    end do

    ! Print the array elements
    do i = 1, 3
```

```
        print *, matrix(i,:)
    end do

    ! Deallocate the array
    deallocate(matrix)
end program dynamic_multi_array
```

Dynamic arrays also support reallocation, which enables resizing an already allocated array. The intrinsic subroutine move_alloc facilitates this by transferring the contents of the old array to a new one with different dimensions.

```
program reallocate_example
    integer, allocatable :: old_array(:), new_array(:)
    integer :: i

    ! Allocate the initial array with 5 elements
    allocate(old_array(5))
    old_array = (/ 1, 2, 3, 4, 5 /)

    ! Allocate the new array with additional 5 elements (total 10)
    allocate(new_array(10))
    new_array(1:5) = old_array
    new_array(6:10) = (/ 6, 7, 8, 9, 10 /)

    ! Transfer contents and deallocate old_array
    call move_alloc(new_array, old_array)

    ! Print the resized array
    print *, old_array

    ! Deallocate the array
    deallocate(old_array)
end program reallocate_example
```

The above example demonstrates how move_alloc transfers values from new_array to old_array, effectively resizing it. This approach is efficient and avoids unnecessary memory copying.

Dynamic arrays are also useful within subroutines and functions, allowing arrays to be allocated and deallocated locally. This ensures that memory is managed effectively and only utilized when necessary.

```
program dynamic_in_subroutine
    call dynamic_array_subroutine(5)
contains
    subroutine dynamic_array_subroutine(n)
        integer, intent(in) :: n
        real, allocatable :: temp_array(:)

        ! Allocate the temporary array
        allocate(temp_array(n))

        ! Initialize the array
        temp_array = (/ (real(i), i=1,n) /)

        ! Print the array elements
```

```
        print *, 'Inside subroutine temp array: ', temp_array

        ! Deallocate the array
        deallocate(temp_array)
    end subroutine dynamic_array_subroutine
end program dynamic_in_subroutine
```

The above code defines a subroutine dynamic_array_subroutine that dynamically allocates an array temp_array. This array is then initialized, used, and deallocated within the subroutine scope, demonstrating memory management within local contexts.

Properly managing dynamic arrays ensures that memory is allocated and freed as required, preventing memory leaks and ensuring efficient resource utilization. By leveraging allocatable arrays, scientists and engineers can build robust Fortran programs that handle varying data sizes dynamically and efficiently.

5.8 Array Intrinsic Functions

Array intrinsic functions in Fortran provide built-in mechanisms to perform common operations on arrays efficiently and succinctly. These functions are an essential feature of Fortran, particularly for scientific computing, as they enhance code readability and performance by minimizing the need for explicit loops. We will explore several key intrinsic functions, including SUM, PRODUCT, MINVAL, MAXVAL, SIZE, MATMUL, and DOT_PRODUCT, providing detailed examples and usage scenarios.

The SUM function calculates the sum of all elements in an array or a specific dimension of an array. Consider the following example:

```
PROGRAM sum_example
  IMPLICIT NONE
  REAL, DIMENSION(3, 3) :: matrix
  REAL :: total_sum, row_sum

  matrix = RESHAPE((/1.0, 2.0, 3.0, 4.0, 5.0, 6.0, 7.0, 8.0, 9.0/), &
           SHAPE(matrix))

  total_sum = SUM(matrix)
  row_sum = SUM(matrix, DIM=1)

  PRINT *, 'Total Sum:', total_sum
  PRINT *, 'Sum of Rows:', row_sum
END PROGRAM sum_example
```

Executing the above program produces the following output:

```
Total Sum:   45.00000
Sum of Rows:   12.00000   15.00000   18.00000
```

The PRODUCT function computes the product of all elements in an array or a specified dimension:

```
PROGRAM product_example
  IMPLICIT NONE
  REAL, DIMENSION(3) :: vector
  REAL :: result

  vector = (/2.0, 3.0, 4.0/)

  result = PRODUCT(vector)

  PRINT *, 'Product of All Elements:', result
END PROGRAM product_example
```

Upon execution, the program yields:

```
Product of All Elements:   24.00000
```

The MINVAL and MAXVAL functions are used to find the minimum and maximum values of an array, respectively. Here's an example demonstrating their usage:

```
PROGRAM minmax_example
  IMPLICIT NONE
  INTEGER, DIMENSION(4) :: array = (/8, 2, 6, 4/)
  INTEGER :: min_value, max_value

  min_value = MINVAL(array)
  max_value = MAXVAL(array)

  PRINT *, 'Minimum Value:', min_value
  PRINT *, 'Maximum Value:', max_value
END PROGRAM minmax_example
```

This yields:

```
Minimum Value:   2
Maximum Value:   8
```

The intrinsic function SIZE returns the number of elements or the size of a specific dimension in an array. Consider the following example:

```
PROGRAM size_example
  IMPLICIT NONE
  REAL, DIMENSION(4, 3) :: matrix
  INTEGER :: total_size, row_size, col_size

  total_size = SIZE(matrix)
  row_size = SIZE(matrix, DIM=1)
  col_size = SIZE(matrix, DIM=2)

  PRINT *, 'Total Size:', total_size
  PRINT *, 'Number of Rows:', row_size
  PRINT *, 'Number of Columns:', col_size
END PROGRAM size_example
```

The resulting output is:

```
Total Size: 12
Number of Rows: 4
Number of Columns: 3
```

For matrix multiplication, the MATMUL function is specifically designed. It performs matrix multiplication on two conformable arrays. Here's an example:

```
PROGRAM matmul_example
  IMPLICIT NONE
  REAL, DIMENSION(2, 2) :: matrix_a, matrix_b, result

  matrix_a = RESHAPE((/1.0, 2.0, 3.0, 4.0/), SHAPE(matrix_a))
  matrix_b = RESHAPE((/5.0, 6.0, 7.0, 8.0/), SHAPE(matrix_b))

  result = MATMUL(matrix_a, matrix_b)

  PRINT *, 'Matrix A:'
  PRINT *, matrix_a
  PRINT *, 'Matrix B:'
  PRINT *, matrix_b
  PRINT *, 'Result (Matrix A * Matrix B):'
  PRINT *, result
END PROGRAM matmul_example
```

Running this program results in:

```
Matrix A:
   1.000000    2.000000
   3.000000    4.000000
Matrix B:
   5.000000    6.000000
   7.000000    8.000000
Result (Matrix A * Matrix B):
  19.00000   22.00000
  43.00000   50.00000
```

Finally, the DOT_PRODUCT function computes the dot product of two vectors. Here's an example:

```
PROGRAM dot_product_example
  IMPLICIT NONE
  REAL, DIMENSION(3) :: vector_a, vector_b
  REAL :: result

  vector_a = (/1.0, 2.0, 3.0/)
  vector_b = (/4.0, 5.0, 6.0/)

  result = DOT_PRODUCT(vector_a, vector_b)

  PRINT *, 'Vector A:'
  PRINT *, vector_a
  PRINT *, 'Vector B:'
  PRINT *, vector_b
  PRINT *, 'Dot Product:', result
END PROGRAM dot_product_example
```

The output displayed will be:

```
Vector A:
  1.000000    2.000000    3.000000
Vector B:
  4.000000    5.000000    6.000000
Dot Product:   32.00000
```

Understanding and leveraging these intrinsic functions is crucial for performing efficient array manipulations in Fortran. These built-in functions reduce code complexity and improve performance by taking advantage of optimized, underlying algorithms provided by the Fortran compiler.

5.9 Array Slicing and Subarrays

Array slicing and subarrays are powerful features in Fortran that enable efficient access and manipulation of segments of arrays without the need for explicit loops. Array slicing allows the programmer to reference sections of an array, which can then be used directly in computations, passed to functions or subroutines, or manipulated as new arrays.

To begin using array slicing in Fortran, one needs to understand the syntax and rules that govern the slicing operations. An array slice is specified by providing a range for each dimension of the array, using the format (start:end), where start and end are the indices of the array segment to be referenced. If omitted, Fortran uses the default values of the array's lower (beginning) and upper (ending) bounds, respectively.

Consider an example where we have a one-dimensional array:

```
INTEGER, DIMENSION(1:10) :: arr
INTEGER :: i

! Initializing the array
DO i = 1, 10
   arr(i) = i
END DO
```

Here, arr is an array of integers ranging from 1 to 10. To extract a subarray consisting of elements 3 through 7, we use slicing:

```
PRINT *, arr(3:7)
```

This operation will output:

```
3 4 5 6 7
```

The key benefit of array slicing lies in its flexibility and the ability to avoid explicit looping. The slicing capability extends to multi-dimensional arrays as well. For example, consider a two-dimensional array:

```
INTEGER, DIMENSION(1:5,1:5) :: mat
INTEGER :: i, j

! Initializing the matrix
DO i = 1, 5
  DO j = 1, 5
    mat(i,j) = i + j
  END DO
END DO
```

To extract a 3x3 subarray starting from the element at position (2,2), we can perform the following slicing operation:

```
PRINT *, mat(2:4,2:4)
```

This will result in the following output:

```
3 4 5
4 5 6
5 6 7
```

In scenarios where only specific rows or columns are required, slicing can be equally effective. For instance, extracting the second row of the matrix can be done as follows:

```
PRINT *, mat(2,:)
```

This outputs:

```
3 4 5 6 7
```

Similarly, extracting the third column is achieved with:

```
PRINT *, mat(:,3)
```

Yielding:

```
4 5 6 7 8
```

Array slicing is not confined to extracting contiguous segments; strides can also be included. The stride parameter, specified using (start:end:stride), indicates the increment between selected indices. For example, to extract every second element from arr:

```
PRINT *, arr(1:10:2)
```

This will produce:

```
1 3 5 7 9
```

Another powerful feature related to array slicing is subarrays. Subarrays are views or references to parts of an existing array, allowing modifications to the subarray to affect the original array directly. Consider:

```
INTEGER, POINTER :: slice(:)

slice => arr(3:7)
slice = 100
PRINT *, arr
```

This code snippet first creates a pointer slice to the subarray from arr(3:7) and then assigns the value 100 to all elements in this subarray. Consequently, the original array arr will be modified:

```
1 2 100 100 100 100 100 8 9 10
```

It is important to adhere to proper array bounds when performing slicing to avoid errors. Fortran provides intrinsic functions LBOUND and UBOUND for determining the lower and upper bounds of arrays, aiding in dynamic slicing operations.

By leveraging array slicing and subarrays, programmers can write more readable, efficient, and concise code, which is particularly useful for large-scale scientific computations. These features reduce the need for complex loop constructions, enhance code clarity, and offer significant performance improvements through implicit, optimized handling by the Fortran runtime.

5.10 Using Arrays in Functions and Subroutines

In Fortran, the ability to use arrays in functions and subroutines is invaluable for modular programming and for reducing code redundancy. This section elucidates how arrays can be passed to functions and subroutines and the potential issues that arise in this process. We will also explore techniques to ensure efficient and error-free code.

Passing arrays to functions and subroutines requires an understanding of Fortran's argument passing mechanisms and array handling. Arrays can be passed as arguments by specifying them in the function or subroutine declaration along with their dimensions if known.

Declaring Functions and Subroutines with Array Arguments

When declaring functions or subroutines that accept arrays, it is crucial to define the array arguments correctly. Fortran supports both explicit shape and assumed shape arrays.

```
subroutine process_array(array)
  integer, dimension(:) :: array
  integer :: i

  do i = 1, size(array)
    array(i) = array(i) * 2
  end do
end subroutine process_array
```

In this example, the subroutine process_array takes an array as an argument. The dimension of the array is indicated by (:), making it an assumed-shape array. Assumed-shape arrays are flexible and allow the subroutine to work with arrays of any size.

For functions, the declaration is similar, but you also need to specify the function's return type and the array type.

```
function sum_elements(array) result(sum)
  integer, dimension(:), intent(in) :: array
  integer :: sum, i

  sum = 0
  do i = 1, size(array)
    sum = sum + array(i)
  end do
end function sum_elements
```

Here, the function sum_elements takes an array, processes it, and returns the sum of its elements. The intent(in) attribute indicates that the array is used for input only and should not be modified within the function.

Using Multi-dimensional Arrays

Handling multi-dimensional arrays in functions and subroutines requires specifying all dimensions accurately. An example of a subroutine that processes a two-dimensional array is shown below:

```
subroutine process_2d_array(array2d)
  integer, dimension(:, :) :: array2d
  integer :: i, j, rows, cols

  rows = size(array2d, 1)
  cols = size(array2d, 2)
```

```
  do i = 1, rows
    do j = 1, cols
      array2d(i, j) = array2d(i, j) * 2
    end do
  end do
end subroutine process_2d_array
```

In this subroutine, process_2d_array, the array argument is specified with two dimensions (:, :), indicating an assumed shape two-dimensional array. The sizes of its dimensions are obtained using the size intrinsic function. This flexibility allows the subroutine to operate on any two-dimensional array.

Allocatable Arrays in Functions and Subroutines

Allocatable arrays can be dynamically allocated within functions and subroutines, enabling the handling of arrays whose size is not known at compile-time. Demonstrating this, consider the following function that allocates and returns an array containing the first n integers.

```
function generate_sequence(n) result(sequence)
  integer, intent(in) :: n
  integer, allocatable, dimension(:) :: sequence
  integer :: i

  allocate(sequence(n))
  do i = 1, n
    sequence(i) = i
  end do
end function generate_sequence
```

In this function, generate_sequence, the array sequence is allocated to the size specified by the input parameter n. The allocatable attribute ensures that the memory for the array is dynamically allocated at runtime.

Best Practices and Common Pitfalls

When passing arrays to functions and subroutines, consider the following best practices to avoid common errors:

- Always use the intent attribute to specify whether the array is for input (intent(in)), output (intent(out)), or both (intent(inout)). This enhances code clarity and helps the compiler perform optimizations.

- Match the array dimensions accurately. Mismatched dimensions between the caller and callee can lead to unexpected behavior or runtime errors.
- Be cautious with array bounds. Accessing elements outside the declared bounds can cause segmentation faults. Use the size function to dynamically obtain array sizes.
- Document the assumptions and expected dimensions of the arrays in your subroutine or function comments.

Consider an example where an array and its bounds are explicitly checked before performing operations:

```
subroutine safe_process_array(array, n)
  integer, intent(inout), dimension(n) :: array
  integer, intent(in) :: n
  integer :: i

  if (n <= 0) return
  do i = 1, n
    array(i) = array(i) * 2
  end do
end subroutine safe_process_array
```

In safe_process_array, the array bounds are explicitly checked to ensure n is positive, which prevents illegal memory access.

Understanding how to effectively use arrays in functions and subroutines is fundamental for modular and reusable code in Fortran. Properly declaring, passing, and manipulating arrays ensures your programs are efficient, reliable, and maintainable.

5.11 Common Errors and Debugging Arrays

To excel in Fortran programming, especially when dealing with arrays, one must develop a keen eye for common errors. Debugging such errors is essential for achieving efficient and accurate scientific computations. This section addresses various errors encountered in array operations and provides strategies for effective debugging.

1. Array Bounds Exceeded
Exceeding array bounds is a frequent error, often leading to undefined behavior or run-time errors. When you attempt to access elements outside the declared range of an array, the bounds are exceeded.

Example:

```
program ArrayBoundsExceeded
    implicit none
    integer :: A(5)
    integer :: i

    do i = 1, 6
        A(i) = i
    end do

end program ArrayBoundsExceeded
```

In this example, the loop iterates from 1 to 6, but A is only declared with 5 elements. Accessing A(6) exceeds the bounds.

Solution: Enable bounds checking during compilation using the -fcheck=bounds or equivalent option in your Fortran compiler. This enforces at runtime that array bounds are respected, which helps identify out-of-bounds errors.

2. Incorrect Array Dimensions
Incorrect array dimensions lead to misalignment of elements and potential logical errors in computations.

Example:

```
program IncorrectArrayDimensions
    implicit none
    integer :: A(5, 5)
    integer :: B(5)
    integer :: i

    do i = 1, 5
        B(i) = A(i, i)
    end do

end program IncorrectArrayDimensions
```

Here, attempting to assign elements from a 2-dimensional array A to a 1-dimensional array B without appropriate handling can lead to confusing logical errors.

Solution: Ensure careful matching of array dimensions. In more complex operations, utilize array intrinsic functions to verify dimensions dynamically.

3. Uninitialized Arrays
Utilizing uninitialized arrays can produce unpredictable outputs since the memory contains residual data from previous operations.

Example:

```
program UninitializedArray
    implicit none
```

```
    integer :: A(5)
    integer :: i

    do i = 1, 5
        print *, 'A(', i, ') = ', A(i)
    end do

end program UninitializedArray
```

If A is not initialized, the printed values are indeterminate.

Solution: Always initialize arrays before use. Use intrinsic functions like ALLOCATE for dynamic arrays and FORALL, or type constructors for static arrays.

4. Misuse of Array Sections
Arrays in Fortran can be sliced, leading to potential errors if not correctly handled.

Example:

```
program MisuseArraySections
    implicit none
    integer :: A(5) = [1, 2, 3, 4, 5]
    integer :: i, B(5)

    B = A(1:4) ! This is incorrect, B requires array sections to match its size.

end program MisuseArraySections
```

The incorrect slicing operation results in a mismatch because the sections are not conformant.

Solution: Ensure that sliced sections are consistent with the dimensions of the target array. Utilize array intrinsic functions like reshape and explicitly verify array bounds during slicing.

5. Incorrect Data Types and Implicit Conversions
Mismatching data types and incorrect implicit conversions dynamically impair precise scientific computations.

Example:

```
program DataConversionError
    implicit none
    real :: A(5)
    integer :: i

    do i = 1, 5
        A(i) = i / 2 ! This results in integer division, not returning desired float.
    end do

end program DataConversionError
```

Dividing integers in this context ignores precision, yielding unexpected results.

Solution: Explicitly manage data types and conversions. Employ intrinsic functions such as REAL or INT for deliberate typecasting. Use IMPLICIT NONE to mandate explicit typing of all variables.

6. Memory Leaks in Dynamic Arrays
Dynamic allocation errors can lead to memory leaks, significantly affecting performance in larger applications.

Example:

```
program MemoryLeak
    implicit none
    integer, allocatable :: A(:)

    allocate(A(100))
    ! Do operations without properly deallocating 'A'

end program MemoryLeak
```

Failure to deallocate A before program termination causes memory not to be released back to the system.

Solution: Consistently deallocate dynamic arrays with DEALLOCATE statements once they are no longer needed. Employ automated tools for memory checking and validation where possible.

Debugging Strategies
Utilizing systematic debugging strategies can significantly enhance error identification and resolution in Fortran programs.

- **Compiler Options:** Enable detailed compiler warnings and runtime checks for bounds and type mismatches.
- **Print Statements:** Insert print statements to track variable values and array content at critical points—ensuring correctness of operations.
- **Debuggers:** Utilize debuggers like gdb and integrated development environments supporting Fortran. Set breakpoints and inspect memory.
- **Unit Testing:** Implement unit tests for functions and subroutines using consistent arrays. Validate results against expected outputs.
- **Code Reviews:** Peer-review code with a focus on array opera-

tions, ensuring correct usage of dimensions, bounds, and initializations.

Through diligent application of these debugging techniques and awareness of common errors, one can significantly enhance the reliability and efficiency of array operations in Fortran programs.

5.12 Best Practices for Using Arrays in Fortran

When working with arrays in Fortran, it is essential to adhere to best practices to ensure efficiency, readability, and correctness of your code. These practices help prevent common errors, make the code more maintainable, and optimize performance.

1. Array Declaration and Initialization: It is recommended to declare arrays with appropriate sizes and initialize them properly. Fortran allows you to combine declaration and initialization for static arrays.

```
real, dimension(10) :: my_array = (/ 0.0, 1.0, 2.0, 3.0, 4.0, 5.0, 6.0, 7.0, 8.0, 9.0 /)
```

Dynamic arrays should be allocated using the allocate statement and deallocated using the deallocate statement to avoid memory leaks.

```
real, allocatable :: dyn_array(:)
integer :: n

! Assuming n is defined and given a value
allocate(dyn_array(n))
dyn_array = 0.0 ! Initialize to zero
deallocate(dyn_array)
```

2. Avoiding Explicit Do-Loops: Although Fortran supports explicit do loops for array operations, it is often more efficient and concise to use array intrinsic functions or array syntax. For example, consider the following operation to add two arrays:

```
real, dimension(100) :: array1, array2, result

! Using array syntax
result = array1 + array2
```

Instead of:

```
integer :: i
do i = 1, 100
    result(i) = array1(i) + array2(i)
```

```
end do
```

3. Array Bounds Checking: When accessing array elements, always ensure that indices are within the defined bounds. Fortran provides a runtime option to check bounds, which can help identify out-of-bounds errors during development. Use the -fcheck=bounds compiler flag for GNU Fortran.

```
gfortran -fcheck=bounds your_program.f90
```

4. Using Array Intrinsic Functions: Fortran provides a suite of intrinsic functions for array operations that are highly optimized. Functions such as sum, product, maxval, and minval are more efficient than manually implementing equivalent operations.

```
real, dimension(100) :: array
real :: total_sum, max_value

total_sum = sum(array)
max_value = maxval(array)
```

5. Memory Management for Large Arrays: For large arrays, consider the memory architecture of the target system. Use dynamic allocation and deallocation to manage memory efficiently and free resources when they are no longer needed. Also, consider using Fortran pointers for references to arrays when handling complex data structures.

```
real, dimension(:), allocatable :: large_array

allocate(large_array(m, n)) ! Allocate a 2D array with dimensions m x n
! Perform operations with large_array
deallocate(large_array) ! Free the memory
```

6. Modular Programming: Encapsulate array operations within modules to improve code clarity and reusability. This allows you to define arrays, intrinsic functions, and procedures in a modular fashion.

```
module array_operations
    implicit none
    contains

    subroutine add_arrays(A, B, C, n)
        real, dimension(:), intent(in) :: A, B
        real, dimension(:), intent(out) :: C
        integer, intent(in) :: n
        C(1:n) = A(1:n) + B(1:n)
    end subroutine add_arrays
end module array_operations
```

7. Use of where and forall Statements: The where and forall statements offer a concise and readable way to perform conditional operations on arrays. The where statement is particularly useful for performing element-wise logical operations.

```
real, dimension(100) :: array1, array2, result

where (array1 > array2)
    result = array1
elsewhere
    result = array2
end where
```

8. Profiling and Optimization: Profile your Fortran programs to identify bottlenecks related to array operations. Use tools such as gprof or built-in compiler profiling options. Based on profiling results, optimize array operations, possibly by reordering computations or minimizing memory access latency.

```
! Assuming gprof is used for profiling
gfortran -pg your_program.f90 -o your_program
./your_program
gprof your_program gmon.out > analysis.txt
```

9. Documentation and Naming Conventions: Use self-explanatory names for arrays, and document the purpose of each array with comments. Consistent naming conventions enhance code readability and facilitate maintenance.

```
! Array containing temperature measurements
real, dimension(100) :: temperature_readings

! Array for storing daily temperature averages
real, dimension(30) :: daily_avg_temperature
```

10. Avoiding Hard-coding Array Sizes: Whenever possible, avoid hard-coding array sizes. Instead, use parameters or constants to define array dimensions.

```
integer, parameter :: n = 100
real, dimension(n) :: my_array
```

These best practices help in creating robust, efficient, and maintainable Fortran programs that effectively leverage array operations.

Chapter 6

Input and Output

This chapter covers the fundamental aspects of input and output (I/O) operations in Fortran, including basic PRINT and READ statements. It explores formatted and list-directed I/O, along with file I/O operations such as OPEN, CLOSE, READ, and WRITE. The chapter also addresses advanced topics like reading and writing records, file positioning, handling I/O errors, and working with unformatted and binary I/O. Additionally, it introduces using internal files and advanced formatting techniques, equipping readers with the skills needed for efficient and effective data management in Fortran programs.

6.1 Introduction to Input and Output in Fortran

Fortran, a language primarily designed for numeric computation and scientific computing, offers various constructs and mechanisms for handling input and output (I/O) operations. These I/O operations are critical for programs that must interact with the outside world, whether through reading data from files or displaying results on a screen.

In Fortran, I/O operations are categorized broadly into two types: **console I/O** and **file I/O**. Console I/O involves reading input from or writing output to the console (typically the screen and keyboard). File I/O is concerned with reading from or writing to files on a storage medium.

PRINT and READ are the most basic statements for console I/O. Whereas OPEN, CLOSE, READ, and WRITE are fundamental for file I/O. Understanding these commands and the mechanisms underlying them is essential for effective Fortran programming.

Basic Console I/O Operations:

For displaying output to the console, the PRINT statement is used. Its typical syntax is:

```
PRINT *, <items>
```

Here, the asterisk (*) indicates that the format is list-directed, which means the compiler decides the format based on the type and value of the <items>.

```
PRINT *, 'The result is:', result
```

For reading inputs from the console, the READ statement is used. Its syntax is similar:

```
READ *, <variables>
```

```
READ *, value
```

Basic File I/O Operations:

Opening a file in Fortran is accomplished with the OPEN statement, which associates a logical unit number with a file. The logical unit number is an integer that serves as an identifier for the file in subsequent I/O operations.

```
OPEN(unit=<unit number>, file='<filename>', status='<status>', iostat=<iostat
    variable>)
```

While reading or writing to a file, the logical unit number is crucial. The basic READ and WRITE statements for file operations resemble those used for console I/O but include the logical unit number:

```
READ(unit, *) <variables>
WRITE(unit, *) <items>
```

For example, to write data to a file:

```
WRITE(10, *) 'Sample data:', data
```

Finally, closing a file ensures that all data is properly saved and resources are freed:

```
CLOSE(unit=<unit number>)
```

Advanced I/O Features:

Fortran also supports more detailed formatting and control in I/O operations. This includes formatted I/O, list-directed I/O, and the use of internal files. These features allow more precise control over how data is inputted and outputted, which is indispensable for tasks that require strict data formatting and processing.

Formatted I/O specify a format for the input or output data. This formatting is specified by a FORMAT statement or inline format specification.

```
WRITE(unit, '(A, I4)') 'Number:', number
```

In this example, (A, I4) is the format, where A represents a string format, and I4 represents an integer format of width 4.

List-directed I/O, indicated by the asterisk (*), allows for simpler and more flexible input and output without specifying a format:

```
WRITE(*, *) 'Enter a number:', number
```

Internal files treat character variables as files. This allows I/O operations to be performed on strings.

```
CHARACTER(len=20) :: line
WRITE(line, '(I4)') 123
PRINT *, line
```

Understanding the right use of these varied I/O capabilities is crucial for efficient Fortran programming. They not only make programs more interactive and user-friendly but also ensure that data is managed and manipulated accurately. The subsequent sections will delve deeper into each of these areas, providing a comprehensive mastery of I/O operations in Fortran.

6.2 Basic PRINT and READ Statements

The PRINT and READ statements form the core of Fortran's input and output operations. Understanding these constructs is crucial for fundamental data management within the language, enabling the developer to interact directly with the program through the console or terminal.

The PRINT Statement

The PRINT statement is utilized to output information to standard output, typically the console. This statement comprises a control list and an optional format descriptor. The basic syntax for the PRINT statement is as follows:

```
PRINT format, item1, item2, ...
```

The format specifier can dictate the appearance of the printed output, providing control over the layout and precision of numerical values, among other aspects. Though not required, it greatly enhances the readability and presentation of output data.

For example:

```
PRINT *, 'Hello, World! This is Fortran.'
PRINT '(A, I3)', 'The value is:', 42
```

In the first example, the asterisk (*) serves as a list-directed format specifier, allowing Fortran to determine the output format automatically. This is straightforward for simple strings. In the second example, (A, I3) is a format descriptor where A represents an alphanumeric output and I3 specifies an integer field of width 3 characters.

The resulting output will appear as:

```
Hello, World! This is Fortran.
The value is: 42
```

The READ Statement

The READ statement facilitates input operations, enabling data to be read from standard input, typically the keyboard. Using READ, a program can store user-provided values into variables.

The basic syntax for the READ statement is:

```
READ format, item1, item2, ...
```

As with PRINT, the format specifier is optional. When included, it guides the reading process, ensuring the data conforms to expected types and sizes.

Consider the following example where we read an integer and a real number from the user:

```
INTEGER :: num
REAL :: val

PRINT *, 'Enter an integer and a real number:'
READ *, num, val
PRINT '(A, I5, A, F10.2)', 'Number: ', num, ', Value: ', val
```

Here, Fortran responds to user-provided input. Suppose the user enters values 25 and 3.14159. The READ statement processes this input, storing 25 into num and 3.14159 into val.

The output would be:

```
Enter an integer and a real number:
Number:    25, Value:      3.14
```

Error Handling in Basic I/O Operations

While essential for basic user interaction, PRINT and READ statements have limited error handling capabilities by default. However, users can enhance them with constructs for better control over input validation.

Consider an example:

```
INTEGER :: num
LOGICAL :: valid

valid = .FALSE.

DO WHILE (.NOT. valid)
    PRINT *, 'Enter an integer value:'
    READ *, num
    IF (IOSTAT == 0) THEN
        valid = .TRUE.
    ELSE
        PRINT *, 'Invalid input. Please enter a valid integer.'
    END IF
END DO

PRINT '(A, I5)', 'You entered: ', num
```

In this code, the loop continues until a valid integer is provided. The IOSTAT intrinsic variable captures the status of the I/O operation, where a value of 0 indicates success. If an invalid entry is detected, an appropriate message prompts the user for new input.

The consistent use of these constructs ensures robust and user-friendly interactions, setting a foundation for more advanced I/O operations in Fortran.

6.3 Formatted Input and Output

Formatted input and output operations in Fortran allow you to control the appearance of the data being read from or written to files or the console. These operations use format specifiers in READ and WRITE statements to ensure the data conforms to a specified layout, which is particularly useful for producing human-readable outputs or reading structured data files.

To use formatted I/O, you need to define format control strings, either directly within the I/O statements or by referencing FORMAT statements. Format specifiers within these strings instruct Fortran on how to handle different data types and control various display options.

Examples of Format Specifiers:

- I - Integer format
- F - Fixed-point real format
- E - Exponential notation for real numbers
- A - Character string
- L - Logical data

Each format specifier can be further refined with additional parameters to control width, precision, and padding.

```
! Example of integer and real number formatted output
PROGRAM formatted_io_example
  INTEGER :: i
  REAL :: x

  i = 256
  x = 123.456

  WRITE(*,'(I6)') i
  WRITE(*,'(F10.3)') x
END PROGRAM formatted_io_example
```

```
   256
   123.456
```

In this example, the integer i is printed in a field of 6 characters wide, and the real number x is printed in a field of 10 characters wide with 3 digits after the decimal point.

Using FORMAT Statements:

Sometimes specifying the format inline can make the code less readable. Instead, you can use FORMAT statements to define reusable format specifiers.

```
PROGRAM format_statement_example
  INTEGER :: i
  REAL :: x

  i = 1256
```

```
  x = 321.654

  WRITE(*,100) i
  WRITE(*,200) x

100 FORMAT(I10)
200 FORMAT(F15.3)
END PROGRAM format_statement_example
```

```
      1256
   321.654
```

FORMAT statements can contain multiple specifiers and can be quite complex, allowing you to achieve sophisticated formatting.

```
PROGRAM complex_format_example
  INTEGER :: i
  REAL :: x

  i = 1234
  x = 5678.12345

  WRITE(*,100) i, x

100 FORMAT('Integer:', I7, ' Real:', F12.5)
END PROGRAM complex_format_example
```

```
Integer:    1234 Real: 5678.12345
```

Repeated Format Specifiers:

You can repeat format specifiers within a FORMAT statement by specifying a repetition count.

```
PROGRAM repeated_format_example
  INTEGER :: i1, i2, i3
  i1 = 10
  i2 = 20
  i3 = 30

  WRITE(*,100) i1, i2, i3

100 FORMAT(3I5)
END PROGRAM repeated_format_example
```

```
   10   20   30
```

Here, the 3I5 format specifier means three integers, each allocated a width of 5 characters.

Controlling Data Alignment and Padding:

To control how data aligns within its field, Fortran provides several options, such as leading zeros for numbers.

```
PROGRAM zero_padding_example
  INTEGER :: i
```

```
  i = 5

  WRITE(*,100) i

100 FORMAT(I5.5)
END PROGRAM zero_padding_example
```

```
00005
```

In the above example, the output integer is padded with leading zeros to ensure it occupies five positions.

String Formatting:

For character strings, the A format specifier provides control over how strings are managed during I/O operations.

```
PROGRAM string_format_example
  CHARACTER(20) :: name
  name = "Fortran"

  WRITE(*,100) name

100 FORMAT(A20)
END PROGRAM string_format_example
```

```
Fortran
```

Here, the string "Fortran" is written in a field of 20 characters, with trailing spaces ensuring it occupies the entire width.

Reading Formatted Data:

Just as with writing, formatted reading operations allow you to precisely control how input data is processed.

```
PROGRAM read_formatted_example
  INTEGER :: i
  REAL :: x

  READ(*,100) i, x

100 FORMAT(I5, F10.2)
  PRINT *, i, x
END PROGRAM read_formatted_example
```

Input for the above program should be structured to match the specified format, such as:

```
  123  45.67
```

```
           123  45.67
```

Using formatted I/O, you can ensure that numeric and character data are arranged and read in an exact manner within your Fortran programs. This enables precise data representation and robust data validation, which are essential for scientific computing and other applications where data accuracy is paramount.

6.4 List-Directed I/O

List-directed I/O in Fortran provides a simplified, yet flexible, method for handling input and output operations. This approach eschews the explicit format specifications required in formatted I/O, allowing the Fortran runtime system to determine the appropriate format based on the context. This section delves into the use of list-directed I/O, commonly invoked through the READ and PRINT statements with an asterisk (*) as the format specifier.

Using List-Directed READ

The READ statement enables the program to accept input from the user or a file. When employing list-directed input, the format specifier is replaced by an asterisk. Consider the following example, which reads three variables from standard input:

```
PROGRAM ListDirectedRead
  IMPLICIT NONE

  INTEGER :: num1
  REAL :: num2, num3

  PRINT *, 'Enter an integer and two real numbers:'
  READ *, num1, num2, num3

  PRINT *, 'You entered: ', num1, num2, num3
END PROGRAM ListDirectedRead
```

In this example, the READ statement with an asterisk reads num1, num2, and num3 from a single input line. The values are separated by spaces, commas, or a combination of both. The list-directed approach automatically handles the appropriate parsing and assignment of these values.

Using List-Directed PRINT

Similarly, the PRINT statement with asterisks outputs the specified variables in a readable format. Here is an illustrative example:

```
PROGRAM ListDirectedPrint
  IMPLICIT NONE

  INTEGER :: num1
  REAL :: num2, num3
```

```
  num1 = 10
  num2 = 20.5
  num3 = -3.14

  PRINT *, 'The values are: ', num1, num2, num3
END PROGRAM ListDirectedPrint
```

This program assigns values to num1, num2, and num3 and then prints them using list-directed output. The format is inferred automatically, and the variables are separated by spaces in the output display.

```
The values are:           10       20.5000000       -3.14000010
```

Handling Character Data

List-directed I/O also simplifies the process of reading and writing character data. When reading strings, the input data must be enclosed in quotes if it contains spaces. Here is an example:

```
PROGRAM ListDirectedChar
  IMPLICIT NONE

  CHARACTER(len=20) :: str

  PRINT *, 'Enter a string:'
  READ *, str

  PRINT *, 'You entered: ', str
END PROGRAM ListDirectedChar
```

When running this program, if the user inputs "Fortran Programming", the quotes ensure the entire string is read into str. Without quotes, only the first word would be assigned. Similarly, list-directed output effectively handles the display of strings.

Reading and Writing Arrays

The power of list-directed I/O extends to arrays, allowing for concise and efficient reading and writing of array data. Consider the following example:

```
PROGRAM ListDirectedArray
  IMPLICIT NONE

  INTEGER, DIMENSION(5) :: array

  PRINT *, 'Enter five integer values:'
  READ *, array

  PRINT *, 'The array values are: ', array
END PROGRAM ListDirectedArray
```

Here, the READ statement populates the array with five integer values from the input. Users can enter the values separated by spaces or commas.

```
Enter five integer values:
1 2 3 4 5
The array values are:           1           2           3           4           5
```

Handling Precision and Type Compatibility

Fortran runtime intelligently manages precision and type compatibility in list-directed I/O operations. When reading real numbers into integer variables, the values are truncated. Conversely, when writing integers as real numbers, the full precision is displayed.

```
PROGRAM ListDirectedType
  IMPLICIT NONE

  INTEGER :: i
  REAL :: r

  PRINT *, 'Enter a real number to be stored as an integer:'
  READ *, r
  i = r

  PRINT *, 'Truncated integer: ', i
  PRINT *, 'Stored as real: ', r
END PROGRAM ListDirectedType
```

```
Enter a real number to be stored as an integer:
123.456
Truncated integer:         123
Stored as real:   123.456001
```

List-directed I/O provides a straightforward and efficient method for input and output operations in Fortran, enabling the dynamic management of data with simplicity and precision. This approach enhances productivity by reducing the need for explicit format specifications, making it an essential tool in the Fortran programmer's repertoire.

6.5 File I/O Basics: OPEN, CLOSE, READ, WRITE

Understanding the basic principles of file I/O operations in Fortran is essential for effective data management in scientific and technical computing. This section delves into the fundamental operations: OPEN, CLOSE, READ, and WRITE.

The OPEN statement is critical for initializing a file connection. It defines how the file will be accessed, whether it is for reading, writing, or both, among other properties. Below is an example of the OPEN statement syntax:

```
OPEN(unit=unit_num, file='filename', status='status', action='action', position='
    position', iostat=ios)
```

Where the key parameters are:

- unit: Specifies the unit number, which is an integer value used to identify the file connection.
- file: The name of the file as a character string.
- status: Specifies the existence of the file. Options include 'old', 'new', 'replace', and 'unknown'.
- action: Specifies the intended operations, such as 'read', 'write', or 'readwrite'.
- position: Specifies the initial position within the file, with options like 'rewind', 'append', or 'asis'.
- iostat: An optional integer variable to store the I/O status. A value of zero indicates success, and non-zero indicates an error.

Consider this example to open an existing file named 'data.txt' for reading:

```
INTEGER :: ios
OPEN(unit=10, file='data.txt', status='old', action='read', iostat=ios)
IF (ios /= 0) THEN
    PRINT *, 'Error opening file'
END IF
```

For file output, the WRITE statement is used. The general form is as follows:

```
WRITE(unit=unit_num, fmt=format_spec) variable_list
```

Here, unit_num is the unit number associated with the open file, format_spec specifies the format of the output, and variable_list contains the list of variables to be written. The format can be either a label of a previously defined FORMAT statement or a format specifier as demonstrated below:

```
WRITE(10, '(*,*)') var1, var2, var3
```

If you reflect back on earlier sections, this statement outputs the values of var1, var2, and var3 to the file connected to unit 10, using list-directed formatting.

To read data from a file, the READ statement is employed. Its syntax is analogous to the WRITE statement:

```
READ(unit=unit_num, fmt=format_spec) variable_list
```

Here is an example that reads integer data from the previously opened file:

```
INTEGER :: number
READ(10, '(*,*)') number
```

It is also crucial to close files after operations to ensure data integrity and release system resources. The CLOSE statement is simple in structure:

```
CLOSE(unit=unit_num, iostat=ios)
```

The parameter iostat remains optional, and its purpose aligns with the OPEN statement: capturing the I/O status.

Here is an example illustrating the closing of the file associated with unit 10:

```
CLOSE(unit=10, iostat=ios)
IF (ios /= 0) THEN
    PRINT *, 'Error closing file'
END IF
```

To solidify these concepts, consider the following complete program. It opens a file named 'input.txt' for reading, processes the data, and writes the results to another file named 'output.txt'.

```
PROGRAM file_io_example
    INTEGER :: ios, num, i
    INTEGER, PARAMETER :: n = 5
    INTEGER :: array(n)
    OPEN(unit=10, file='input.txt', status='old', action='read', iostat=ios)
    IF (ios /= 0) THEN
        PRINT *, 'Error opening input file'
        STOP
    END IF

    DO i = 1, n
        READ(10, '(*,*)') array(i)
    END DO

    CLOSE(unit=10, iostat=ios)
    IF (ios /= 0) THEN
        PRINT *, 'Error closing input file'
        STOP
    END IF

    OPEN(unit=20, file='output.txt', status='replace', action='write', iostat=ios)
    IF (ios /= 0) THEN
        PRINT *, 'Error opening output file'
```

```
        STOP
    END IF

    DO i = 1, n
        WRITE(20, '(*,*)') array(i)
    END DO

    CLOSE(unit=20, iostat=ios)
    IF (ios /= 0) THEN
        PRINT *, 'Error closing output file'
        STOP
    END IF
END PROGRAM file_io_example
```

The example demonstrates reading five integers from input.txt and writing them to output.txt. It encapsulates the core elements of file I/O operations in Fortran, showcasing the practical application of OPEN, CLOSE, READ, and WRITE statements.

6.6 Reading and Writing Records in Files

Fortran's record-based I/O capabilities are instrumental when dealing with files that contain structured data. This section delves into the mechanisms to read and write records efficiently, illustrating various techniques and considerations for effective use.

In Fortran, a record represents a contiguous set of variables stored in a file. Records facilitate the management of data when dealing with fixed-format files or when the files contain structured, repeated data units.

To begin with, the basic concepts related to records in Fortran:

- RECORD: A logical entity that groups related data items.
- Fixed-Length Records: Each record is of the same size. Common in legacy systems and flat-file databases.
- Sequential Access: Records are accessed in a linear order.
- Direct Access: Records can be accessed directly using an index or key.

Writing Records to Files

When writing records to a file, you typically open the file in a mode that supports record writing, such as DIRECT or SEQUENTIAL for unformatted access.

```
PROGRAM WriteRecords
  IMPLICIT NONE
  INTEGER :: iounit, i, rec_length
  CHARACTER(LEN=80) :: rec

  ! Open file for direct access
  OPEN(UNIT=10, FILE='records.dat', ACCESS='DIRECT', RECL=80, STATUS='
      NEW', IOSTAT=iounit)
  IF (iounit /= 0) THEN
      PRINT *, 'Error opening file'
      STOP
  END IF

  ! Writing records to file
  rec_length = 80
  DO i = 1, 10
     WRITE(rec, '(A,I2,A)') 'Record number ', i, CHAR(10)
     WRITE(10, REC=i, IOSTAT=iounit) rec
     IF (iounit /= 0) THEN
         PRINT *, 'Error writing to file'
         STOP
     END IF
  END DO

  ! Close file
  CLOSE(UNIT=10, IOSTAT=iounit)
  IF (iounit /= 0) THEN
      PRINT *, 'Error closing the file'
  END IF

END PROGRAM WriteRecords
```

In the above example, the OPEN statement specifies ACCESS='DIRECT' for direct access I/O. The RECL parameter indicates the length of each record. The WRITE statement includes the REC keyword to specify the record number.

Reading Records from Files

Reading involves similar operations, where we identify the record to be read. Direct access files allow efficient random access to records by specifying record numbers, while sequential access requires reading each record in sequence.

```
PROGRAM ReadRecords
  IMPLICIT NONE
  INTEGER :: iounit, i, rec_length
  CHARACTER(LEN=80) :: rec

  ! Open file for direct access
  OPEN(UNIT=10, FILE='records.dat', ACCESS='DIRECT', RECL=80, STATUS='
      OLD', IOSTAT=iounit)
  IF (iounit /= 0) THEN
      PRINT *, 'Error opening file'
      STOP
  END IF

  ! Reading records from file
```

```
  rec_length = 80
  DO i = 1, 10
     READ(10, REC=i, IOSTAT=iounit) rec
     IF (iounit /= 0) THEN
        PRINT *, 'Error reading from file'
        STOP
     ELSE
        PRINT *, 'Read:', TRIM(rec)
     END IF
  END DO

  ! Close file
  CLOSE(UNIT=10, IOSTAT=iounit)
  IF (iounit /= 0) THEN
     PRINT *, 'Error closing the file'
  END IF

END PROGRAM ReadRecords
```

In this example, the READ statement is used with the REC keyword to specify the record number to be read. This directs the system to retrieve specific records, bypassing unnecessary ones.

Formatted vs Unformatted Records

Formatted I/O operations involve converting internal data representations into a human-readable format, such as ASCII text, whereas unformatted I/O retains the binary form. Formatted I/O is more portable but incurs conversion overhead, while unformatted I/O is faster and more storage-efficient but lacks portability.

Formatted write example:

```
WRITE(10, '(A)') 'This is a formatted record'
```

Unformatted write example:

```
WRITE(10) some_data_structure
```

Error Handling

Robust applications must account for potential I/O errors. Commonly used parameters include IOSTAT, which captures the I/O status after an operation—the value zero for success, non-zero for failure—and ERR, which specifies a label to branch to in case of an error.

```
WRITE(10, REC=rec_num, IOSTAT=iounit, ERR=999) rec
IF (iounit /= 0) THEN
   PRINT *, 'Encountered an error-writing the record'
   GOTO 999
END IF
999 CONTINUE
```

Practical Considerations

Careful selection between sequential and direct access modes affects performance and ease of data management. When records will be accessed frequently in random order, direct access may offer substantial efficiency gains. Conversely, sequential access is suitable for scenarios where records are processed in the order saved.

Code readability and maintainability benefit from consistent and meaningful record lengths (RECL). It is advisable to document the structure and purpose of each record layout for broader comprehension by future maintainers.

Understanding these concepts ensures efficient and effective data management in Fortran programs, equipping readers with essential skills for handling structured data within files.

6.7 Navigating Files: REWIND, BACKSPACE, and END FILE

Navigating files efficiently is a critical skill in Fortran programming, particularly when dealing with large datasets or complex I/O operations. In Fortran, we have powerful intrinsic functions to manage file positioning: REWIND, BACKSPACE, and END FILE. Understanding how to use these commands properly can greatly enhance your ability to manipulate files, especially in situations where random access or specific record manipulation is required.

REWIND sets the position to the beginning of the file, BACKSPACE moves the position backward by one record, and END FILE marks the end of the file. Together, these commands facilitate a robust file navigation mechanism.

REWIND Statement

The REWIND statement is used to position the file pointer at the start of a file, ensuring subsequent I/O operations begin from the first record. The syntax for REWIND is straightforward:

```
REWIND(unit)
```

Here, unit refers to the logical unit number associated with the file. For example:

```
! Open a file for reading
OPEN(unit=10, file='data.txt', status='old')

! Read the first record
READ(10, *) record1
PRINT *, record1

! Rewind the file to read from the beginning again
REWIND(10)

! Read the first record once more
READ(10, *) record2
PRINT *, record2

! Close the file
CLOSE(10)
```

This simple example demonstrates how REWIND allows the same record to be read twice by resetting the file position.

BACKSPACE Statement

The BACKSPACE statement is essential when you need to move the file pointer one record backward. This can be useful if you need to re-read or skip back in the file. The syntax is:

```
BACKSPACE(unit)
```

Again, unit denotes the logical unit number. Example:

```
! Open a file for reading
OPEN(unit=20, file='dataset.txt', status='old')

! Read the first and second records
READ(20, *) record1
READ(20, *) record2
PRINT *, 'First record:', record1
PRINT *, 'Second record:', record2

! Backspace to re-read the second record
BACKSPACE(20)
READ(20, *) record2_again
PRINT *, 'Re-read second record:', record2_again

! Close the file
CLOSE(20)
```

In this example, after reading the first two records, the BACKSPACE command allows us to move the file pointer back to the position before the second record, enabling us to re-read it.

END FILE Statement

The END FILE statement designates the current position in the file as the end-of-file marker. This is particularly useful when writing file truncation or signaling the termination of valid data in a file. The syntax is:

```
END FILE(unit)
```

Here's a practical scenario:

```
! Open a file for writing
OPEN(unit=30, file='output.txt', status='unknown')

! Write some records into the file
WRITE(30, *) 'Record 1'
WRITE(30, *) 'Record 2'
WRITE(30, *) 'Record 3'

! Mark the current position as the end of the file
END FILE(30)

! Write additional records (this will not be visible beyond the end-of-file marker)
WRITE(30, *) 'Record beyond EOF'

! Close the file
CLOSE(30)

! Re-open the file to read contents
OPEN(unit=30, file='output.txt', status='old')

! Read until EOF
DO
  READ(30, *, IOSTAT=ios) line
  IF (ios /= 0) EXIT
  PRINT *, line
END DO

! Close the file
CLOSE(30)
```

In this case, even though 'Record beyond EOF' is physically written to the file, it will not be accessible once END FILE sets the end-of-file marker.

When using these commands, it is essential to handle I/O statements properly, ensuring that the file operations maintain data integrity and achieve the intended navigation and manipulation.

6.8 Handling Errors in I/O Operations

Handling errors efficiently in I/O operations is crucial for ensuring the robustness and reliability of a Fortran program. Fortran provides mechanisms to detect and manage errors that may occur during file operations such as reading, writing, opening, or closing files. Understanding these mechanisms helps prevent unexpected program behavior and facilitates debugging.

Fortran's I/O statements incorporate error handling capabilities through the IOSTAT and IOMSG specifiers. The IOSTAT specifier is used to store an integer error code, while the IOMSG specifier holds an error message string. By checking the values assigned to these specifiers after an I/O operation, a program can determine whether an error occurred and respond appropriately.

```
INTEGER :: io_status
CHARACTER(len=256) :: io_message

OPEN(UNIT=10, FILE='data.txt', STATUS='OLD', IOSTAT=io_status, IOMSG
     =io_message)
IF (io_status /= 0) THEN
   PRINT *, 'Error opening file: ', TRIM(io_message)
ELSE
   PRINT *, 'File opened successfully.'
END IF
```

In the example above, the OPEN statement attempts to open an existing file named data.txt. The IOSTAT specifier captures the status of the operation, and IOMSG holds a descriptive error message. If an error occurs (indicated by io_status not being zero), the error message is printed to the console.

Error detection is essential for several I/O operations, such as reading from or writing to a file. The following code snippet demonstrates error handling in a READ statement:

```
INTEGER :: number

READ(UNIT=10, FMT=*, IOSTAT=io_status, IOMSG=io_message) number
IF (io_status /= 0) THEN
   PRINT *, 'Error reading from file: ', TRIM(io_message)
ELSE
   PRINT *, 'Read number: ', number
END IF
```

Here, the program attempts to read an integer from the file associated with unit 10. If an error occurs, the error message provides detailed information, helping identify the cause.

Fortran's error-handling specifiers can also be utilized with other I/O operations like WRITE:

```
WRITE(UNIT=10, FMT=*, IOSTAT=io_status, IOMSG=io_message) "Hello,
    World!"
IF (io_status /= 0) THEN
   PRINT *, 'Error writing to file: ', TRIM(io_message)
ELSE
   PRINT *, 'Write successful.'
END IF
```

This example writes a string to a file and checks for errors. The status and descriptive message provide insights if the operation fails.

Additionally, Fortran allows for non-blocking I/O, which can be monitored for completion using the PENDING specifier in combination with IOSTAT and IOMSG. This approach is particularly useful for handling large I/O operations without stalling the program.

For advanced error handling, programs can utilize END and ERR labels in I/O statements. The END label directs the program to a specific statement if an end-of-file condition is detected, while the ERR label handles other errors.

```
   READ(UNIT=10, FMT=*, END=999, ERR=888) number
   PRINT *, 'Read number: ', number
   GOTO 1000

888 CONTINUE
   PRINT *, 'Error reading from file.'
   GOTO 1000

999 CONTINUE
   PRINT *, 'End of file reached.'
1000 CONTINUE
```

In the above code, if an error occurs during the READ operation, control is transferred to the statement labeled 888. If the end-of-file condition is encountered, the control moves to the statement labeled 999. This method provides a clear pathway for handling different conditions and enables consistent error management.

When handling I/O errors, understanding system-specific error codes provided in the ISO_FORTRAN_ENV module is vital. This module defines named constants for common error codes, enhancing code readability and maintainability.

```
USE ISO_FORTRAN_ENV, ONLY: IOSTAT_END, IOSTAT_EOR

INTEGER :: io_status

READ(UNIT=10, FMT=*, IOSTAT=io_status) number
IF (io_status == IOSTAT_END) THEN
```

```
    PRINT *, 'End of file encountered.'
ELSE IF (io_status == IOSTAT_EOR) THEN
    PRINT *, 'End of record encountered.'
ELSE IF (io_status /= 0) THEN
    PRINT *, 'An error occurred during reading.'
ELSE
    PRINT *, 'Read number: ', number
END IF
```

In this example, the named constants IOSTAT_END and IOSTAT_-EOR represent specific error conditions for end-of-file and end-of-record, respectively. Utilizing these constants makes the code more understandable and less prone to errors compared to using numeric error codes directly.

Effective error handling in I/O operations not only prevents program crashes but also helps in identifying issues swiftly, thus significantly improving the overall quality and reliability of the software. Proper use of error detection and handling mechanisms in Fortran empowers programmers to build robust applications capable of gracefully managing unexpected I/O conditions.

6.9 Unformatted and Binary I/O

Unformatted and binary Input/Output (I/O) operations are crucial in Fortran for efficiently managing data storage and retrieval. Unformatted I/O involves reading from or writing to files without explicit formatting, which ensures speed and minimizes storage overhead. Binary I/O further streamlines these processes by handling raw binary data, essential for high-performance applications demanding large-scale data management.

In Fortran, unformatted I/O operations can be performed using the READ and WRITE statements. The syntax for these statements in the unformatted mode is:

```
READ(unit, *) variable_list
WRITE(unit, *) variable_list
```

Here, unit is the logical unit number associated with the file, and variable_list is a list of variables to be read or written. To utilize binary I/O, the file must be opened in an unformatted mode:

```
OPEN(unit=unit_number, file='filename.dat', access='stream', form='unformatted')
```

Using access='stream' allows for the manipulation of files on a byte-by-

byte basis, ideal for binary data operations. The form='unformatted' attribute ensures that no extra formatting characters are added to the data.

To illustrate unformatted I/O, consider the following example where data is written to and read from a binary file:

```
PROGRAM BinaryIOExample
    IMPLICIT NONE
    INTEGER :: unit_number = 10
    REAL :: data_write(5) = [1.0, 2.0, 3.0, 4.0, 5.0]
    REAL :: data_read(5)
    INTEGER :: i

    ! Open the file for unformatted, stream access
    OPEN(unit=unit_number, file='data.bin', access='stream', form='unformatted')

    ! Write the data to the file
    WRITE(unit_number) data_write

    ! Rewind the file pointer to the beginning
    REWIND(unit_number)

    ! Read the data back from the file
    READ(unit_number) data_read

    ! Close the file
    CLOSE(unit_number)

    ! Print the data to verify
    PRINT *, "Data read from binary file:"
    DO i = 1, 5
        PRINT *, data_read(i)
    END DO
END PROGRAM BinaryIOExample
```

In this example, an array of real numbers, data_write, is written to a binary file named data.bin. The READ and WRITE statements specifically employ unformatted mode. After writing, the file pointer is rewound with the REWIND statement to enable reading the data back into data_read.

It is critical to ensure data consistency between the writing and reading processes. Mismatches in data types or array dimensions can lead to erroneous results or runtime errors. Therefore, validation and verification steps, such as printing the read data for confirmation, as demonstrated above, are essential.

Unformatted I/O, in essence, eliminates additional characters like spaces or line breaks, resulting in more compact and faster data handling. However, it necessitates cautious implementation to maintain data integrity and compatibility, particularly across different systems or Fortran compilers. Initialization of appropriate variables and a consistent file handling strategy bolster the efficacy of unformatted and binary I/O operations, ensuring that the data flow remains seamless and robust throughout the program execution.

Finally, it is sometimes beneficial to align binary data with certain structures or record lengths for specific applications. Properly understanding and implementing these structures can further optimize performance and reliability in data-intensive tasks.

6.10 Using Internal Files

Internal files in Fortran provide a flexible mechanism for manipulating data in memory without the need for external files. An internal file is essentially a string variable or an array of strings that you can use for input/output (I/O) operations. This feature is particularly useful for formatting data or creating test data within the program. The syntax and behavior closely resemble those used with external files, but internal files exist only for the duration of program execution and do not involve the file system.

To use an internal file, we need to understand the following Fortran constructs: character strings (or arrays of character strings), the READ and WRITE statements adapted for internal files, and the corresponding format specifications.

```
character(len=50) :: internal_string
character(len=50), dimension(5) :: internal_array
```

Character variables defined in this manner can serve as internal files. Before delving deeper, let's explore an example where an internal string is used for formatted I/O operations.

```
program internal_file_example
   implicit none
   character(len=50) :: buffer
   integer :: num1, num2, io_stat

   ! Write formatted data into the internal string buffer
   write(buffer, '(I5, 1X, I5)', IOSTAT=io_stat) 123, 456

   ! Check for any I/O errors
   if (io_stat /= 0) then
      print *, 'Error occurred during WRITE operation to internal file.'
      stop
   end if

   print *, 'Internal file content:', buffer

   ! Read the data back from the internal string buffer
```

```
    read(buffer, '(I5, 1X, I5)', IOSTAT=io_stat) num1, num2

    ! Check for any I/O errors
    if (io_stat /= 0) then
        print *, 'Error occurred during READ operation from internal file.'
        stop
    end if

    print *, 'Read values from internal file - num1:', num1, ', num2:', num2
end program internal_file_example
```

The above example demonstrates writing and reading integers from an internal string buffer. The WRITE statement formats the integers into the string, and the READ statement parses the formatted data back into numerical variables. Using the IOSTAT specifier, we handle any potential I/O errors by checking the status code.

Internal arrays of strings can also be utilized as internal files, providing even more flexibility. This can be useful when handling multi-line data.

```
program internal_array_example
    implicit none
    character(len=50), dimension(3) :: buffer_lines
    real :: value1, value2, value3
    integer :: io_stat

    ! Write formatted data into the internal string array
    write(buffer_lines(1), '(F8.2)', IOSTAT=io_stat) 123.45
    write(buffer_lines(2), '(F8.2)', IOSTAT=io_stat) 678.90
    write(buffer_lines(3), '(F8.2)', IOSTAT=io_stat) 234.56

    ! Check for any I/O errors
    if (io_stat /= 0) then
        print *, 'Error occurred during WRITE operation to internal file array.'
        stop
    end if

    ! Output the content of the internal file array
    print *, 'Internal file array content:'
    print *, buffer_lines

    ! Read the data back from the internal string array
    read(buffer_lines(1), '(F8.2)', IOSTAT=io_stat) value1
    read(buffer_lines(2), '(F8.2)', IOSTAT=io_stat) value2
    read(buffer_lines(3), '(F8.2)', IOSTAT=io_stat) value3
    ! Check for any I/O errors
    if (io_stat /= 0) then
        print *, 'Error occurred during READ operation from internal file array.'
        stop
    end if

    ! Output the read values
    print *, 'Read values from internal file array:', value1, value2, value3
end program internal_array_example
```

In this example, three real numbers are written to and read from an array of character strings. Each element in the array functions as a separate line in the internal file. This method is particularly useful when dealing with tabular or multi-line input/output scenarios.

When working with internal files, paying close attention to format specifications is crucial since format strings must match the data types and structures within the character variables.

Handling errors in internal file operations is similar to external files. Employing the IOSTAT specifier within READ and WRITE statements allows programmers to detect and handle any anomalies gracefully. Proper error checking ensures robustness, especially in complex applications where data consistency and integrity are paramount.

The use of internal files simplifies certain programming tasks, such as generating formatted output for debugging purposes or simulating file I/O without the overhead of actual file operations. These internalized operations remain internal to the program, providing an efficient and controlled environment for data manipulation and format testing.

6.11 Advanced Formatting Techniques

Advanced formatting techniques in Fortran enable precise control over how input and output operations render data. These techniques are crucial for creating user-friendly and readable outputs, especially in applications demanding high levels of data presentation accuracy.

Character Edit Descriptors: Fortran provides several edit descriptors for formatting character type data. These include:

- A: Outputs character data as is.
- Aw: Outputs at most w characters, where w is a positive integer.

For example:

```
CHARACTER(LEN=20) :: name = "FORTRAN"
PRINT '(A)', name
PRINT '(A10)', name
```

The output will be:

```
FORTRAN
FORTRAN
```

In the output, the first PRINT statement outputs the entire string "FORTRAN" whereas the second PRINT statement pads the output to make it 10 characters long.

Numeric Edit Descriptors: Numeric data formatting in Fortran is handled using several edit descriptors such as I, F, E, G, D, and L.

- Iw: Outputs an integer in a field of width w.
- Fw.d: Outputs a real number in a field of width w with d digits after the decimal point.
- Ew.dE: Outputs a real number in scientific notation, where E specifies the exponent field width.
- Gw.d: General format for real numbers, choosing between F and E notation based on the value's magnitude.
- Lw: Logical edit descriptor for a logical variable.

For example:

```
INTEGER :: i = 12345
REAL :: x = 678.901
PRINT '(I8)', i
PRINT '(F10.2)', x
PRINT '(E12.3E3)', x
```

The output will be:

```
   12345
    678.90
0.679E+03
```

The first PRINT statement outputs the integer i with a width of 8, right-justified. The second PRINT statement formats the real number x with two decimal places, and the third line outputs x in scientific notation with three digits in the exponent.

Positioning Edit Descriptors: To control output positioning, Fortran provides several positioning edit descriptors:

- Tn: Moves to the nth position of the current record.
- TLn: Moves n positions to the left from the current position.
- TRn: Moves n positions to the right from the current position.
- /: Advances to the next line.

For example:

```
PRINT '(T7, A)', "Right"
PRINT '(A, TR5, A)', "Start", "End"
PRINT '(A, /, A)', "Line 1", "Line 2"
```

The output will be:

```
      Right
Start     End
Line 1
Line 2
```

Controlling String Size: Fortran allows control over string size, especially useful when dealing with substrings or specific string lengths.

```
CHARACTER(LEN=12) :: str = "FORTRAN"
PRINT '(A)', str
PRINT '(A8)', str
PRINT '(A3)', str(1:3)
```

The output will be:

```
FORTRAN
FORTRAN
FOR
```

Zero-Padding Output: Zero-padding is critical for certain numeric output formats for alignment or specific display requirements.

```
INTEGER :: num = 42
PRINT '(I5.5)', num
REAL :: fnum = 3.1415
PRINT '(F10.4)', fnum
PRINT '(F10.4)', 0.1234
```

The output will be:

```
00042
    3.1415
    0.1234
```

The first PRINT statement zero-pads the integer to occupy exactly five positions. The second PRINT format outputs the real number with four decimal places, including a width descriptor ensuring proper spacing.

Advanced Integer and Real Output with Descriptors: More complex scenarios often require combining various descriptors to achieve the desired formatting.

```
INTEGER :: a = 7, b = 1234
REAL :: pi = 3.1416, e = 2.71828
PRINT '(I5, I10)', a, b
PRINT '(F8.2, F12.5)', pi, e
```

The output will be:

```
7       1234
3.14       2.71828
```

Multi-Line Formatting: For complex formatting that spans multiple lines, use slashes in format strings to break lines deliberately.

```
CHARACTER(LEN=6) :: lang1 = "Python", lang2 = "Fortran"
INTEGER :: year1 = 1991, year2 = 1957
PRINT '(A, I5, /, A, I5)', lang1, year1, lang2, year2
```

The output will be:

```
Python 1991
Fortran 1957
```

In this example, Fortran inserts a line break between the output of lang1 and year1, and lang2 and year2, demonstrating multi-line formatting effectively.

These advanced formatting techniques allow Fortran programmers to harness the full power of its I/O capabilities, leading to cleaner and more controlled data presentation.

6.12 Best Practices for Efficient I/O Operations

Efficient I/O operations are crucial for high-performance Fortran applications, especially when working with large datasets or performing computations that require significant reading from or writing to files. This section presents best practices aimed at optimizing I/O operations to minimize execution time and resource utilization.

When implementing I/O operations in Fortran, consider the following guidelines:

- **Minimize I/O Operations**: Consolidate multiple reads or writes into single, larger operations whenever possible. For example, instead of reading or writing data in small chunks within a loop, prefer bulk operations to reduce the overhead latency associated with each I/O call.

- **Buffering**: Leverage buffering techniques to store intermediate data in memory before performing actual I/O operations. This reduces the number of disk accesses and enhances throughput. For instance, read inputs into an array and then process the array in memory:

```
integer, parameter :: n = 1000
real :: data(n)
open(unit=10, file='input.dat', status='old')
read(10, *) data
close(10)
```

- **Formatted vs Unformatted I/O**: Opt for unformatted I/O for performance-critical applications. Formatted I/O involves additional processing to convert data between its binary representation and a human-readable form, which can be computationally expensive:

```
! Example of unformatted write
real :: data(1000)
open(unit=20, file='unformatted_output.dat', status='new', form='
    unformatted')
write(20) data
close(20)

! Example of formatted write
open(unit=30, file='formatted_output.txt', status='new', form='formatted')
write(30, '(F10.4)') data
close(30)
```

- **Efficient Use of Internal Files**: Internal files are useful for generating formatted output that will be consumed internally by the program. This avoids unnecessary file operations:

```
character(len=20) :: line
real :: value = 123.456
write(line, '(F8.3)') value
! line now contains the formatted output " 123.456"
```

- **File Positioning Operations**: Minimize the use of file positioning operations such as REWIND or BACKSPACE. These commands can be expensive, as they require repositioning the file pointer, which can be time-consuming for large files:

```
open(unit=40, file='datafile.dat', status='old')
! Avoid unnecessary REWINDs
do i = 1, n
   read(40, *) value
   ! process value
end do
close(40)
```

- **Error Handling**: Implement robust error handling to gracefully manage I/O errors. This prevents the program from crashing and allows for better debugging and logging:

```
integer :: ios
```

```
open(unit=50, file='important_data.dat', status='old', iostat=ios)
if (ios /= 0) then
    write(*, *) 'Error opening file, IOSTAT = ', ios
    stop
endif
! Continue with I/O operations
close(50)
```

- **Optimize Open and Close Operations**: Avoid frequently opening and closing files within loops. Instead, open a file once before entering the loop and close it after exiting the loop:

```
open(unit=60, file='results.dat', status='new')
do i = 1, n
    write(60, *) data(i)
end do
close(60)
```

- **Asynchronous I/O**: For large-scale applications, consider utilizing asynchronous I/O operations, which allow computations to proceed while I/O operations are still in progress. This feature, available in later iterations of Fortran, enables overlapping computation with I/O, thereby enhancing performance:

```
async integer :: req
real :: buffer(1000)
open(unit=70, file='async_output.dat', status='new')
write(70, asynchronous='yes') buffer
wait(70, id=req) ! Ensure I/O is complete
close(70)
```

Integrating these best practices into your Fortran programs will help in achieving optimal performance in I/O operations. Properly managing file I/O not only enhances the efficiency of data handling but also contributes to the overall robustness and scalability of your applications.

Chapter 7

File Handling

This chapter delves into the specifics of file handling in Fortran, detailing operations such as opening and closing files, and reading and writing data. It covers various file positioning techniques like REWIND, BACKSPACE, and END FILE, and differentiates between formatted and unformatted files, as well as direct access and stream I/O. The chapter also discusses handling file status and errors, utilizing file I/O in subroutines and functions, and advanced file management techniques, providing readers with a comprehensive understanding of effective file operations in Fortran.

7.1 Introduction to File Handling

File handling is a crucial aspect of programming that enables the storage, retrieval, and manipulation of data external to the program's immediate execution environment. In Fortran, efficient file handling is essential for tasks ranging from simple data storage to complex scientific computations that require the management of large datasets. This section introduces basic concepts and operations related to file handling in Fortran, providing a foundation for understanding subsequent sections on advanced file operations.

Fortran supports several file operations, including opening and closing files, reading and writing data, and positioning within files. These operations are facilitated through specific Fortran constructs and intrinsic functions, ensuring that file handling is both robust and flexible.

When dealing with files in Fortran, it is important to understand the file I/O statements and intrinsic routines. One of the primary statements used for file handling is the OPEN statement, which establishes a connection between a file on the disk and a unit number within the program. The syntax for the OPEN statement is as follows:

```
OPEN(UNIT=unit, FILE='filename', STATUS='status', ACTION='action',
     POSITION='position', IOSTAT=iostat, ERR=err_label)
```

Here are the main components of the OPEN statement:

- UNIT: An integer expression specifying the unit number to be associated with the file.
- FILE: A character expression specifying the name of the file.
- STATUS: A character expression that indicates the status of the file. The possible values are 'OLD', 'NEW', 'REPLACE', 'UNKNOWN' for files to be opened.
- ACTION: A character expression indicating the allowed operations on the file, such as 'READ', 'WRITE', or 'READWRITE'.
- POSITION: Specifies the position within the file where I/O operations begin. This can be 'ASIS', 'REWIND', or 'APPEND'.
- IOSTAT: An integer variable that stores the status code of the I/O operation. If the operation is successful, IOSTAT is zero; otherwise, it is a non-zero error code.
- ERR: A label to transfer control if an error occurs during the OPEN operation.

For example, to open an existing file named 'data.txt' for reading, you would use:

```
INTEGER :: iostat
OPEN(UNIT=10, FILE='data.txt', STATUS='OLD', ACTION='READ', IOSTAT=
    iostat)
IF (iostat /= 0) THEN
   PRINT *, 'Error opening file'
END IF
```

Once a file is opened, various I/O operations can be performed. To read data from a file, Fortran provides the READ statement. The READ statement is used to transfer data from a file into variables. Its basic syntax is:

```
READ(UNIT=unit, FMT=format, IOSTAT=iostat, ERR=err_label) variable_list
```

The main components of the READ statement include:

- UNIT: Specifies the unit number associated with the file.
- FMT: Defines the format of the input data. It can be a format label, a character expression specifying a format string, or an asterisk (*) for list-directed input.
- IOSTAT and ERR: Optional components to handle I/O status and errors similar to the OPEN statement.
- variable_list: A comma-separated list of variables where the data will be read into.

To read a series of integers from a file, you might use:

```
INTEGER :: num1, num2, iostat
READ(UNIT=10, FMT='(I5, I5)', IOSTAT=iostat) num1, num2
IF (iostat /= 0) THEN
    PRINT *, 'Error reading file'
END IF
```

Writing data to a file is accomplished using the WRITE statement, which has a similar structure to the READ statement:

```
WRITE(UNIT=unit, FMT=format, IOSTAT=iostat, ERR=err_label) variable_list
```

To append integers num1 and num2 to a file, the code could be written as:

```
INTEGER :: num1, num2, iostat
num1 = 10
num2 = 5
OPEN(UNIT=10, FILE='data.txt', STATUS='OLD', ACTION='WRITE', POSITION
      ='APPEND', IOSTAT=iostat)
IF (iostat == 0) THEN
    WRITE(UNIT=10, FMT='(I5, I5)', IOSTAT=iostat) num1, num2
    IF (iostat /= 0) THEN
        PRINT *, 'Error writing to file'
    END IF
ELSE
    PRINT *, 'Error opening file'
END IF
```

Finally, closing a file is an important operation to free resources and ensure data integrity. The CLOSE statement is employed for this purpose, with the following syntax:

```
CLOSE(UNIT=unit, IOSTAT=iostat, ERR=err_label)
```

To close the previously opened file, the code would be:

```
CLOSE(UNIT=10, IOSTAT=iostat)
IF (iostat /= 0) THEN
    PRINT *, 'Error closing file'
END IF
```

An understanding of these basic operations forms the bedrock of proficient file handling in Fortran. Subsequent sections will build on these foundations, diving deeper into more advanced aspects such as file positioning, direct access files, stream I/O, handling file status and errors, and integrating file I/O within subroutines and functions.

7.2 Opening and Closing Files

File handling begins with understanding how to open and close files in Fortran, which is essential for performing any subsequent file operations. Files in Fortran are associated with unit numbers, which are integers that act as file identifiers within a given program. It is crucial to use appropriate syntax and options for the OPEN and CLOSE statements to ensure robust file handling.

Opening Files:

The OPEN statement is used to open a file and associate it with a unit number. The basic syntax of the OPEN statement is as follows:

```
OPEN(unit=unit_number, file='filename', status='file_status', action='read_action',
     iostat=iostat_variable, err=error_label)
```

Key components of the OPEN statement:

- unit=unit_number: Specifies the unit number (an integer) to associate with the file.
- file='filename': Provides the name of the file to open.
- status='file_status': Indicates the status of the file. Possible values are:
  - 'old': The file must already exist.
  - 'new': The file does not exist and will be created.
  - 'replace': An existing file with the same name will be deleted and a new file created.

  - 'scratch': A temporary file that will be deleted upon program termination.
  - 'unknown': The file status is not specified.

- action='read_action': Specifies the allowed operations on the file. Possible values are:
  - 'read': The file is opened for reading only.
  - 'write': The file is opened for writing only.
  - 'readwrite': The file is opened for both reading and writing.

- iostat=iostat_variable: Stores the status of the I/O operation. A zero value indicates success, while a non-zero value indicates an error.

- err=error_label: Specifies a label to jump to in the event of an error.

An example of opening a file for reading is shown below:

```
INTEGER :: unit_number, iostat
unit_number = 10
OPEN(unit=unit_number, file='data.txt', status='old', action='read', iostat=iostat)
IF (iostat /= 0) THEN
    PRINT *, 'Error opening file: ', iostat
END IF
```

Closing Files:

The CLOSE statement is used to close a file that has been opened. The basic syntax is:

```
CLOSE(unit=unit_number, iostat=iostat_variable, err=error_label, status='
    file_status')
```

Key components of the CLOSE statement:

- unit=unit_number: Specifies the unit number associated with the file to be closed.

- iostat=iostat_variable: Stores the status of the close operation. Similar to the OPEN statement, a zero value indicates success, while a non-zero value indicates an error.

- err=error_label: Specifies a label to jump to in the event of an error.

- status='file_status': Specifies the status of the file after closing. Possible values are:
  - 'keep': The file is retained (default behavior for permanent files).
  - 'delete': The file is deleted upon closing.

An example of closing a file is shown below:

```
INTEGER :: unit_number, iostat
unit_number = 10
CLOSE(unit=unit_number, iostat=iostat, status='keep')
IF (iostat /= 0) THEN
    PRINT *, 'Error closing file: ', iostat
END IF
```

Appropriate opening and closing of files in Fortran prevent resource leaks and other potential issues. For example, failing to close a file may result in reaching a system-specific limit on the number of open files, leading to errors in subsequent file operations.

Careful handling of the iostat variable helps in diagnosing file operation errors without abruptly terminating the program. This practice is particularly important in robust and resilient Fortran applications that may require complex file handling logic across multiple files and operations.

7.3 Reading Data from Files

In Fortran, reading data from files is an essential function that enables efficient data processing and file handling. This section elucidates the methodologies and syntax involved in extracting data from files. The material presumes familiarity with basic Fortran constructs and file opening operations discussed in preceding sections.

The primary statement used for reading data in Fortran is the READ statement, which facilitates input from both standard input devices and external files. The syntax for the READ statement is presented as follows:

```
READ (unit, format, options) list-of-variables
```

Here, unit specifies the logical unit number of the file from which data is to be read, format denotes the format specification (which can be a label, character constant, or an asterisk for list-directed I/O), and options may include parameters such as ERR=label, END=label, or IOSTAT=i-var for error handling and I/O status reporting.

1. Basic READ Statement Usage

Consider a file named data.txt containing the following formatted data:

```
10 20 30
40 50 60
```

The corresponding Fortran program to read these values would be:

```
PROGRAM ReadFile
  IMPLICIT NONE
  INTEGER :: i, j, k, unit

  unit = 10 ! Define the logical unit number

  OPEN(unit, FILE='data.txt', STATUS='OLD')

  READ(unit, *) i, j, k
  PRINT *, i, j, k

  READ(unit, *) i, j, k
  PRINT *, i, j, k

  CLOSE(unit)
END PROGRAM ReadFile
```

In this example, data is read sequentially. The first READ statement extracts the first line of integers, storing 10, 20, and 30 in the variables i, j, and k, respectively. The second READ retrieves the next line, with 40, 50, and 60 assigned similarly.

2. Reading Data with Explicit Format

For formatted input, an explicit FORMAT statement can define the input structure:

```
PROGRAM ReadFileFormatted
  IMPLICIT NONE
  INTEGER :: a, b, c, unit

  unit = 20
  OPEN(unit, FILE='data.txt', STATUS='OLD')

  READ(unit, '(I5, I5, I5)') a, b, c
  PRINT *, a, b, c

  CLOSE(unit)
END PROGRAM ReadFileFormatted
```

Here, the format (I5, I5, I5) indicates three integers, each occupying five columns. This format should match the data layout in the file.

3. Error Handling During Reading

To handle potential errors during reading operations, the ERR=label and IOSTAT options are crucial. The ERR=label option transfers control to a specified statement label if an error occurs. The IOSTAT option stores a status code, allowing the program to check the success of the I/O operation:

```
PROGRAM ReadWithErrorHandling
  IMPLICIT NONE
  INTEGER :: x, y, z, unit, iostat

  unit = 30

  OPEN(unit, FILE='data.txt', STATUS='OLD', IOSTAT=iostat)
  IF (iostat /= 0) THEN
    PRINT *, 'Error opening file'
    STOP
  END IF

  READ(unit, *, IOSTAT=iostat) x, y, z
  IF (iostat /= 0) THEN
    PRINT *, 'Error reading data'
  ELSE
    PRINT *, x, y, z
  END IF

  CLOSE(unit)
END PROGRAM ReadWithErrorHandling
```

In this program, the IOSTAT parameter captures the status of the OPEN and READ operations, enabling proactive error messages if issues arise.

4. Reading Data from Formatted Files with Different Data Types

For files containing mixed data types, it is imperative to read with appropriate formats. Consider mixeddata.txt:

```
100 'Fortran' 3.14
200 'Programming' 2.71
```

Reading such a file would require the following code:

```
PROGRAM ReadMixedData
  IMPLICIT NONE
  INTEGER :: num, unit
  REAL :: value
  CHARACTER(LEN=15) :: text

  unit = 40
  OPEN(unit, FILE='mixeddata.txt', STATUS='OLD')

  READ(unit, '(I3, A15, F5.2)') num, text, value
  PRINT *, num, TRIM(text), value

  CLOSE(unit)
END PROGRAM ReadMixedData
```

The format (I3, A15, F5.2) specifies an integer, a character string of length 15, and a real number with two decimal places. This structure should encompass the data layout precisely.

Reading data from files in Fortran involves mastering the READ statement, understanding the intricacies of format specifiers, and handling potential errors judiciously. The above examples provide a foundational approach to efficiently reading a variety of formatted and mixed-type data from files, ensuring that data input operations are both precise and robust.

7.4 Writing Data to Files

Writing data to files in Fortran is a fundamental task that allows the storage of processed information, results, and other data for later use. The primary statement used for writing data to files is the WRITE statement. This section explores the syntax of the WRITE statement, various methods for writing both formatted and unformatted data, and best practices to ensure efficient and error-free file operations.

The WRITE statement syntax can be expressed as follows:

```
WRITE(unit, format) [io-list]
```

Here, unit is an integer expression representing the logical unit number of the file. The format can be a label of a FORMAT statement, an asterisk * for list-directed formatting, or a character literal specifying the format directly. The io-list consists of the variables or expressions to be written to the file.

Example: Writing Formatted Data

Consider a Fortran program that writes an array of integers to a file, each element on a new line.

```
PROGRAM WriteFormattedData
  INTEGER :: i, unit
  INTEGER, DIMENSION(5) :: data = (/ 1, 2, 3, 4, 5 /)

  unit = 10
  OPEN(unit, FILE='output.txt', STATUS='REPLACE')

  DO i = 1, SIZE(data)
    WRITE(unit, '(I5)') data(i)
  END DO

  CLOSE(unit)
END PROGRAM WriteFormattedData
```

After executing the above program, the content of output.txt will be:

```
1
2
3
4
5
```

Writing Data with List-directed Formatting

List-directed formatting, specified by an asterisk *, allows Fortran to determine the format based on the data type of each element. This method is simpler but provides less control over the output format.

```
PROGRAM WriteListDirected
  INTEGER :: unit
  REAL :: a = 1.23, b = 4.56, c = 7.89

  unit = 20
  OPEN(unit, FILE='output_list.txt', STATUS='REPLACE')

  WRITE(unit, *) a, b, c

  CLOSE(unit)
END PROGRAM WriteListDirected
```

The resulting file output_list.txt will contain:

```
 1.2300000      4.5600000      7.8900000
```

Writing Unformatted Data

Unformatted data provides a more efficient way to write and read binary data files without the overhead of formatting characters. This method is useful for large datasets and when precise control over data representation is necessary.

```
PROGRAM WriteUnformattedData
  INTEGER :: i, unit
  INTEGER, DIMENSION(5) :: data = (/ 1, 2, 3, 4, 5 /)

  unit = 30
  OPEN(unit, FILE='output_unformatted.dat', STATUS='REPLACE', FORM='
       UNFORMATTED')

  WRITE(unit) data

  CLOSE(unit)
END PROGRAM WriteUnformattedData
```

Unformatted files store data in a binary format, and their content is typically not human-readable. This approach is particularly useful for interchanging data between programs or for performance-critical applications where processing speed is paramount.

Best Practices

- **File Status:** Always specify the STATUS parameter when opening files to avoid accidental overwriting of important data. Use STATUS='REPLACE' to overwrite and STATUS='NEW' to prevent accidental overwriting.
- **Error Handling:** Implement error handling for file operations by checking the IOSTAT parameter to manage runtime errors gracefully.
- **Close Files:** Ensure that all opened files are properly closed using the CLOSE statement to release system resources.

Sample program demonstrating error handling:

```
PROGRAM WriteWithErrorHandling
  INTEGER :: unit, ios
  REAL :: data = 1.23
  CHARACTER(LEN=20) :: filename = 'output_error.txt'

  unit = 40
  OPEN(unit, FILE=filename, STATUS='NEW', IOSTAT=ios)

  IF (ios /= 0) THEN
    PRINT *, 'Error opening file', filename
  ELSE
    WRITE(unit, *) data
    CLOSE(unit)
  END IF
END PROGRAM WriteWithErrorHandling
```

This program incorporates checking of the IOSTAT parameter to capture any errors during the file opening process, thereby ensuring that the program can handle errors without crashing.

Understanding the WRITE statement in its various forms enables the creation of efficient programs for data storage in Fortran. Proper handling of file operations and adherence to best practices not only enhances program reliability but also contributes to better resource management.

7.5 File Positioning: REWIND, BACKSPACE, and END FILE

File positioning in Fortran is critical for controlling the point of data access in file operations. The REWIND, BACKSPACE, and END

FILE statements provide granular control over file position, facilitating non-sequential data access and streamlining file handling procedures. Here, we delve into these essential Fortran file positioning commands, elucidating their syntax, usage, and practical implications.

REWIND Statement

The REWIND statement resets the position of a file to the beginning. This operation is particularly useful for re-reading files or restarting file-based processes without closing and reopening the file. The syntax for the REWIND statement is simple and straightforward:

```
REWIND (unit = iunit [, iostat = ios] [, err = err_label])
```

- unit - Specifies the logical unit number associated with the file.
- iostat - (Optional) Variable that stores the status return value. It will be zero if the operation is successful, non-zero otherwise.
- err - (Optional) Specifies the label to which control is transferred if an error occurs.

```
! Example of REWIND usage
PROGRAM rewind_example
  INTEGER :: ios
  OPEN (UNIT=10, FILE='data.txt', STATUS='OLD')
  REWIND (UNIT=10, IOSTAT=ios)
  IF (ios /= 0) THEN
    PRINT *, 'Error rewinding file.'
  END IF
  CLOSE (UNIT=10)
END PROGRAM rewind_example
```

BACKSPACE Statement

The BACKSPACE statement is used to move the file position indicator backward by one record. This command is valuable in scenarios where you need to reprocess or reconsider the last read or written record. The syntax for the BACKSPACE statement is as follows:

```
BACKSPACE (unit = iunit [, iostat = ios] [, err = err_label])
```

- unit - Specifies the logical unit number associated with the file.
- iostat - (Optional) Variable that stores the status return value. It will be zero if the backspace operation is successful, non-zero otherwise.

- err - (Optional) Specifies the label to which control is transferred if an error occurs.

```
! Example of BACKSPACE usage
PROGRAM backspace_example
  INTEGER :: ios
  OPEN (UNIT=10, FILE='data.txt', STATUS='OLD')
  BACKSPACE (UNIT=10, IOSTAT=ios)
  IF (ios /= 0) THEN
    PRINT *, 'Error performing backspace.'
  END IF
  CLOSE (UNIT=10)
END PROGRAM backspace_example
```

END FILE Statement

The END FILE statement is utilized to indicate the end of a file. This command essentially marks the end of data writing and, when read, signals the end-of-file condition. The syntax for the END FILE statement is:

```
END FILE (unit = iunit [, iostat = ios] [, err = err_label])
```

- unit - Specifies the logical unit number associated with the file.
- iostat - (Optional) Variable that stores the status return value. It will be zero if the end file operation is successful, non-zero otherwise.
- err - (Optional) Specifies the label to which control is transferred if an error occurs.

```
! Example of END FILE usage
PROGRAM endfile_example
  INTEGER :: ios
  OPEN (UNIT=10, FILE='data.txt', STATUS='NEW')
  WRITE (UNIT=10, FMT='(A)') 'Sample Data Line 1'
  WRITE (UNIT=10, FMT='(A)') 'Sample Data Line 2'
  END FILE (UNIT=10, IOSTAT=ios)
  IF (ios /= 0) THEN
    PRINT *, 'Error writing end of file.'
  END IF
  CLOSE (UNIT=10)
END PROGRAM endfile_example
```

Correct application of REWIND, BACKSPACE, and END FILE statements streamlines file handling, ensuring logical and efficient data access and manipulation. Understanding these commands facilitates more versatile and robust file processing routines in Fortran programs.

7.6 Formed and Unformed Files

In Fortran, files can be categorized into two types: *formatted* and *unformatted*. Understanding the distinction between these two types of files is essential for effective file handling and data processing. This section will discuss these concepts in detail, providing examples and explanations of when to use each file type.

Formatted files, also known as text files, store data in a human-readable format. Each data element is converted to its character representation, and records are typically delineated by newline characters. Formatted files are often used for data interchange, logging, and configurations because they can be easily read and modified using standard text editors.

Unformatted files, also known as binary files, store data in its native binary representation. This method of storage is more efficient in terms of both speed and space, as it avoids the overhead of converting data to and from text. However, unformatted files are not human-readable and are often used for tasks requiring fast I/O operations or where data integrity and precision are critical, such as in scientific computations.

When working with formatted files, the data is typically accessed through the use of format specifiers. These specifiers dictate how the data should be interpreted and presented. In contrast, unformatted file I/O bypasses the need for such specifiers as the data is written and read exactly as it is stored in memory.

```
program write_formatted
    implicit none
    integer :: unit_no
    character(len=20) :: filename
    real :: pi

    pi = 3.14159
    filename = 'data_formatted.txt'

    open(unit_no, file=filename, status='unknown', action='write', form='formatted')
    write(unit_no, '(F8.5)') pi
    close(unit_no)
end program write_formatted
```

In this example, the value of pi is written to a formatted file named data_formatted.txt. The write statement uses the format specifier F8.5 to indicate that the value should be written as a floating-point number with three digits before the decimal point and five digits after.

Reading from formatted files involves specifying how the data should be interpreted and read from the file, as shown in the example below:

```
program read_formatted
    implicit none
    integer :: unit_no
    character(len=20) :: filename
    real :: pi

    filename = 'data_formatted.txt'

    open(unit_no, file=filename, status='old', action='read', form='formatted')
    read(unit_no, '(F8.5)') pi
    close(unit_no)

    print *, 'Value of pi:', pi
end program read_formatted
```

In this example, the file data_formatted.txt is opened for reading. The read statement retrieves the value stored in the file using the same format specifier F8.5.

Conversely, with unformatted files, data is written and read in its binary form without any format specification. This type of file I/O is accomplished using statements that directly transfer data between memory and the file system.

```
program write_unformatted
    implicit none
    integer :: unit_no
    character(len=20) :: filename
    real :: pi

    pi = 3.14159
    filename = 'data_unformatted.dat'

    open(unit_no, file=filename, status='unknown', action='write', form='unformatted'
        )
    write(unit_no) pi
    close(unit_no)
end program write_unformatted
```

In this example, the value of pi is written to an unformatted file named data_unformatted.dat. No format specifier is needed as the data is stored in its binary form.

Reading from unformatted files requires the data read operation to match the data write operation exactly, in terms of both data type and structure:

```
program read_unformatted
    implicit none
    integer :: unit_no
    character(len=20) :: filename
    real :: pi

    filename = 'data_unformatted.dat'
```

```
    open(unit_no, file=filename, status='old', action='read', form='unformatted')
    read(unit_no) pi
    close(unit_no)

    print *, 'Value of pi:', pi
end program read_unformatted
```

In the corresponding read operation, the binary data is read back into the variable pi, preserving its original binary structure.

Choosing between formatted and unformatted files depends largely on the intended use-case and the requirements for data interpretation and manipulation. Formatted files are ideal for scenarios where human readability and data interchange are important, while unformatted files are better suited for high-performance computation, where speed and precision are paramount.

7.7 Direct Access Files

Direct access files in Fortran provide a mechanism for reading and writing records at arbitrary positions within a file. Unlike sequential access files, where data is processed in a predetermined order, direct access allows for non-linear data retrieval and storage, greatly enhancing flexibility and efficiency for certain applications.

File Opening Syntax

To utilize direct access files, the OPEN statement must specify the ACCESS parameter as 'DIRECT'. Additionally, the RECL (record length) parameter must be defined, indicating the size of each record in the file. This record length is critical as it dictates how the data will be segmented and accessed within the file.

```
OPEN(UNIT=10, FILE='datafile.dat', STATUS='NEW', ACCESS='DIRECT', RECL
     =80)
```

In the example above, datafile.dat is opened as a new direct access file with records of 80 characters (or bytes) in length.

Reading and Writing Direct Access Files

Direct access file operations use the READ and WRITE statements similarly to sequential files, but they include an REC parameter to specify the record number for the operation.

```
WRITE(10, REC=5) variable1, variable2
```

```
READ(10, REC=15) variable3, variable4
```

The above statements write variable1 and variable2 to record number 5 and read variable3 and variable4 from record number 15, respectively.

Example: Direct Access File Operations

Consider an example where we need to store and retrieve information about employees in a company. Each record contains an employee's ID, name, and salary. The file operations include writing employee data and reading it back based on the employee ID.

```
PROGRAM DirectAccessDemo
  IMPLICIT NONE
  INTEGER :: emp_id, rec_num
  CHARACTER(LEN=30) :: emp_name
  REAL :: emp_salary
  INTEGER, PARAMETER :: recl = 44 ! Record Length (4 + 30 + 4 + 4 + 2)

  ! Open the direct access file
  OPEN(UNIT=20, FILE='employees.dat', STATUS='NEW', ACCESS='DIRECT',
       RECL=recl)

  ! Writing employee data
  DO rec_num = 1, 3
    PRINT *, "Enter Employee ID, Name, and Salary:"
    READ(*,*) emp_id, emp_name, emp_salary
    WRITE(20, REC=rec_num) emp_id, emp_name, emp_salary
  END DO

  ! Reading employee data
  DO rec_num = 1, 3
    READ(20, REC=rec_num) emp_id, emp_name, emp_salary
    PRINT *, "Record", rec_num, ": ID=", emp_id, ", Name=", emp_name, ", Salary
         =", emp_salary
  END DO

  ! Close the file
  CLOSE(20)
END PROGRAM DirectAccessDemo
```

```
Sample Output:
Enter Employee ID, Name, and Salary:
1 John_Doe 55000.00

Enter Employee ID, Name, and Salary:
2 Jane_Smith 60000.00

Enter Employee ID, Name, and Salary:
3 Alan_Turing 120000.00

Record 1 : ID= 1 , Name= John_Doe , Salary= 55000.00
Record 2 : ID= 2 , Name= Jane_Smith , Salary= 60000.00
Record 3 : ID= 3 , Name= Alan_Turing , Salary= 120000.00
```

Error Handling in Direct Access Files

Error handling is crucial in file operations to ensure robustness. The

IOSTAT variable can be used to capture error codes from I/O operations. If an error occurs, the ERR label directs the program flow to an error-handling segment.

```
INTEGER :: ios
OPEN(UNIT=30, FILE='records.dat', STATUS='UNKNOWN', ACCESS='DIRECT',
      RECL=100)

READ(30, REC=10, IOSTAT=ios) var1, var2
IF (ios /= 0) THEN
  PRINT *, "Error reading record 10"
  ! Error handling code here
END IF

CLOSE(30)
```

Performance Considerations

Direct access files provide significant performance advantages for applications requiring frequent, arbitrary record retrieval. By allowing direct positioning within the file, they eliminate the need to sequentially search through preceding data, thus reducing I/O overhead. However, the fixed record length requirement might introduce padding, leading to potential storage inefficiencies.

When designing applications that leverage direct access files, it is crucial to balance the benefits of rapid, random data access against potential file space utilization inefficiencies. Selecting an appropriate RECL based on the exact data requirements helps mitigate some of the padding issues, ensuring optimal storage and performance.

Direct access file operations are invaluable for certain classes of problems, offering flexibility and efficiency, especially in applications where rapid, non-sequential data access is paramount.

7.8 Stream I/O

Stream I/O in Fortran offers a more flexible approach to file handling than traditional record-based I/O operations. This method allows for reading and writing data in a continuous byte stream, making it particularly useful for handling large files or binary data where record boundaries are either non-existent or irrelevant.

Stream I/O operations are particularly significant when the file contains complex data structures or mixed data types, where the position and size of the data are critical.

Opening Files for Stream I/O

To perform stream I/O, a file must be opened with the ACCESS specifier set to STREAM. The following is an example of how to open a file for stream access:

```
OPEN(UNIT=10, FILE='data.bin', STATUS='OLD', ACCESS='STREAM', &
    ACTION='READWRITE', FORM='UNFORMATTED')
```

UNIT specifies the unit number, FILE gives the name of the file, and STATUS indicates the status of the file (e.g., 'OLD', 'NEW'). The ACCESS specifier must be set to 'STREAM' to indicate stream access. The ACTION specifier determines whether the file can be read, written, or both. In this case, 'READWRITE' allows both operations. The FORM specifier is set to 'UNFORMATTED' to indicate binary data.

Reading Data with Stream I/O

To read data in stream mode, the POS specifier is used to indicate the position within the file from which to start reading. Here's an example demonstrating how to read an integer array starting from the 21st byte position:

```
INTEGER :: array(10)
READ(UNIT=10, POS=21) array
```

In this case, the file starts reading at the 21st byte. The variable array is filled with the data read from the file starting at that position.

Writing Data with Stream I/O

Similarly, to write data using stream I/O, one must specify the UNIT, the data to write, and the POS specifier if positioning is required. Here's an example of writing an integer array starting at the 11th byte position:

```
INTEGER :: newData(10) = (/1, 2, 3, 4, 5, 6, 7, 8, 9, 10/)
WRITE(UNIT=10, POS=11) newData
```

This writes the contents of newData to the file, beginning at the 11th byte position.

Determining File Size

When working with stream I/O, determining the file size or the position within the file is often necessary. For binary files, this can be achieved using the INQUIRE statement with the POS and SIZE specifiers. Here is an example:

```
INTEGER :: fileSize
INQUIRE(UNIT=10, SIZE=fileSize)
```

This sets fileSize to the size of the file connected to unit 10.

Error Handling in Stream I/O

Error handling is crucial to ensure data integrity during file operations. The IOSTAT specifier can be used to check the success of a read or write operation. Here is an example:

```
INTEGER :: ioError, array(10)
READ(UNIT=10, POS=21, IOSTAT=ioError) array
IF (ioError /= 0) THEN
    PRINT *, 'Error reading the file, IOSTAT = ', ioError
END IF
```

This code checks the ioError variable after attempting to read from the file. If an error occurs, it prints the error code.

Stream I/O provides powerful capabilities for handling complex and large-scale data files in Fortran. By allowing byte-level file positioning, it offers an approach that is more flexible than traditional record-oriented I/O, making it suitable for a broad range of applications. Proper error handling and awareness of file positioning greatly enhance the robustness of stream I/O operations.

7.9 Handling File Status and Errors

Understanding and effectively managing file status and errors in Fortran is crucial for robust and reliable programming. Proper handling ensures that data operations are executed correctly, and potential issues are identified and resolved promptly.

File Status Inquiry

Fortran provides several built-in functions that allow you to query the status of a file. These functions are essential for verifying the existence of a file, checking its accessibility, and obtaining other pertinent information. The INQUIRE statement is widely used for this purpose.

```
INQUIRE(FILE='data.txt', EXIST=fileExists, OPENED=fileOpened, NUMBER=
      unitNumber, READ=readable, WRITE=writable)
```

In this example, INQUIRE checks various attributes of the file data.txt. The variables fileExists, fileOpened, unitNumber, readable, and writable will be set according to the file's status. Here is what each of these variables represents:

- fileExists: Logical variable indicating whether the file exists.

- fileOpened: Logical variable indicating whether the file is currently open.
- unitNumber: Integer variable that will hold the unit number if the file is open.
- readable: Logical variable indicating whether the file is readable.
- writable: Logical variable indicating whether the file is writable.

Error Handling with IOSTAT and IOMSG

Fortran offers mechanisms to handle errors during file operations, primarily through the IOSTAT and IOMSG specifiers. These specifiers can be used within read, write, open, close, and inquire statements, among others.

```
INTEGER :: ioStatus
CHARACTER(len=100) :: ioMessage

OPEN(UNIT=10, FILE='data.txt', STATUS='OLD', IOSTAT=ioStatus, IOMSG=
    ioMessage)

IF (ioStatus /= 0) THEN
   PRINT *, 'Error opening file: ', ioMessage
   STOP
ENDIF
```

In this code, IOSTAT captures the error status of the operation, while IOMSG provides a descriptive error message. If IOSTAT is non-zero, an error has occurred, prompting the program to print the error message and terminate execution.

Common IOSTAT Error Codes:

- +1: End-of-file was reached.
- -1: End-of-record was reached.
- -2: Input conversion error.
- Other non-zero values indicate different kinds of errors.

Checking for File Existence

Before attempting to open a file for reading or writing, it is often advisable to check whether the file already exists to avoid unintended data loss or read errors. This can be achieved using the INQUIRE statement.

```
LOGICAL :: fileExists
INQUIRE(FILE='dataOutput.txt', EXIST=fileExists)

IF (.NOT. fileExists) THEN
   PRINT *, 'File does not exist.'
   STOP
ENDIF
```

Handling End-of-File Condition

While reading data from a file, it is important to handle the end-of-file (EOF) condition correctly. Fortran allows you to detect EOF using the IOSTAT specifier during read operations.

```
INTEGER :: unitNumber, ioStatus
unitNumber = 20
OPEN(UNIT=unitNumber, FILE='inputData.txt', STATUS='OLD')

DO
   READ(unitNumber, *, IOSTAT=ioStatus) :: variable
   IF (ioStatus == -1) EXIT ! End of record
   IF (ioStatus == 0) THEN
      ! Process the read data
   ELSE
      PRINT *, 'Error reading file'
      EXIT
   ENDIF
ENDDO

PRINT *, 'Reached end of file.'
CLOSE(unitNumber)
```

In this example, the DO loop continues to read entries from the file until IOSTAT equals -1, indicating the end of the file.

Error Handling in File Operations

Robust error handling in file operations can be implemented by checking the IOSTAT value after each file operation. This ensures the program can gracefully handle errors and provide informative feedback to the user.

For instance, when writing data to a file, error handling should be incorporated to manage write failures.

```
INTEGER :: ioStatus
CHARACTER(len=100) :: ioMessage

OPEN(UNIT=30, FILE='outputData.txt', STATUS='NEW', IOSTAT=ioStatus,
     IOMSG=ioMessage)

IF (ioStatus /= 0) THEN
   PRINT *, 'Error opening file: ', ioMessage
   STOP
ENDIF
```

```
WRITE(UNIT=30, FMT='(A)', IOSTAT=ioStatus, IOMSG=ioMessage) 'Sample data
    line.'
IF (ioStatus /= 0) THEN
   PRINT *, 'Error writing to file: ', ioMessage
ENDIF

CLOSE(UNIT=30, IOSTAT=ioStatus, IOMSG=ioMessage)
IF (ioStatus /= 0) THEN
   PRINT *, 'Error closing file: ', ioMessage
ENDIF
```

This code snippet demonstrates comprehensive error handling by checking the IOSTAT value after opening the file, writing data to it, and closing it. This ensures that all file operations are monitored for errors, making the program more robust and reliable.

Effective file status and error handling in Fortran not only prevents program failures but also provides meaningful diagnostic messages, facilitating easier debugging and maintenance.

7.10 File I/O in Subroutines and Functions

File input/output (I/O) in Fortran is not restricted solely to the main program; it can be efficiently managed within subroutines and functions. This provides modularity, code reusability, and ease of maintenance. Managing file operations within subroutines and functions requires careful consideration to ensure that the file states and error handling are accurately implemented. This section discusses best practices for incorporating file I/O in subroutines and functions, including the use of file I/O statements such as OPEN, READ, WRITE, and CLOSE, parameter passing, and error handling.

When designing a subroutine or function that performs file I/O, it is crucial to pass sufficient information to these procedures so they can carry out their tasks properly. This often includes file names, unit numbers, I/O modes (such as read or write), and potential error handling parameters.

Consider the following example where a subroutine named read_data is responsible for reading data from a file:

```
SUBROUTINE read_data(file_name, unit_num, data, size, ierr)
  CHARACTER(LEN=*), INTENT(IN) :: file_name
  INTEGER, INTENT(IN) :: unit_num
  REAL, DIMENSION(:), INTENT(OUT) :: data
  INTEGER, INTENT(OUT) :: size
  INTEGER, INTENT(OUT) :: ierr
```

```
  INTEGER :: i, ios
  OPEN(UNIT=unit_num, FILE=file_name, STATUS='OLD', IOSTAT=ios)
  IF (ios /= 0) THEN
    ierr = ios
    RETURN
  END IF

  size = 0
  DO
    READ(unit_num, *, IOSTAT=ios) data(size + 1)
    IF (ios /= 0) EXIT
    size = size + 1
  END DO
  ierr = 0
  CLOSE(unit_num)
END SUBROUTINE read_data
```

In this example, the subroutine read_data takes as arguments the file name (file_name), the unit number to use for the file (unit_num), the array to which the data will be read (data), the actual number of elements read (size), and an integer variable for error reporting (ierr). Within the subroutine, the OPEN statement attempts to open the specified file. If the file cannot be opened (indicated by a non-zero ios), the subroutine sets the ierr and returns immediately. Otherwise, it proceeds to read the data from the file into the data array until EOF or an error occurs.

For more advanced operations, consider handling both reading and writing in subroutines. For instance, a subroutine can manage both tasks based on an additional parameter indicating the operation type:

```
SUBROUTINE manage_file(file_name, unit_num, data, size, mode, ierr)
  CHARACTER(LEN=*), INTENT(IN) :: file_name
  INTEGER, INTENT(IN) :: unit_num
  REAL, DIMENSION(:), INTENT(INOUT) :: data
  INTEGER, INTENT(INOUT) :: size
  CHARACTER(LEN=*), INTENT(IN) :: mode
  INTEGER, INTENT(OUT) :: ierr

  INTEGER :: ios
  IF (mode == 'READ') THEN
    OPEN(UNIT=unit_num, FILE=file_name, STATUS='OLD', IOSTAT=ios)
    IF (ios /= 0) THEN
      ierr = ios
      RETURN
    END IF

    size = 0
    DO
      READ(unit_num, *, IOSTAT=ios) data(size + 1)
      IF (ios /= 0) EXIT
      size = size + 1
    END DO
    ierr = 0
    CLOSE(unit_num)

  ELSE IF (mode == 'WRITE') THEN
    OPEN(UNIT=unit_num, FILE=file_name, STATUS='UNKNOWN', ACTION='
```

```
      WRITE', IOSTAT=ios)
    IF (ios /= 0) THEN
      ierr = ios
      RETURN
    END IF

    DO i = 1, size
      WRITE(unit_num, *) data(i)
    END DO
    ierr = 0
    CLOSE(unit_num)
  ELSE
    ierr = -1 ! Invalid mode
  END IF
END SUBROUTINE manage_file
```

This subroutine manage_file employs a mode parameter to determine whether to read from or write to the file specified by file_name. The logic for each operation is encapsulated within the corresponding IF blocks, ensuring that proper file handling and error checking are performed for each mode.

For error handling, it is essential to check the IOSTAT returns after every file operation. This provides robustness to the subroutine and ensures that any issues (such as an inability to open a file or read errors) are promptly communicated to the calling program via the ierr parameter.

To invoke these subroutines effectively, consider the context of the calling program. Here is an example of a main program utilizing the manage_file subroutine:

```
PROGRAM file_io_example
  CHARACTER(LEN=20) :: file_name
  INTEGER :: unit_num, ierr, size
  REAL, DIMENSION(100) :: data

  file_name = 'example.dat'
  unit_num = 10

  CALL manage_file(file_name, unit_num, data, size, 'READ', ierr)
  IF (ierr /= 0) THEN
    PRINT *, 'Error occurred during file read:', ierr
    STOP
  END IF

  ! Process data
  ! (Data processing logic would go here)

  CALL manage_file(file_name, unit_num, data, size, 'WRITE', ierr)
  IF (ierr /= 0) THEN
    PRINT *, 'Error occurred during file write:', ierr
    STOP
  END IF
END PROGRAM file_io_example
```

This program calls the manage_file subroutine twice: first to read data from a file and then to write data back. Any errors encountered are checked and reported immediately, ensuring the program halts gracefully if an issue arises.

By encapsulating file I/O operations within subroutines and functions, code modularity is significantly enhanced, which allows for clearer and more maintainable code. Additionally, it simplifies error management and ensures a standardized approach to handling files across the entire program.

7.11 Advanced File Handling Techniques

Fortran offers sophisticated mechanisms for handling files that go beyond the basic operations of opening, reading, writing, and closing. This section explores advanced file handling techniques that can help improve efficiency, manage large datasets, and handle complex file management tasks. Topics covered include file pointers, asynchronous I/O, memory mapping, and error recovery techniques.

Efficient file handling is critical in high-performance computing and large-scale data processing tasks. Understanding and leveraging advanced techniques can lead to substantial performance improvements.

File Pointers and Offsets

File pointers point to a location within a file from which data can be read or to which data can be written. In Fortran, file pointers can be managed using the INQUIRE statement. The INQUIRE statement can provide information about the current position of the file pointer, which can be used to implement custom file navigation.

```
PROGRAM FilePointerExample
  INTEGER :: iUnit, Position
  CHARACTER(len=100) :: Buffer

  iUnit = 10
  OPEN(UNIT=iUnit, FILE='example.txt', STATUS='OLD')

  ! Read initial data
  READ(iUnit, '(A)') Buffer
  PRINT *, 'Initial Data: ', TRIM(Buffer)

  ! Get current position
  INQUIRE(UNIT=iUnit, POS=Position)
  PRINT *, 'Current File Position: ', Position

  ! Reposition the file pointer
  BACKSPACE iUnit
```

```
  ! Read data again
  READ(iUnit, '(A)') Buffer
  PRINT *, 'Data after BACKSPACE: ', TRIM(Buffer)

  CLOSE(iUnit)
END PROGRAM FilePointerExample
```

```
Initial Data: Hello World
Current File Position: 12
Data after BACKSPACE: Hello World
```

In this example, the INQUIRE(UNIT=iUnit, POS=Position) statement retrieves the current position of the file pointer. The BACKSPACE statement moves the file pointer back, allowing data to be reread.

Asynchronous I/O

Asynchronous I/O operations allow a program to continue executing while a file operation is in progress, rather than waiting for the file operation to complete. This technique is essential in scenarios where I/O operations are time-consuming, as it enhances performance by overlapping computation and communication.

Fortran 2008 introduced support for asynchronous I/O. The ASYNCHRONOUS attribute and the WAIT statement are key components in implementing asynchronous I/O.

```
PROGRAM AsynchronousIOExample
  INTEGER :: iUnit, IOStat
  CHARACTER(len=100) :: Buffer

  iUnit = 20
  OPEN(UNIT=iUnit, FILE='async_example.txt', STATUS='NEW', ACTION='
      WRITE')

  ! Initiate an asynchronous write operation
  WRITE(UNIT=iUnit, FMT='(A)', ASYNCHRONOUS='YES') 'Hello World', POS=
      IOStat

  ! Perform other computations
  PRINT *, 'Performing simultaneous computations...'

  ! Ensure the I/O operation is complete
  WAIT(UNIT=iUnit)

  CLOSE(iUnit)
END PROGRAM AsynchronousIOExample
```

```
Performing simultaneous computations...
```

The WRITE statement includes the ASYNCHRONOUS='YES' attribute, and the WAIT statement ensures the I/O operation completes before continuing program execution.

Memory Mapping

Memory mapping a file maps a file or a portion of a file into the address space of the process, enabling file contents to be accessed via pointers. While Fortran does not provide direct support for memory-mapped files, interfaces to system calls or external libraries (such as POSIX mmap) can be used.

The following example illustrates how to use the ISO_C_BINDING module to interface with the C mmap function:

```
MODULE MemoryMap
  USE, INTRINSIC :: ISO_C_BINDING
  IMPLICIT NONE
  INTERFACE
    FUNCTION mmap(address, length, prot, flags, fd, offset) BIND(C, NAME='mmap'
        )
      USE ISO_C_BINDING, ONLY : C_PTR, C_SIZE_T, C_INT, C_OFF_T
      TYPE(C_PTR) :: mmap
      TYPE(C_PTR), VALUE :: address
      INTEGER(C_SIZE_T), VALUE :: length
      INTEGER(C_INT), VALUE :: prot, flags, fd
      INTEGER(C_OFF_T), VALUE :: offset
    END FUNCTION mmap
  END INTERFACE
END MODULE MemoryMap

PROGRAM MemoryMappingExample
  USE MemoryMap
  USE, INTRINSIC :: ISO_C_BINDING
  IMPLICIT NONE

  INTEGER(C_INT) :: file_desc
  TYPE(C_PTR) :: map_address
  INTEGER(C_SIZE_T) :: length
  CHARACTER(len=100), PARAMETER :: filename = 'map_example.txt'

  ! Assume file_desc and length are assigned appropriately
  ! Calling mmap function
  map_address = mmap(0_C_PTR, length, 1, 2, file_desc, 0)

  ! Access the mapped file via map_address
  ! Implementation specific to system and file

END PROGRAM MemoryMappingExample
```

Error Recovery

Error handling in file operations is indispensable for developing robust programs. Fortran provides several mechanisms to capture and handle I/O errors. The ERR and IOSTAT specifiers in READ and WRITE statements, and the IOMSG specifier, allow detection and graceful recovery from errors.

```
PROGRAM ErrorRecoveryExample
  INTEGER :: iUnit, IOStat
  CHARACTER(len=100) :: Buffer, IOMessage
```

```
  iUnit = 30
  OPEN(UNIT=iUnit, FILE='nonexistent.txt', STATUS='OLD', IOSTAT=IOStat,
        IOMSG=IOMessage)

  IF (IOStat /= 0) THEN
    PRINT *, 'Error opening file: ', TRIM(IOMessage)
  ELSE
    READ(UNIT=iUnit, FMT='(A)', IOSTAT=IOStat, IOMSG=IOMessage) Buffer
    IF (IOStat /= 0) THEN
      PRINT *, 'Error reading file: ', TRIM(IOMessage)
    ELSE
      PRINT *, 'File Data: ', TRIM(Buffer)
    END IF
    CLOSE(iUnit)
  END IF
END PROGRAM ErrorRecoveryExample
```

```
Error opening file: No such file or directory
```

Incorporating error handling ensures the program can respond appropriately to various errors without terminating unexpectedly. The IOSTAT and IOMSG specifiers capture error codes and messages, providing context for remedial actions.

These advanced techniques form a critical part of developing efficient, reliable, and high-performance Fortran applications. By mastering these methods, programmers can handle more complex file processing tasks with greater ease and reliability.

7.12 Best Practices for File Management in Fortran

Effective file management in Fortran is crucial for ensuring data integrity, optimizing performance, and maintaining code readability and maintainability. The following best practices provide guidelines and techniques to achieve these goals.

- **Consistent Naming Conventions**: Adopt a naming convention for files that is clear, consistent, and ideally self-explanatory. For example, files holding input data can be named with a prefix input_, and output data files with a prefix output_.
- **File Path Management**: Always use full paths or properly handle relative paths to avoid ambiguity. Considering cross-platform compatibility, use system functions to check and format paths appropriately.

```
character(len=100) :: filepath
filepath = 'data/input_data.txt'
```

- **Check File Existence**: Before attempting to open a file, check if the file exists to prevent runtime errors. This can be done using the INQUIRE statement.

```
logical :: file_exists
call inquire(file='data/input_data.txt', exist=file_exists)
if (.not. file_exists) then
    print *, 'Error: File does not exist.'
    stop
endif
```

- **Proper File Opening Modes**: Use appropriate file access modes ('READ', 'WRITE', 'APPEND') based on the operation required to prevent reading from an uninitialized file or overwriting critical data inadvertently.

- **Error Handling**: Implement robust error handling for all file operations. Check the IOSTAT variable after each critical I/O statement to manage runtime errors effectively.

```
integer :: iostat, unit
open(unit=unit, file='data/input_data.txt', status='old', action='read', iostat=
      iostat)
if (iostat /= 0) then
    print *, 'Error: Unable to open file.'
    stop
endif
```

- **Closing Files**: Always close files as soon as operations are complete to free system resources.

```
close(unit=unit)
```

- **Resource Management**: Assign logical unit numbers dynamically using loop constructs for large scale projects, ensuring resource management is handled cleanly.

```
integer :: unit, iostat
do unit=10, 30
    open(unit=unit, file='data/output_data.txt', status='unknown', iostat=
          iostat)
    if (iostat == 0) then
        write(unit, *) 'Data written successfully'
        close(unit)
        exit
    endif
end do
```

- **Buffer Management**: Manage the buffer sizes appropriately for the application size and memory constraints to optimize I/O operations.
- **Use of Modular Code**: Encapsulate file handling routines into modular, reusable subroutines and functions to promote code reuse and clarity.

```
module file_io
contains
  subroutine open_file(filename, unit)
    character(len=*), intent(in) :: filename
    integer, intent(out) :: unit
    integer :: iostat
    open(unit=unit, file=filename, status='old', iostat=iostat)
    if (iostat /= 0) then
        print *, 'Error opening file: ', filename
    endif
  end subroutine open_file
end module file_io

program main
    use file_io
    integer :: unit
    call open_file('data/input_data.txt', unit)
    ! Perform file I/O operations and then close
    close(unit=unit)
end program main
```

- **Documentation and Comments**: Clearly comment file operations to specify their purpose and expected behavior to aid in code maintenance and readability.

Attention to these best practices will assist in creating robust, efficient, and maintainable Fortran programs.

Chapter 8

Modules and Packages

This chapter introduces the concepts of modules and packages in Fortran, essential tools for organizing and managing complex programs. Readers will learn how to create and use modules, utilize public and private access specifiers, and implement module procedures. The chapter also covers the basics of packages, including their creation and usage, and managing dependencies. It addresses compiling and linking modules and packages, as well as best practices for modular programming and debugging, ensuring efficient and organized code development in Fortran.

8.1 Introduction to Modules

Modules in Fortran are a pivotal feature introduced in Fortran 90 to enhance the modularity, readability, and maintainability of code. They provide a mechanism to encapsulate data definitions, subprograms, and other entities, overcoming the limitations of common blocks used in older Fortran versions. By using modules, programmers can achieve better data abstraction, information hiding, and namespace management.

To define a module, the keyword module is employed, followed by the module name. A module can contain variable declarations, parameter definitions, procedures (both subroutines and functions), and other modules. The end of the module definition is signaled using the end module statement.

```
module myModule
  implicit none
  integer :: var
  contains
  subroutine printVar
    print *, "The value of var is ", var
  end subroutine printVar
end module myModule
```

In the example above, myModule contains an integer variable var and a subroutine printVar that prints the value of var. Unlike common blocks, modules allow for grouping such related entities, making Fortran programs more modular and legible.

To use a module in a program or another module, the use statement is employed. This allows for the seamless integration of the module's entities into the scope where it is needed.

```
program main
  use myModule
  implicit none
  var = 10
  call printVar
end program main
```

In the main program demonstrated above, the use myModule statement imports all accessible entities from myModule. Consequently, the variable var and the subroutine printVar can be utilized directly in the program. This exemplifies one of the core advantages of modules: namespace management, enabling the encapsulation and reuse of code across different parts of a Fortran application.

Modules provide essential mechanisms to avoid name conflicts. With modules, variables and procedures can be declared as either public or private. By default, all module entities are public, but they can be explicitly restricted to be private using the private attribute.

```
module moduleDataHiding
  implicit none
  private
  integer, public :: publicVar
  integer, private :: privateVar
  contains
  public :: showPublicVar
  private :: showPrivateVar

  subroutine showPublicVar
    print *, "The value of publicVar is ", publicVar
  end subroutine showPublicVar

  subroutine showPrivateVar
    print *, "The value of privateVar is ", privateVar
  end subroutine showPrivateVar
```

```
end module moduleDataHiding
```

In moduleDataHiding, the usage of private as the default attribute restricts access to the module's entities. publicVar and showPublicVar are explicitly made public. In this way, restrictive access to sensitive parts of the module is controlled, ensuring encapsulation and data security.

When utilizing the module moduleDataHiding, only publicVar and showPublicVar will be accessible to the program or module that imports moduleDataHiding:

```
program main
  use moduleDataHiding
  implicit none
  publicVar = 42
  call showPublicVar
  !privateVar = 5 ! This will cause a compilation error
  !call showPrivateVar ! This will also cause a compilation error
end program main
```

This mechanism exemplifies the importance of data hiding and access control, crucial for managing complex Fortran programs. It prevents unintended or unauthorized access to critical variables and subprograms, promoting robust and error-resistant code development.

Moreover, modules in Fortran support the concept of module procedures. Procedures defined within modules can be referenced and used just like any stand-alone procedures, but they carry the additional benefits of module encapsulation and abstraction.

```
module mathOperations
  implicit none
  contains
  function square(x)
    integer, intent(in) :: x
    integer :: square
    square = x * x
  end function square

  function cube(x)
    integer, intent(in) :: x
    integer :: cube
    cube = x * x * x
  end function cube
end module mathOperations
```

In the mathOperations module, two functions square and cube are defined, providing common mathematical operations. By encapsulating these functions within a module, they become reusable across various programs without the risk of naming conflicts or repetitive code.

Modules also facilitate the use of data types in Fortran. Derived types and user-defined types can be declared within modules, providing a structured manner to handle complex data constructs.

```
module geometry
  implicit none
  type :: Point
    real :: x
    real :: y
    real :: z
  end type Point
  contains
  subroutine printPoint(p)
    type(Point), intent(in) :: p
    print *, "Point coordinates: (", p%x, ", ", p%y, ", ", p%z, ")"
  end subroutine printPoint
end module geometry
```

The geometry module illustrates the declaration of a derived type Point and a subroutine printPoint that prints the coordinates of a Point. Such modular structuring is pivotal for handling multidimensional data, simplifying the development and maintenance of scientific and engineering applications.

As an evolution from traditional techniques, modules in Fortran represent an indispensable feature, fostering modular programming practices that enhance code organization, reusability, and maintainability.

8.2 Creating and Using Modules

The creation and use of modules in Fortran facilitate better organization and maintainability of complex programs. Modules encapsulate variables, parameters, and procedures, providing an efficient way to manage dependencies and promote code reuse. This section delineates the steps required to create and utilize modules effectively, with illustrative examples to elucidate the concepts.

Modules in Fortran are defined using the module and endmodule statements. The general structure of a module is as follows:

```
module module_name
  ! Declarations
contains
  ! Procedures
endmodule module_name
```

Each module starts with the module keyword and ends with endmodule. Declarations of variables, constants, and other data types are stated before the contains keyword, which is followed by module-specific procedures.

Consider a simple example where a module named math_operations is created to encapsulate basic mathematical operations:

```
module math_operations
  implicit none
  private
  public :: add, subtract

contains
  function add(a, b)
    real :: add
    real, intent(in) :: a, b
    add = a + b
  end function add

  function subtract(a, b)
    real :: subtract
    real, intent(in) :: a, b
    subtract = a - b
  end function subtract

end module math_operations
```

In this module: - The implicit none statement ensures that all variables must be explicitly declared. - The private statement specifies that all module entities are by default private. - The public :: add, subtract statement makes only the add and subtract functions accessible from outside the module.

To use the functionalities provided by the math_operations module in a Fortran program, the use statement is employed:

```
program use_math_operations
  use math_operations
  implicit none

  real :: num1, num2, result

  num1 = 5.0
  num2 = 3.0

  result = add(num1, num2)
  print *, 'Addition: ', result

  result = subtract(num1, num2)
  print *, 'Subtraction: ', result

end program use_math_operations
```

The use math_operations statement imports the module, making its public entities available within the program scope. The program then utilizes the add and subtract functions to perform mathematical operations, and the results are printed to the screen.

```
Addition:    8.0000000
Subtraction: 2.0000000
```

Modules can also include derived types and parameters. For instance, consider a module managing complex numbers:

```
module complex_math
  implicit none
  private
  public :: complex_number, add_complex, subtract_complex

  type complex_number
    real :: real_part
    real :: imag_part
  end type complex_number

contains
  function add_complex(a, b) result(c)
    type(complex_number), intent(in) :: a, b
    type(complex_number) :: c

    c%real_part = a%real_part + b%real_part
    c%imag_part = a%imag_part + b%imag_part
  end function add_complex

  function subtract_complex(a, b) result(c)
    type(complex_number), intent(in) :: a, b
    type(complex_number) :: c

    c%real_part = a%real_part - b%real_part
    c%imag_part = a%imag_part - b%imag_part
  end function subtract_complex

end module complex_math
```

In this example, the complex_math module defines a derived type complex_number and procedures to add and subtract complex numbers. The use of modules not only organizes the code but also enhances its readability and maintainability.

Using the module in a program follows the same principles as before:

```
program use_complex_math
  use complex_math
  implicit none

  type(complex_number) :: num1, num2, result

  num1 = complex_number(1.0, 2.0)
  num2 = complex_number(3.0, 4.0)

  result = add_complex(num1, num2)
  print *, 'Addition of complex numbers: ', result

  result = subtract_complex(num1, num2)
  print *, 'Subtraction of complex numbers: ', result

end program use_complex_math
```

The expected output demonstrates the correct working of complex number operations:

```
Addition of complex numbers: (4.0000000, 6.0000000)
Subtraction of complex numbers: (-2.0000000, -2.0000000)
```

By encapsulating related procedures and data within modules, Fortran programmers achieve better modularization, promoting code reuse and simplifying the management of large codebases.

8.3 Public and Private Access Specifiers

In Fortran, managing the visibility and accessibility of procedures, variables, and other entities within a module is crucial for creating maintainable and modular code. The concept of access specifiers allows developers to control which parts of a module can be accessed by other program units. The two primary access specifiers in Fortran are **public** and **private**.

Entities declared with the public attribute are accessible from outside the module, making them part of the module's interface. This allows other program units to use these entities. Conversely, entities declared with the private attribute are hidden from outside the module, ensuring that they can only be accessed from within the module itself. Proper use of these specifiers enhances encapsulation and reduces the risk of unintended interactions between different parts of a program.

public and private access specifiers can be applied to both data objects and procedures within the module. They can be specified in two main ways: using general statements that apply to the entire module or specifically for individual entities.

The general form for setting all entities to be public or private by default is:

```
module example_module
    implicit none
    private ! All entities are private by default
    public :: public_procedure ! Exception: this procedure is public
contains
    subroutine public_procedure
        print *, "This is a public procedure."
    end subroutine public_procedure

    subroutine private_procedure
        print *, "This is a private procedure."
    end subroutine private_procedure
end module example_module
```

In this example, the private statement at the beginning of the module sets all entities to be private by default. The public declaration for public_procedure then explicitly makes that particular procedure available to other program units. The private_procedure, on the other hand, remains private to the module.

To fine-tune access control, you may also use private and public declarations directly with individual entities. This approach is useful when the access specification of each entity needs to be managed with precision:

```
module precise_control_module
    implicit none
    integer, public :: available_variable
    integer, private :: hidden_variable
contains
    subroutine available_subroutine
        print *, "This is a subroutine accessible from outside the module."
    end subroutine available_subroutine

    subroutine hidden_subroutine
        print *, "This subroutine is private to the module."
    end subroutine hidden_subroutine
end module precise_control_module
```

In this case, available_variable and available_subroutine are accessible from outside the module, while hidden_variable and hidden_subroutine are restricted to module-internal use. This selective exposure is beneficial for adhering to the principle of least privilege, ensuring that only necessary components are exposed to the broader program.

The access specifiers play a significant role when using modules within other program units. Consider the following program that utilizes the example_module defined earlier:

```
program use_modules
    use example_module
    implicit none

    call public_procedure ! This call is valid
    ! call private_procedure ! This would result in a compilation error
end program use_modules
```

Attempting to call the private_procedure from outside the module would lead to a compilation error since it is not accessible due to its private status.

Let's examine another practical example where module access specifiers enhance encapsulation and modularity:

```
module bank_account
    implicit none
    private
    real :: balance
```

```
    public :: deposit, withdraw, get_balance

contains
    subroutine deposit(amount)
        real, intent(in) :: amount
        balance = balance + amount
    end subroutine deposit

    subroutine withdraw(amount)
        real, intent(in) :: amount
        if (amount <= balance) then
            balance = balance - amount
        else
            print *, "Insufficient funds"
        end if
    end subroutine withdraw

    function get_balance() result(current_balance)
        real :: current_balance
        current_balance = balance
    end function get_balance

end module bank_account
```

In this bank_account module, the balance variable is kept private to prevent direct manipulation from outside the module. Instead, public subroutines deposit, withdraw, and get_balance provide controlled access to the balance. This approach enhances data integrity and encapsulation.

Efficient use of public and private access specifiers is foundational for building robust, secure, and maintainable Fortran programs. By carefully managing visibility and access within modules, developers can encapsulate functionality, reduce interdependencies, and protect sensitive data.

8.4 Module Procedures

Module procedures in Fortran are fundamentally subroutines or functions that are defined within a module. They provide a structured means to encapsulate procedures that can be reused across different program units, promoting code modularity and reusability. This section delves into defining, using, and managing module procedures, thereby laying the groundwork for sophisticated and organized code development.

To define a procedure within a module, one can use either subroutines or functions, depending on the required functionality. Below is an example of a simple module that contains a subroutine and a function.

```
module math_operations
```

```
  implicit none
  contains
    subroutine add_numbers(a, b, result)
      real, intent(in) :: a, b
      real, intent(out) :: result
      result = a + b
    end subroutine add_numbers

    function multiply_numbers(a, b) result(product)
      real, intent(in) :: a, b
      real :: product
      product = a * b
    end function multiply_numbers
end module math_operations
```

In this example, the module math_operations defines two procedures: add_numbers and multiply_numbers. The subroutine add_numbers takes two real input arguments and an output argument to store the result. The function multiply_numbers takes two real input arguments and returns their product.

To incorporate these module procedures in a program, the program must use the respective module. Here is an example of a Fortran program that utilizes the math_operations module:

```
program test_math_operations
  use math_operations
  implicit none
  real :: x, y, sum, product

  x = 5.0
  y = 10.0

  call add_numbers(x, y, sum)
  product = multiply_numbers(x, y)

  print *, 'Sum: ', sum
  print *, 'Product: ', product
end program test_math_operations
```

Upon execution, this program will produce the following output:

```
Sum:          15.0000000
Product:      50.0000000
```

When defining module procedures, it is possible to include internal subprograms - subprograms defined inside other subprograms. This can enhance modularization by encapsulating helper functions or subroutines that are only relevant within the scope of the main procedure. Here is an example:

```
module advanced_math_operations
  implicit none
  contains
```

```
    subroutine compute_statistics(data, mean, stdev)
      real, dimension(:), intent(in) :: data
      real, intent(out) :: mean, stdev
      real :: sum, variance
      integer :: n, i
      n = size(data)
      sum = 0.0

      do i = 1, n
        sum = sum + data(i)
      end do
      mean = sum / n

      sum = 0.0
      do i = 1, n
        sum = sum + (data(i) - mean) ** 2
      end do
      variance = sum / n
      stdev = sqrt(variance)
    end subroutine compute_statistics
end module advanced_math_operations
```

The subroutine compute_statistics computes the mean and standard deviation of an array of real numbers. It demonstrates the use of loops and mathematical operations within a module procedure, further enhancing your understanding of their practical applications.

When working with module procedures, one must also be mindful of the access specifiers. By default, all entities defined in a module have public access, meaning they are accessible from outside the module. However, one can explicitly define the access specifiers using public or private attributes. Here is an improved version of the advanced_math_operations module with access specifiers:

```
module advanced_math_operations
  implicit none
  private
  public :: compute_statistics
  contains
    subroutine compute_statistics(data, mean, stdev)
      real, dimension(:), intent(in) :: data
      real, intent(out) :: mean, stdev
      real :: sum, variance
      integer :: n, i
      n = size(data)
      sum = 0.0

      do i = 1, n
        sum = sum + data(i)
      end do
      mean = sum / n

      sum = 0.0
      do i = 1, n
        sum = sum + (data(i) - mean) ** 2
      end do
      variance = sum / n
```

```
    stdev = sqrt(variance)
  end subroutine compute_statistics
end module advanced_math_operations
```

Here, compute_statistics is explicitly declared as public, making it accessible from programs using this module, while other entities (if any) will remain private unless explicitly specified otherwise.

When using module procedures, it is also vital to manage dependencies to ensure that the modules are compiled and linked efficiently. Systems such as makefiles or build systems like CMake can assist in managing these dependencies. Moreover, consistent and clear documentation is critical when dealing with complex modules to facilitate maintenance and understandability.

The effective use of module procedures underpins the concept of modular programming in Fortran. By encapsulating subroutines and functions within modules, programmers can create more organized, reusable, and maintainable code, ultimately leading to robust software design.

8.5 Using Modules in Programs

The utilization of modules in programs allows for efficient code organization and reuse, enhancing readability and maintainability. In Fortran, integrating modules into programs involves understanding how to declare, access, and manipulate modules and their components. This section delves into the practical aspects of incorporating modules within Fortran programs, emphasizing syntax and best practices.

Declaring Modules in a Program

To use a module in a Fortran program, the use statement is employed. This statement should precede the program's main code section but follow any implicit none statements. The general syntax is:

```
program main_program
  use module_name
  implicit none
  ! Variable declarations
  ! Program code
end program main_program
```

Here, module_name should be replaced with the actual name of the module being utilized. Multiple modules can be included by adding multiple use statements.

Example: Using a Simple Module

Consider the following module, which defines a set of mathematical functions:

```
module math_operations
  implicit none
  contains
    real function add(a, b)
      real, intent(in) :: a, b
      add = a + b
    end function add

    real function subtract(a, b)
      real, intent(in) :: a, b
      subtract = a - b
    end function subtract
end module math_operations
```

The module math_operations is included in the main program as follows:

```
program use_math_operations
  use math_operations
  implicit none
  real :: x, y, result

  ! Initialize variables
  x = 10.0
  y = 5.0

  ! Perform operations
  result = add(x, y)
  print *, 'Addition result: ', result

  result = subtract(x, y)
  print *, 'Subtraction result: ', result
end program use_math_operations
```

Execution of this program yields:

```
Addition result: 15.000000
Subtraction result: 5.000000
```

Selective Importing with the only Clause

For larger modules, there may be situations where only a subset of procedures or variables is needed. In such cases, the only clause can be used to import specific components:

```
use math_operations, only: add
```

In the example above, only the add function from the math_operations module is made available in the program. This practice helps avoid namespace pollution and potential conflicts.

Renaming Module Components

To prevent naming conflicts between module components and program variables or other modules, Fortran allows for renaming imported entities via the use statement:

```
use math_operations, only: add => module_add
```

Here, the add function is renamed to module_add within the program's scope. This ensures that calls to module_add refer to the function within math_operations, avoiding any potential conflicts with other entities named add.

Intrinsic Modules

Fortran provides several intrinsic modules containing pre-defined procedures and functions, which can be directly used in programs. Examples include iso_fortran_env and iso_c_binding. To use an intrinsic module, the use statement is applied similarly:

```
use iso_fortran_env
```

This inclusion makes constants such as int8, int16, and int32 available for describing variable kinds, enhancing interoperability and precision control.

Avoiding Circular Dependencies

When using multiple modules, it is crucial to avoid circular dependencies, where two or more modules depend on each other. Such dependencies can cause compilation errors and complicate program structure. A modular design should strive for independence and clear dependency hierarchies.

To illustrate, consider two modules modA and modB:

```
module modA
  use modB ! Potential for circular dependency if modB also uses modA
  implicit none
  ! Module contents
end module modA

module modB
  use modA ! This creates a circular dependency
  implicit none
  ! Module contents
end module modB
```

This structure causes a circular dependency and should be refactored to eliminate such recursion. One solution is to consolidate shared procedures or data into a separate module, reducing direct interdependencies among primary modules.

Best Practices for Using Modules in Programs

When integrating modules into programs, consider the following practices:

- Use clear and descriptive names for modules to enhance readability.
- Prefer selective importing to avoid unnecessary components being loaded.
- Regularly refactor the code to minimize interdependencies and maintain modularity.
- Write comprehensive documentation for each module, detailing its purpose and usage.
- Test modules independently to ensure their reliability before integrating them into larger programs.

Through these practices, Fortran programs become more organized, maintainable, and scalable. The principles discussed lay a foundation for effective modular programming, enabling the creation of complex and robust software systems.

8.6 Advanced Features of Modules

The Fortran language provides a sophisticated means of managing complex programs through modules. Beyond the basic functionalities, several advanced features enhance modular programming by promoting code reuse, maintainability, and extensibility. We will explore three fundamental advanced features: module submodules, generic procedures, and overloading operators. Applicability of these features significantly optimizes the structure and functionality of Fortran code.

Module Submodules

Submodules allow for the separation of the module interface from its implementation, enabling clearer and more maintainable code. A module can declare specifications, and its implementation details can be separately defined in submodules. This approach promotes encapsulation and simplifies the modification and extension of module functionalities.

Consider the following example, where a module named $\mathrm{math\_utils}$ is created with a submodule defining the implementation of a function.

```
module math_utils
  implicit none
  interface
    module function add(a, b)
      real :: add
      real, intent(in) :: a, b
    end function add
  end interface
end module math_utils
```

The implementation of the add function is provided within a submodule.

```
submodule (math_utils) math_utils_impl
  contains
    module function add(a, b)
      real :: add
      real, intent(in) :: a, b
      add = a + b
    end function add
end submodule math_utils_impl
```

The separation ensures that the module's interface is clearly defined in the main module file, while the implementation details are handled independently. Modifications to the function implementation do not affect the module's interface, thus preserving the integrity of dependent code.

Generic Procedures

Generic procedures provide a means to define a procedure interface that can adapt to different data types or arguments. This feature enhances code flexibility and reuse by allowing a unified interface for procedures that perform similar operations but with different inputs.

Consider a scenario where operations need to be performed on both integer and real numbers. A module can specify a generic interface to handle these different types.

```
module operations
  implicit none
  interface add
    module procedure add_int, add_real
  end interface
contains
  integer function add_int(a, b)
    integer, intent(in) :: a, b
    add_int = a + b
  end function add_int

  real function add_real(a, b)
    real, intent(in) :: a, b
    add_real = a + b
  end function add_real
end module operations
```

Here, the generic interface add maps to two specific procedures: add_int for integers and add_real for real numbers. This generic definition allows the same interface to be used with different data types, providing a flexible and elegant approach to method overloading.

Overloading Operators

Operator overloading extends the capability of intrinsic operators to work with user-defined types, enabling intuitive and natural expressions in code that manipulates complex data structures.

As an example, consider a module that defines a user-defined type vector and overloads the addition operator for this type.

```
module vector_operations
  implicit none
  type :: vector
    real :: x, y, z
  end type vector

  interface operator(+)
    module procedure add_vectors
  end interface
contains
  function add_vectors(v1, v2) result(res)
    type(vector), intent(in) :: v1, v2
    type(vector) :: res
    res%x = v1%x + v2%x
    res%y = v1%y + v2%y
    res%z = v1%z + v2%z
  end function add_vectors
end module vector_operations
```

By overloading the addition operator, vectors can be added using the familiar + symbol, making the code that uses vectors more readable and easier to understand.

```
use vector_operations
type(vector) :: vec1, vec2, vec3
vec1 = vector(1.0, 2.0, 3.0)
vec2 = vector(4.0, 5.0, 6.0)
vec3 = vec1 + vec2
```

This code snippet demonstrates how the custom-defined operator makes vector addition straightforward and intuitive, enhancing code clarity and maintainability.

These advanced features of modules – submodules, generic procedures, and operator overloading – enable efficient modular programming in Fortran. They facilitate the creation of flexible, maintainable, and extensible code, essential for managing large and complex scientific and technical computations.

8.7 Introduction to Packages

In Fortran, packages represent a powerful feature designed to manage and organize related-modules systematically. The notion of packages extends the modular capabilities of Fortran by allowing collections of modules to be grouped together and treated as a cohesive unit. This approach facilitates efficient code management, improves readability, and streamlines the compilation and linking process.

A package is essentially a directory or archive containing Fortran modules, along with optional metadata that describes the contents and dependencies. By grouping related modules into packages, developers can ensure a more logical organization of their code, simplify the deployment process, and enhance reusability. Packages also enable the separation of interface and implementation, promoting better encapsulation and information hiding.

To create a package in Fortran, follow these general steps:

- Define the package structure.
- Create and include the relevant modules.
- Write a package configuration file (optional).
- Compile and distribute the package.

Consider a package named linear_algebra containing modules for matrix operations, vector operations, and utility functions. The directory structure for this package might look like:

```
linear_algebra/
   matrix_operations.f90
   vector_operations.f90
   utilities.f90
   linear_algebra.pkg
```

The package configuration file, linear_algebra.pkg, serves to document the package's contents and dependencies. While Fortran does not mandate a specific format for package configuration files, adopting a consistent and clear structure is a good practice.

```
# linear_algebra.pkg
Package: linear_algebra
Version: 1.0
Modules:
    - matrix_operations.f90
    - vector_operations.f90
    - utilities.f90
```

```
Dependencies:
    - none
Description: A package providing matrix and vector operations for linear algebra
        computations.
```

Next, implement each of the modules with appropriate functionalities. For illustration, the matrix_operations.f90 module might include procedures for matrix multiplication and transposition:

```
module matrix_operations
  implicit none

  contains

  subroutine matrix_multiply(A, B, C, n, m, p)
    real, intent(in) :: A(n, m), B(m, p)
    real, intent(out) :: C(n, p)
    integer, intent(in) :: n, m, p
    integer :: i, j, k

    C = 0.0
    do i = 1, n
      do j = 1, p
        do k = 1, m
          C(i, j) = C(i, j) + A(i, k) * B(k, j)
        end do
      end do
    end do
  end subroutine matrix_multiply

  subroutine transpose(A, B, n, m)
    real, intent(in) :: A(n, m)
    real, intent(out) :: B(m, n)
    integer, intent(in) :: n, m
    integer :: i, j

    do i = 1, n
      do j = 1, m
        B(j, i) = A(i, j)
      end do
    end do
  end subroutine transpose
end module matrix_operations
```

After defining the modules, compile them using the Fortran compiler. The package can then be shared and used in other Fortran projects. Other developers can include the linear_algebra package in their projects by adding the path to the package directory and using the modules within it.

To compile and link a main program with the linear_algebra package, utilize the include directive and compilation commands:

```
! main_program.f90
program main_program
  use matrix_operations
```

```
  implicit none

  real :: A(2, 2) = reshape([1.0, 2.0, 3.0, 4.0], [2, 2])
  real :: B(2, 2) = reshape([5.0, 6.0, 7.0, 8.0], [2, 2])
  real :: C(2, 2)

  call matrix_multiply(A, B, C, 2, 2, 2)
  print *, "Matrix C: ", C
end program main_program
```

Typically, the compilation command will link all necessary modules from the package:

```
gfortran -c matrix_operations.f90 vector_operations.f90 utilities.f90
gfortran main_program.f90 matrix_operations.o vector_operations.o utilities.o -o main_program
./main_program
```

Output of program execution:

```
Matrix C:    19.0000000    22.0000000    43.0000000    50.0000000
```

By adopting packages, Fortran developers can achieve a more organized and maintainable codebase, particularly for larger projects.

8.8 Creating and Using Packages

In Fortran, packages and modules are essential for structuring code and managing dependencies effectively. They promote code reuse by encapsulating functionalities into reusable components. This section elaborates on the process of creating and using packages, focusing on the steps to define, compile, and link packages. We will use practical examples to demonstrate how packages can streamline code organization and enhance maintainability.

A package in Fortran can be seen as a collection of modules and related resources bundled together. Packages simplify the distribution and integration of complex numerical libraries and applications.

```
! math_operations.f90
module math_operations
  public :: add, multiply
contains

  function add(a, b)
    real :: add
    real, intent(in) :: a, b
    add = a + b
  end function add

  function multiply(a, b)
    real :: multiply
```

```
    real, intent(in) :: a, b
    multiply = a * b
  end function multiply

end module math_operations
```

The above example defines a Fortran module math_operations with two public functions, add and multiply. These functions can be accessed by any program or other modules that use math_operations.

To create a package containing the above module, follow these steps:

- **Organize the Package Directory Structure**

  A well-structured directory layout is crucial for managing packages. Place your Fortran source files in directories corresponding to their purpose.

  ```
  my_package/
    src/
      math_operations.f90
      other_modules.f90
    include/
  ```

- **Compiling the Package Modules**

  Compile each module separately to generate object files (.o) and module files (.mod). This allows for incremental compilation, where only modified source files need to be recompiled.

  ```
  $ gfortran -c src/math_operations.f90 -o src/math_operations.o
  $ gfortran -c src/other_modules.f90 -o src/other_modules.o
  ```

  After this step, you should have math_operations.o and math_operations.mod files in your src directory.

- **Creating a Static Library**

  Aggregate the compiled object files into a static library using the ar command. This static library can be linked with other Fortran programs.

  ```
  $ ar rcs libmypackage.a src/math_operations.o src/other_modules.o
  ```

  This command creates a static library libmypackage.a, encapsulating all the object files.

- **Linking the Package with a Program**

  To use the functions contained within the package, link the static library with your Fortran program during the compilation.

```
! main_program.f90
program main_program
  use math_operations
  implicit none

  real :: x, y, result

  x = 2.0
  y = 3.0

  result = add(x, y)
  print *, 'Add result: ', result

  result = multiply(x, y)
  print *, 'Multiply result: ', result

end program main_program
```

The above program main_program.f90 illustrates how to use the math_operations module. To compile and link it with the static library, use the following command:

```
$ gfortran main_program.f90 -L. -lmypackage -o main_program
```

The -L. flag tells the compiler to look in the current directory for libraries, and -lmypackage specifies the library name.

- **Running the Program**

  After successfully compiling the program, run the executable to verify that the linked package operates correctly.

```
$ ./main_program
 Add result:    5.000000
 Multiply result:    6.000000
```

These steps outline the process of creating and using a Fortran package. Properly managing directories, compiling modules, creating libraries, and linking them with your programs ensures a modular and reusable codebase, enabling easier maintenance and scalability.

When developing larger projects, it is common to use build automation tools such as Makefile to streamline the compilation process. Here is a basic Makefile for the above example:

```
FC = gfortran
SRC = src
OBJ = $(SRC)/math_operations.o $(SRC)/other_modules.o
LIB = libmypackage.a
```

```
all: $(LIB) main_program

$(SRC)/math_operations.o: $(SRC)/math_operations.f90
	$(FC) -c $< -o $@

$(SRC)/other_modules.o: $(SRC)/other_modules.f90
	$(FC) -c $< -o $@

$(LIB): $(OBJ)
	ar rcs $@ $^

main_program: main_program.f90 $(LIB)
	$(FC) $< -L. -lmypackage -o $@

clean:
	rm -f $(SRC)/*.o $(SRC)/*.mod $(LIB) main_program
```

This Makefile automates the compilation of modules, creation of the static library, and linking with the main program. The clean target is useful for removing all generated files, ensuring a fresh rebuild. Using Makefile not only simplifies the build process but also minimizes human errors during compilation, especially in large projects.

8.9 Managing Dependencies with Packages

Managing dependencies effectively is critical for maintaining clean and efficient Fortran projects. When working with packages, dependencies can become more complex, necessitating robust strategies to keep the project organized and manageable. This section delves into the intricacies of managing dependencies within Fortran packages, considering both internal and external dependencies.

Dependencies in Fortran are handled by organizing code into modules and packages, thus breaking down the program into smaller, reusable components. Each package can depend on other packages or modules, and these dependencies need to be declared and resolved accurately to ensure the program compiles and runs correctly.

Dependencies primarily fall into two categories:

- **Internal Dependencies:** These are dependencies between modules within the same package.
- **External Dependencies:** These include dependencies on other packages or libraries not part of the current package.

Internal Dependencies

Internal dependencies are usually straightforward, requiring the importing of one module into another within the same package. Consider the following example, where module_a utilizes module_b within the same package:

```
module module_b
  implicit none
  contains
    subroutine hello_b()
      print *, "Hello from module B"
    end subroutine hello_b
end module module_b

module module_a
  use module_b
  implicit none
  contains
    subroutine hello_a()
      call hello_b()
    end subroutine hello_a
end module module_a
```

In this example, module_a depends on module_b as it calls hello_b() from within hello_a(). The use statement is employed to import module_b into module_a. When compiling, it is crucial to compile module_b before module_a to resolve dependencies correctly.

External Dependencies

External dependencies are slightly more complex, as they involve importing modules or libraries that are not part of the current package. These could be standard libraries or third-party libraries that provide additional functionalities. Consider the example below, which utilizes an external library, lib_math, to perform mathematical operations.

```
module math_operations
  use lib_math
  implicit none
  contains
    function add_two_numbers(x, y)
      real, intent(in) :: x, y
      real :: add_two_numbers
      add_two_numbers = x + y
    end function add_two_numbers
end module math_operations
```

Here, lib_math is an external library providing additional mathematical routines. The project must ensure that lib_math is available and correctly linked during compilation. This is typically handled via the compiler flags, where the include paths and library paths are specified.

Managing Dependencies Using make

The make utility is a straightforward and efficient tool for managing dependencies and automating the build process. A Makefile specifies how modules and packages should be compiled and linked, ensuring that dependencies are resolved in the correct order.

Consider a project structure where we have two modules, module_a and module_b, and an external library, lib_math. Here is an example Makefile to manage the dependencies:

```
# Variables
FC = gfortran
LIBS = -L/path/to/libs -llib_math
INCLUDES = -I/path/to/includes

# Targets
all: program

module_b.o: module_b.f90
  $(FC) -c module_b.f90 $(INCLUDES)

module_a.o: module_a.f90 module_b.o
  $(FC) -c module_a.f90 $(INCLUDES)

math_operations.o: math_operations.f90
  $(FC) -c math_operations.f90 $(INCLUDES)

program: module_a.o module_b.o math_operations.o
  $(FC) -o program module_a.o module_b.o math_operations.o $(LIBS)

clean:
  rm -f *.o program
```

This Makefile specifies the compilation process, indicating the dependencies between modules and ensuring they are compiled in the correct order. The LIBS and INCLUDES variables help manage external dependencies, linking the necessary libraries during the final compilation step.

Best Practices for Dependency Management

Effective dependency management ensures that the project remains maintainable, reducing the risk of errors and improving build efficiency. Here are some best practices:

- Modular Design: Break down the program into smaller, well-defined modules and packages.

- Explicit Imports: Always specify module dependencies explicitly using the use statement.
- Version Control: Maintain version control over dependencies, particularly external libraries, to ensure compatibility.
- Automated Builds: Use build automation tools like make to streamline the compilation process and handle dependencies efficiently.
- Documentation: Provide comprehensive documentation for the package dependencies, including installation and configuration instructions for external libraries.

Adhering to these practices will lead to a clear and organized project structure, facilitating maintenance and scaling of the Fortran projects.

8.10 Compiling and Linking Modules and Packages

Fortran has specific mechanisms for compiling and linking modules and packages, which are essential for ensuring that complex programs are efficiently organized and executed correctly. This section details the process, providing clear instructions and examples to facilitate understanding.

Compiling modules in Fortran involves generating object files (.o or .obj) and module files (.mod), which are then linked to create an executable. The modules encapsulate procedures and data definitions, simplifying code reuse and maintenance. We will start by compiling standalone modules and move on to compiling and linking entire packages comprising multiple modules.

First, consider a simple module definition:

```
module math_operations
  implicit none
  public :: add
contains
  function add(x, y)
    implicit none
    integer, intent(in) :: x, y
    integer :: add
    add = x + y
```

```
  end function add
end module math_operations
```

To compile this module, the Fortran compiler (e.g., gfortran) can be used as follows:

```
gfortran -c math_operations.f90
```

The -c flag tells the compiler to compile the code without linking, producing math_operations.o and math_operations.mod files. The object file contains the compiled code, while the module file contains the module-related information.

Next, consider a program that uses this module:

```
program test_math
  use math_operations
  implicit none
  integer :: result
  result = add(5, 3)
  print *, 'The result is: ', result
end program test_math
```

This program can be compiled and linked with the module as follows:

```
gfortran -o test_math test_math.f90 math_operations.o
```

The -o flag specifies the name of the executable, and both the program source file and the object file of the module are provided to the compiler.

Creating and Linking Packages:

A package may contain multiple modules, necessitating a more intricate compilation and linking process. Consider the following structure for a package named mypack:

- mypack/
  - math_operations.f90
  - io_operations.f90
  - main.f90

The math_operations.f90 can be the module described earlier. The io_operations.f90 might look like this:

```
module io_operations
  implicit none
  public :: print_result
contains
  subroutine print_result(result)
    implicit none
```

```
    integer, intent(in) :: result
    print *, 'The result from io_operations module is: ', result
  end subroutine print_result
end module io_operations
```

The main.f90 integrates these modules:

```
program main
  use math_operations
  use io_operations
  implicit none
  integer :: result
  result = add(7, 8)
  call print_result(result)
end program main
```

To compile and link these files, perform the following steps:

1. Compile each module separately:

```
gfortran -c mypack/math_operations.f90
gfortran -c mypack/io_operations.f90
```

The above commands generate math_operations.o, math_operations.mod, io_operations.o, and io_operations.mod files.

2. Compile the main program and link it with the module object files:

```
gfortran -o main mypack/main.f90 mypack/math_operations.o mypack/io_operations.o
```

This command compiles main.f90 and links it with the object files, creating the executable main.

Proper dependency management ensures that changes in modules trigger only necessary recompilations. Tools like make can automate this process. Consider the following Makefile:

```
# Makefile for compiling the mypack package

FC = gfortran
OBJ = math_operations.o io_operations.o
MODS = math_operations.mod io_operations.mod

all: main

%.o: %.f90
	$(FC) -c $<

main: main.o $(OBJ)
	$(FC) -o $@ main.o $(OBJ)

clean:
	rm -f *.o *.mod main

.PHONY: clean
```

Running make executes the necessary commands to compile and link the program, ensuring efficient development and management of dependencies.

The intricate but automated process of compiling and linking Fortran modules and packages ensures that larger programs are maintainable, modular, and scalable. Properly compiled object files and correctly managed module dependencies result in a streamlined and efficient development process.

8.11 Best Practices for Modular Programming

Effective modular programming in Fortran, or any programming language, requires adherence to a set of best practices designed to enhance code readability, maintainability, and reusability. This section discusses several key principles and practices that should be followed to achieve these goals.

1. Cohesive Module Design

Modules should be designed to perform a specific set of related tasks. A highly cohesive module contains procedures and variables that are closely related by their functionality. This not only makes the module easier to understand but also enhances maintenance. For example, a module for matrix operations should include procedures such as matrix multiplication, addition, and inversion, but not unrelated operations like sorting an array.

2. Encapsulation

Encapsulation is a fundamental principle of modular programming. It involves bundling the data (variables) and the code (procedures) that operate on the data into a single unit, known as a module. Encapsulation helps to protect the internal state of the module from unintended interference. In Fortran, you can control the visibility of module components using the public and private access specifiers.

```
module matrix_operations
  implicit none
  private
  public :: matrix_add, matrix_multiply

  ! Internal variables and procedures
  real, dimension(:,:), allocatable :: internal_matrix

contains

  subroutine matrix_add(A, B, C)
```

```
    real, intent(in) :: A(:,:), B(:,:)
    real, intent(out) :: C(:,:)
    C = A + B
  end subroutine matrix_add

  subroutine matrix_multiply(A, B, C)
    real, intent(in) :: A(:,:), B(:,:)
    real, intent(out) :: C(:,:)
    C = matmul(A, B)
  end subroutine matrix_multiply

end module matrix_operations
```

internal_matrix is private and thus inaccessible to code outside the module, ensuring that only the module's procedures can modify its value.

3. Minimizing Dependencies

Minimizing dependencies between modules is crucial for modular programming. High coupling between modules can lead to a tightly intertwined codebase, making it difficult to modify one module without affecting others. To minimize dependencies:

- Use explicit interfaces and avoid using global variables.
- Where possible, pass parameters through arguments rather than relying on module-wide variables.
- Design modules to have clear, well-defined APIs.

Consider the following example where parameters are passed explicitly:

```
module math_utils
  implicit none
  private
  public :: quadratic_solver

contains

  subroutine quadratic_solver(a, b, c, root1, root2)
    real, intent(in) :: a, b, c
    real, intent(out) :: root1, root2
    real :: discriminant
    discriminant = b**2 - 4.0*a*c

    if (discriminant < 0) then
      print *, 'No real roots.'
      root1 = 0.0
      root2 = 0.0
    else
      root1 = (-b + sqrt(discriminant)) / (2.0*a)
      root2 = (-b - sqrt(discriminant)) / (2.0*a)
    end if
```

```
  end subroutine quadratic_solver

end module math_utils
```

By explicitly passing a, b, c, root1, and root2, this subroutine avoids introducing unnecessary dependencies.

4. Descriptive Naming Conventions

Use meaningful names for modules, procedures, variables, and constants. Good naming conventions improve code readability and help other programmers (or your future self) quickly understand the purpose of each element.

```
module geometry_operations
  implicit none
  private
  public :: compute_area_triangle, compute_area_circle

contains

  function compute_area_triangle(base, height) result(area)
    real, intent(in) :: base, height
    real :: area
    area = 0.5 * base * height
  end function compute_area_triangle

  function compute_area_circle(radius) result(area)
    real, intent(in) :: radius
    real :: area
    area = 3.14159 * radius**2
  end function compute_area_circle

end module geometry_operations
```

Names like compute_area_triangle and compute_area_circle clearly describe the functions' purposes.

5. Documentation and Comments

Thorough documentation and comments within modules and procedures are vital. Comments should explain the purpose of the code, the logic behind complex operations, and the use of specific parameters. Modules should have a header comment describing the overall functionality and purpose.

```
module linear_algebra
  ! This module contains functions for basic linear algebra operations
  implicit none
  private
  public :: vector_add, vector_dot_product

contains

  ! Computes the sum of two vectors
  subroutine vector_add(vec1, vec2, result)
```

```
    real, intent(in) :: vec1(:), vec2(:)
    real, intent(out) :: result(size(vec1))
    result = vec1 + vec2
  end subroutine vector_add

  ! Computes the dot product of two vectors
  function vector_dot_product(vec1, vec2) result(dot_product)
    real, intent(in) :: vec1(:), vec2(:)
    real :: dot_product
    dot_product = sum(vec1 * vec2)
  end function vector_dot_product
end module linear_algebra
```

6. Testing and Validation

Rigorous testing and validation are essential to ensure the module works as expected. Unit tests should be written to verify each procedure within a module, ideally covering a wide range of cases. This can be facilitated using automated testing frameworks.

Consider the following example of how to test the vector_add procedure:

```
program test_vector_add
  use linear_algebra
  implicit none

  real :: vec1(3), vec2(3), result(3)

  vec1 = (/1.0, 2.0, 3.0/)
  vec2 = (/4.0, 5.0, 6.0/)

  call vector_add(vec1, vec2, result)
  print *, 'Result: ', result

end program test_vector_add
```

Expected Output:

Result: 5.0 7.0 9.0

7. Modular Code Review

Regular code reviews involving multiple developers can help identify potential issues and improvements in module design. They can also ensure that the code adheres to the defined best practices and standards.

8. Consistent Style Guidelines

Maintaining a consistent style within modules and across the codebase is vital to improve readability and maintainability. This includes consistent indentation, line length, naming conventions, and comment style. Configuring an editor with linting tools and using formatting tools can help enforce these guidelines.

The successful application of these best practices will greatly enhance the quality, scalability, and robustness of Fortran programs.

8.12 Debugging Modules and Packages

Efficient debugging of modules and packages is crucial for ensuring the correctness and reliability of Fortran programs. This section delves into methodologies and tools that facilitate the debugging of modular Fortran code. Understanding the nuances of debugging in the context of Fortran modules and packages will enhance the developer's ability to identify and rectify errors effectively.

Using Compiler Options for Debugging

Fortran compilers provide various options that aid in the debugging process. Common compiler flags include -g, which enables debugging information, and -check all, which enables runtime checks. Here is an example of compiling a Fortran module with debugging information:

```
gfortran -g -check all -o my_program my_module.f90 my_program.f90
```

The -g flag is essential as it allows tools such as the GNU Debugger (GDB) to provide meaningful information during debugging sessions.

Using GDB for Debugging Fortran Code

GDB is a powerful debugging tool that can be used to debug Fortran programs. To debug a program with GDB, compile it with the -g flag and then start GDB as follows:

```
gdb ./my_program
```

Within GDB, several commands can be useful:

- break: Sets a breakpoint at a specified line or function.
- run: Starts the program within GDB.
- next: Executes the next line of code, stepping over any function calls.
- step: Executes the next line of code, stepping into any function calls.

- print: Prints the value of a variable.
- backtrace: Displays the call stack at the point where the program is paused.
- continue: Resumes execution until the next breakpoint or the program finishes.

Here is an example GDB session with a Fortran program that includes a module:

```
(gdb) break my_module.f90:42
(gdb) run
(gdb) print my_variable
(gdb) next
(gdb) continue
```

Tracing Module Procedures

When debugging module procedures, it is often helpful to trace their execution. This can be achieved by setting breakpoints at the beginning of module procedures using GDB or by adding print statements in the code to log procedure calls. An example of adding a print statement to trace a module procedure:

```
module my_module
implicit none
contains
subroutine my_procedure(x)
    real :: x
    print*, 'Entering my_procedure with x = ', x
    ! Procedure logic
    print*, 'Exiting my_procedure with x = ', x
end subroutine my_procedure
end module my_module
```

Handling Private and Public Access Specifiers

When debugging issues relating to access specifiers, ensure that variables and procedures are correctly labeled public or private. Misuse of these specifiers can lead to difficult-to-diagnose access violations. For instance, if a private variable is accessed unintentionally from outside a module, it can result in compilation errors. Verify the scope of variables and procedures by reviewing the module's interface:

```
module my_module
public :: public_variable
private :: private_procedure

real :: public_variable
contains
subroutine private_procedure()
    ! Only accessible within this module
end subroutine private_procedure
```

```
end module my_module
```

Using Static Analysis Tools

Static analysis tools such as flint or forcheck can examine Fortran source code for errors, potential bugs, and adherence to coding standards without executing the program. These tools are particularly useful for identifying issues in complex modules and packages that are not easily detected during runtime.

Dynamic Analysis Using Valgrind

Valgrind is a tool that can detect memory management errors and memory leaks in programs:

```
valgrind --leak-check=full ./my_program
```

For Fortran programs, Valgrind can detect invalid reads, invalid writes, and provide detailed diagnostic messages that help in identifying memory-related bugs within modules and packages.

```
==12345== Invalid read of size 4
==12345==    at 0x4009A8: my_procedure (my_module.f90:23)
==12345==    by 0x400AF2: main (my_program.f90:15)
```

Ensuring meticulous management of pointers and memory allocations within modules and packages can preempt many of these common errors.

Lastly, careful examination of dependencies within packages, ensuring correct linking and resolution of module interfaces, is essential. Mismanaged dependencies can prevent successful compilation or lead to runtime errors. Understanding module dependencies and maintaining a clear organization within packages will support a smoother debugging process and foster a more manageable codebase.

Chapter 9

Memory Management and Pointers

This chapter focuses on memory management and the use of pointers in Fortran. It explains the concepts of dynamic memory allocation and pointer usage, including declaring and manipulating pointers. Readers will learn about pointer arithmetic, using pointers with arrays and derived types, and avoiding memory leaks through proper memory management practices. The chapter also covers advanced pointer features, pointer association and disassociation, and debugging memory-related issues, equipping readers with the knowledge to manage memory efficiently in Fortran applications.

9.1 Introduction to Memory Management

Memory management is a fundamental aspect of developing efficient and robust Fortran programs. It pertains to the process of handling memory allocation, utilization, and deallocation during the lifecycle of a program. Understanding memory management is crucial for optimizing performance and ensuring that applications use system resources effectively without causing memory leaks or other related issues.

Memory in a computer system can be broadly categorized into static memory and dynamic memory. Static memory is allocated at compile time and remains fixed throughout the execution of the program. In contrast, dynamic memory is allocated at runtime, providing greater flexibility and efficient use of memory resources.

Dynamic memory allocation allows programs to request the amount of memory needed during execution, which is essential when dealing with data of varying sizes or when the amount of memory required is not known beforehand. This is where pointers play an integral role. Pointers are variables that store memory addresses, and they can be used to dynamically allocate and deallocate memory.

Efficient memory management involves several key concepts:

- **Memory Allocation:** The process of reserving a portion of memory for use by a program. In Fortran, this can be done statically (at compile time) or dynamically (at runtime).
- **Memory Deallocation:** The process of releasing previously allocated memory back to the system to avoid memory leaks.
- **Pointers:** Variables that hold memory addresses and are used to manipulate and navigate through allocated memory.
- **Memory Leaks:** Situations where dynamically allocated memory is not properly deallocated, leading to wasted memory resources.
- **Garbage Collection:** The automatic reclaiming of memory that is no longer in use, which is not natively supported in Fortran but can be managed manually.

In Fortran, the ALLOCATE and DEALLOCATE statements are pivotal for dynamic memory management. The ALLOCATE statement requests memory for a variable or an array, while the DEALLOCATE statement frees the allocated memory.

Consider the following example which demonstrates basic memory allocation and deallocation in Fortran:

```
PROGRAM dynamic_memory_example
  IMPLICIT NONE
  INTEGER, POINTER :: ptr(:)
  INTEGER :: size

  ! Determine the size of the array at runtime
  PRINT *, 'Enter the size of the array:'
  READ *, size

  ! Allocate memory for the array dynamically
  ALLOCATE(ptr(size))
```

```
  ! Assign values to the allocated array
  ptr = [(i, i=1, size)]

  ! Output the values
  PRINT *, 'Array values: ', ptr

  ! Deallocate the memory
  DEALLOCATE(ptr)
END PROGRAM dynamic_memory_example
```

In this program, the size of the array ptr is determined at runtime based on user input. The ALLOCATE statement allocates the memory, and the DEALLOCATE statement ensures that the memory is released back to the system.

Attention must be paid to the following best practices when managing memory in Fortran:

- Always ensure that dynamically allocated memory is deallocated using the DEALLOCATE statement to prevent memory leaks.
- Use the ASSOCIATED intrinsic function to check if a pointer is associated with a target before deallocating memory.
- Avoid dangling pointers by nullifying pointers using the NULLIFY statement after deallocation.
- Monitor memory usage to detect potential issues such as insufficient memory or unexpected growth in memory footprint.

Here is an example emphasizing the use of the ASSOCIATED function and NULLIFY statement:

```
PROGRAM memory_management_practices
  IMPLICIT NONE
  INTEGER, POINTER :: ptr(:)

  ! Example memory allocation
  ALLOCATE(ptr(10))
  ptr = [(i, i=1, 10)]

  ! Check if the pointer is associated before deallocation
  IF (ASSOCIATED(ptr)) THEN
     PRINT *, 'Deallocating memory'
     DEALLOCATE(ptr)
  ELSE
     PRINT *, 'Pointer is not associated'
  END IF

  ! Nullify the pointer to avoid dangling pointer
  NULLIFY(ptr)
```

```
  ! Check status of the pointer
  IF (.NOT. ASSOCIATED(ptr)) THEN
     PRINT *, 'Pointer has been nullified'
  END IF
END PROGRAM memory_management_practices
```

By adhering to these principles, developers can manage memory effectively, preventing issues such as memory leaks and ensuring that applications run efficiently. The concepts introduced here form the foundation for exploring more advanced topics in memory management and pointers within Fortran.

9.2 Understanding Pointers

Pointers in Fortran serve as variables that store the address of another variable. This ability allows for dynamic memory allocation, efficient handling of memory, and the creation of complex data structures. Understanding pointers is essential for advanced Fortran programming, especially when dealing with large-scale applications.

A pointer in Fortran can be declared using the POINTER attribute. This attribute indicates that the variable can hold the memory address of another variable or an array. The syntax for declaring a pointer is as follows:

```
INTEGER, POINTER :: ptr
```

In this example, ptr is an integer pointer, which can hold the address of an integer variable. For pointers to different data types, the declaration would follow a similar pattern:

```
REAL, POINTER :: ptr_real
CHARACTER(LEN=10), POINTER :: ptr_char
```

The characteristics of pointers in Fortran can be summarized as follows:

- Pointers store the address of another variable or array element.
- Pointers can be associated and disassociated with target variables.
- Pointers facilitate dynamic memory allocation and deallocation.
- Pointers provide flexibility in managing memory for data structures.

To use a pointer, it must be associated with a target. This can be done using the TARGET attribute, which specifies that a variable can be pointed to by a pointer. Here is an example:

```
INTEGER, TARGET :: target_var
INTEGER, POINTER :: ptr

ptr => target_var
```

In the above example, the pointer ptr is associated with target_var. The symbol => is used to establish this association, indicating that ptr now holds the address of target_var. It is possible to modify the value of the target variable through the pointer:

```
ptr = 5
PRINT*, target_var ! Output will be 5
```

Dynamic memory allocation is achieved using the ALLOCATE statement. This can be done for pointers, allowing the programmer to allocate memory at runtime. For example:

```
INTEGER, POINTER :: ptr
ALLOCATE(ptr)
ptr = 10
PRINT*, ptr ! Output will be 10
DEALLOCATE(ptr)
```

When ALLOCATE is called, memory is dynamically allocated for the pointer ptr. It is crucial to deallocate the memory using the DEALLOCATE statement to avoid memory leaks, ensuring that the allocated memory is properly released.

Pointers can also be used with arrays, enabling dynamic array manipulation. For example:

```
REAL, POINTER :: arr(:)
ALLOCATE(arr(5))
arr = [1.0, 2.0, 3.0, 4.0, 5.0]
PRINT*, arr
DEALLOCATE(arr)
```

In this case, arr is a pointer to a one-dimensional real array. Memory is allocated for an array of five elements, and the array values are initialized and printed. Subsequently, the memory is deallocated.

Pointers can also be used with derived types, which are custom data structures defined by the programmer. This allows for the creation of complex data structures such as linked lists or trees. Here is an example with a derived type:

```
TYPE Node
```

```
    INTEGER :: value
    TYPE(Node), POINTER :: next
END TYPE Node

TYPE(Node), POINTER :: head, temp

! Allocate and initialize the head node
ALLOCATE(head)
head%value = 1
head%next => NULL()

! Allocate and initialize the next node
ALLOCATE(temp)
temp%value = 2
temp%next => NULL()
head%next => temp

! Output the value of the second node
PRINT*, head%next%value ! Output will be 2

! Deallocate memory
DEALLOCATE(temp)
DEALLOCATE(head)
```

In this example, Node is a derived type representing a node in a linked list. Each node has an INTEGER value and a pointer next to the next node. Memory is dynamically allocated for the nodes, and they are properly initialized and linked to form a simple linked list. The PRINT* statement confirms the correct value of the second node, and the DEALLOCATE statements release the allocated memory.

Understanding pointers in Fortran is vital for efficient memory management and the construction of dynamic data structures. With correct usage, they offer significant flexibility and control over memory resources, ensuring the robust and efficient execution of Fortran programs.

9.3 Declaring and Using Pointers

In Fortran, pointers provide a powerful way to reference and manipulate memory locations directly. This section delves into the syntax and semantics of declaring pointers, performing pointer assignment, and effectively using them in various programming contexts.

A pointer in Fortran is essentially a variable that holds the address of another variable. Fortran pointers can point to scalars, arrays, or the elements of derived types. Proper declaration and usage of pointers are critical for dynamic memory manipulation and for creating complex data structures.

Declaring Pointers

The declaration of a pointer involves specifying the POINTER attribute in the declaration statement. The general syntax for declaring a pointer is as follows:

```
TYPE, POINTER :: pointer_variable
```

Here, TYPE represents the data type of the pointer, which can be any intrinsic or derived data type.

```
INTEGER, POINTER :: ptr
DOUBLE PRECISION, POINTER :: d_ptr
```

In the above examples, ptr is a pointer to an integer and d_ptr is a pointer to a double precision floating-point number.

Pointer Initialization and Association

Pointers can be associated with target variables using the => operator. This association can be direct or through dynamic memory allocation.

To associate a pointer with a static variable:

```
INTEGER, TARGET :: target_var = 10
INTEGER, POINTER :: ptr

ptr => target_var
```

In this example, target_var is declared with the TARGET attribute, allowing it to be associated with the pointer ptr. Now, any modification through ptr will affect target_var directly.

Dynamic memory allocation involves the use of the ALLOCATE statement, as shown below:

```
INTEGER, POINTER :: ptr

ALLOCATE(ptr)
ptr = 42
```

Here, memory is allocated dynamically to the pointer ptr, and it is subsequently assigned a value of 42.

Pointer Nullification

A pointer can be nullified using the NULLIFY statement, effectively disassociating it from any target or allocated memory:

```
NULLIFY(ptr)
```

After nullification, routines should include checks to ensure pointers aren't dereferenced when unassociated. This can be done using the ASSOCIATED intrinsic function.

```
IF (ASSOCIATED(ptr)) THEN
  ! Pointer is associated; safe to use
ELSE
  ! Pointer is not associated; do not dereference
ENDIF
```

Using Pointers with Arrays

Pointers are equally useful with arrays, allowing dynamic allocation and flexible memory management. For an array pointer, the syntax extends the pointer declaration to include array bounds.

```
INTEGER, POINTER :: array_ptr(:)
```

Dynamic memory for array pointers can then be allocated as follows:

```
ALLOCATE(array_ptr(1:10))
array_ptr = (/ 1, 2, 3, 4, 5, 6, 7, 8, 9, 10 /)
```

To demonstrate the usage of pointers with arrays more contextually, consider the following example:

```
INTEGER, TARGET :: arr(5) = (/ 1, 2, 3, 4, 5 /)
INTEGER, POINTER :: p_arr(:)

p_arr => arr
p_arr(3) = 10
PRINT *, arr
```

Here, p_arr is a pointer to the array arr. Modifying p_arr(3) updates the third element of arr, highlighting how pointers allow for indirect array manipulation.

Pointers with Derived Types

Using pointers with derived types enables the creation of complex and flexible data structures. Consider a scenario where we use pointers to link nodes in a simple linked list.

```
TYPE :: Node
  INTEGER :: value
  TYPE(Node), POINTER :: next
END TYPE Node

TYPE(Node), POINTER :: head, current

ALLOCATE(head)
head%value = 1
ALLOCATE(head%next)
head%next%value = 2
```

In this example, Node is a derived type with an integer value and a pointer to the next node. Memory for each node is allocated dynamically, creating a basic linked list structure.

Understanding and effectively employing pointers in Fortran programs significantly enhances the ability to manage memory and create dynamic data structures. Equally important is the proper management of pointers, including regular checks for valid associations and appropriate deallocation procedures, to prevent memory leaks and ensure robust application performance.

9.4 Dynamic Memory Allocation

Dynamic memory allocation is essential for efficiently managing memory in applications where the size of data structures is not known at compile time. In Fortran, dynamic memory allocation allows the programming of applications with flexible and adaptive memory usage, catering to varying data structures sizes during runtime. This section delves into the mechanisms and methodologies involved in dynamically allocating and deallocating memory in Fortran.

Dynamic memory allocation in Fortran is primarily managed through the ALLOCATE and DEALLOCATE statements, used for allocating and deallocating memory, respectively. These statements enable the allocation of memory for arrays and derived types at runtime.

```
PROGRAM DynamicMemoryExample
    IMPLICIT NONE
    INTEGER, ALLOCATABLE :: array(:)
    INTEGER :: n

    ! Prompt user for the number of elements
    PRINT *, 'Enter the number of elements:'
    READ *, n

    ! Allocate memory for the array
    ALLOCATE(array(n))

    ! Initialize the array with values
    array = (/ (i, i=1, n) /)

    ! Print the values in the array
    PRINT *, 'Values in the array: ', array

    ! Deallocate the array
    DEALLOCATE(array)
END PROGRAM DynamicMemoryExample
```

In this example, the program allocates memory for an array based on user input, initializes the array with sequential values, prints the values, and deallocates the memory afterward. The ALLOCATABLE attribute declares that the variable array will be dynamically allocated.

Dynamic allocation is particularly crucial when working with multi-dimensional arrays or when the required memory size cannot be statically predefined. For example, consider allocating a 2D array where dimensions are provided by the user:

```
PROGRAM Dynamic2DArray
   IMPLICIT NONE
   INTEGER, ALLOCATABLE :: matrix(:,:)
   INTEGER :: rows, cols, i, j

   ! Prompt user for the number of rows and columns
   PRINT *, 'Enter number of rows and columns:'
   READ *, rows, cols

   ! Allocate memory for the 2D array
   ALLOCATE(matrix(rows, cols))

   ! Initialize the matrix with values
   DO i = 1, rows
      DO j = 1, cols
         matrix(i, j) = i * j
      END DO
   END DO

   ! Print the matrix
   PRINT *, 'Values in the matrix:'
   DO i = 1, rows
      PRINT *, matrix(i, :)
   END DO

   ! Deallocate the matrix
   DEALLOCATE(matrix)
END PROGRAM Dynamic2DArray
```

Here, the program dynamically allocates memory for a 2D array, initializes each element based on the product of its indices, prints the matrix, and subsequently deallocates the memory.

It's important to note that failing to deallocate dynamically allocated memory can lead to memory leaks, where allocated memory is not returned to the system once it is no longer needed. This can degrade system performance over time and lead to inefficient memory usage. Therefore, always ensure that DEALLOCATE statements are used appropriately.

When dynamically allocating derived types, the principles remain similar. Consider a derived type Person with allocatable components:

```
MODULE PersonModule
   IMPLICIT NONE
   TYPE :: Person
```

```
        CHARACTER(LEN=:), ALLOCATABLE :: name
        INTEGER :: age
    END TYPE Person
END MODULE PersonModule

PROGRAM DerivedTypeAllocation
    USE PersonModule
    IMPLICIT NONE
    TYPE(Person), ALLOCATABLE :: people(:)
    INTEGER :: n, i

    ! Prompt user for the number of people
    PRINT *, 'Enter number of people:'
    READ *, n

    ! Allocate memory for the array of Person types
    ALLOCATE(people(n))

    ! Initialize each person's data
    DO i = 1, n
        ALLOCATE(CHARACTER(LEN=20) :: people(i)%name)
        people(i)%name = 'Person_' // TRIM(ADJUSTL(CHAR(i)))
        people(i)%age = 20 + i
    END DO

    ! Print each person's data
    PRINT *, 'People data:'
    DO i = 1, n
        PRINT *, 'Name: ', people(i)%name, ', Age: ', people(i)%age
    END DO

    ! Deallocate each person's name and the people array
    DO i = 1, n
        DEALLOCATE(people(i)%name)
    END DO
    DEALLOCATE(people)
END PROGRAM DerivedTypeAllocation
```

In this example, we define a derived type Person with a dynamically allocatable component name. The main program dynamically allocates an array of Person types, initializes each one's name and age, prints their data, and deallocates each name and the array itself.

Proper dynamic memory management ensures efficient use of resources and avoids memory leaks, which can be critical for the performance and reliability of sophisticated Fortran applications.

9.5 Pointer Arithmetic

Pointer arithmetic is a fundamental aspect of using pointers in Fortran. It facilitates the movement through memory locations in a controlled and predictable manner. This section covers how to perform arithmetic operations with pointers and discusses the underlying principles that govern these operations.

In Fortran, pointer arithmetic is less conventional compared to languages like C or C++, owing to its high-level abstractions and array-oriented nature. The basic operations we can perform on pointers include association, disassociation, comparisons, and shifting (moving between different memory locations).

To understand pointer arithmetic, consider a pointer p of a particular data type, such as an integer:

```
INTEGER, POINTER :: p
```

Pointer p can point to a single integer or an array of integers. When p points to an array, we can navigate through the array's elements using arithmetic operations.

Pointer Assignment and Association

Initially, a pointer needs to be associated with a target. This association is performed using the => operator. Below is an example where the pointer p is associated with an integer variable a:

```
INTEGER, TARGET :: a
INTEGER, POINTER :: p
a = 10
p => a ! Associate pointer p with the target a
```

When dealing with arrays, the pointer can be associated with the array's starting memory location:

```
INTEGER, TARGET :: array(5)
INTEGER, POINTER :: p
array = (/1, 2, 3, 4, 5/)
p => array(1)
```

Arithmetic Operations

Fortran does not allow direct arithmetic operations like adding an integer to a pointer to move it across array elements, as seen in lower-level languages. Instead, we utilize array sectioning and striding to achieve similar outcomes.

Array Sectioning

Array sectioning allows pointers to reference specific parts of an array. Consider the following:

```
p => array(2:4)
```

Here, p now references the subsection of array from the second to the fourth element.

Striding

Striding is another powerful feature in Fortran that can be used within pointer arithmetic to skip elements. The general form is array(start:end:stride). For example, if we wish to reference every second element:

```
p => array(1:5:2)
```

This results in p referencing array elements at indices 1, 3, and 5.

Manipulating Elements through Pointers

Once a pointer is associated with an array or a section of it, manipulating elements becomes straightforward. Consider our previous array:

```
array = (/1, 2, 3, 4, 5/)
p => array(2:4) ! p references array(2), array(3), array(4)

p(1) = 20 ! array(2) is now 20
p(2) = 30 ! array(3) is now 30
p(3) = 40 ! array(4) is now 40

! On printing array, we will see: 1 20 30 40 5
```

```
Output:
1 20 30 40 5
```

Pointer arithmetic in this case allows us to modify segments of the array directly through the pointer reference.

Using Pointers in Derived Types

Pointers within derived types present additional utility by enabling dynamic data structures such as linked lists and trees.

```
TYPE Node
  INTEGER :: value
  TYPE(Node), POINTER :: next
END TYPE Node

TYPE(Node), POINTER :: head, current

! Creating nodes and linking them

ALLOCATE(head)
head%value = 1
NULLIFY(head%next)

ALLOCATE(head%next)
head%next%value = 2

! Traversing the linked list
```

```
current => head
DO WHILE (ASSOCIATED(current))
  PRINT *, current%value
  current => current%next
END DO
```

Pointer Comparisons

Comparing pointers is pivotal in certain algorithms, especially in linked structures.

```
IF (ASSOCIATED(p, array(3))) THEN
  PRINT *, "Pointer is associated with array element 3"
ENDIF
```

Properly understanding and utilizing pointer arithmetic ensures efficient memory management and manipulation of dynamic data structures, enhancing the performance and capability of Fortran applications.

9.6 Pointers with Arrays and Derived Types

In Fortran, pointers offer powerful capabilities for handling dynamic arrays and derived types, allowing programmers to create flexible and memory-efficient applications. This section delves into the use of pointers with arrays and derived types, explaining their declaration, allocation, and manipulation. Readers will gain an understanding of how pointers can be used to interface with complex data structures, enhancing both the performance and maintainability of their code.

Pointers with Arrays:

In Fortran, arrays are a fundamental data structure. We can use pointers to dynamically allocate and manage the memory for arrays. Consider the following example wherein we demonstrate how to declare, allocate, and use a pointer to an array:

```
program pointer_with_arrays
  implicit none
  integer, pointer :: p_array(:)
  integer :: i

  ! Allocate memory for a 10-element integer array
  allocate(p_array(10))

  ! Populate the array with values
  do i = 1, 10
    p_array(i) = i * 2
  end do

  ! Output the contents of the array
```

```
  do i = 1, 10
    print *, "p_array(", i, ") = ", p_array(i)
  end do

  ! Deallocate the memory to avoid memory leaks
  deallocate(p_array)
end program pointer_with_arrays
```

When this program is executed, it will produce the following output:

```
p_array( 1 ) =  2
p_array( 2 ) =  4
p_array( 3 ) =  6
p_array( 4 ) =  8
p_array( 5 ) =  10
p_array( 6 ) =  12
p_array( 7 ) =  14
p_array( 8 ) =  16
p_array( 9 ) =  18
p_array(10) =  20
```

Here, p_array is a pointer to an integer array. The memory for the array is allocated using the allocate statement. After using the array, we use the deallocate statement to free the allocated memory, which helps in preventing memory leaks.

Pointers with Derived Types:

Derived types in Fortran allow the creation of complex data structures. Pointers can be associated with these derived types for dynamic memory allocation and flexible data handling. Consider the following derived type definition and its usage with pointers:

```
module derived_type_module
  implicit none
  type :: person
    character(len=50) :: name
    integer :: age
  end type person
end module derived_type_module

program pointer_with_derived_types
  use derived_type_module
  implicit none
  type(person), pointer :: p_person

  ! Allocate memory for a person object
  allocate(p_person)

  ! Populate the object with data
  p_person%name = "John Doe"
  p_person%age = 30

  ! Output the contents of the object
  print *, "Name: ", p_person%name
  print *, "Age: ", p_person%age

  ! Deallocate the memory to avoid memory leaks
  deallocate(p_person)
```

```
end program pointer_with_derived_types
```

When this program is executed, the output will be:

```
Name: John Doe
Age: 30
```

In this example, we define a derived type person containing two components: name and age. A pointer to an object of type person, named p_person, is declared and allocated memory using the allocate statement. The object's data members are populated and then printed. Finally, memory is deallocated to prevent memory leaks.

Pointers with Arrays of Derived Types:

Combining pointers with arrays of derived types further enhances flexibility. Consider the following case where we handle an array of derived type objects:

```
module derived_type_module
  implicit none
  type :: person
    character(len=50) :: name
    integer :: age
  end type person
end module derived_type_module

program pointer_with_array_of_derived_types
  use derived_type_module
  implicit none
  type(person), pointer :: p_persons(:)
  integer :: i

  ! Allocate memory for an array of 3 person objects
  allocate(p_persons(3))

  ! Populate the array with data
  p_persons(1)%name = "Alice"
  p_persons(1)%age = 28

  p_persons(2)%name = "Bob"
  p_persons(2)%age = 32

  p_persons(3)%name = "Charlie"
  p_persons(3)%age = 25

  ! Output the contents of the array
  do i = 1, 3
    print *, "Person ", i, ":"
    print *, "Name: ", p_persons(i)%name
    print *, "Age: ", p_persons(i)%age
  end do

  ! Deallocate the memory to avoid memory leaks
  deallocate(p_persons)
end program pointer_with_array_of_derived_types
```

Executing this program will result in the following output:

```
Person 1 :
 Name: Alice
 Age: 28
Person 2 :
 Name: Bob
 Age: 32
Person 3 :
 Name: Charlie
 Age: 25
```

In this example, p_persons is a pointer to an array of person objects. The array is allocated memory for three elements. Each element's data members are populated, printed, and finally, the memory is deallocated. This example demonstrates the combination of array handling capabilities and the flexibility of derived types using pointers.

Understanding and utilizing pointers with arrays and derived types allows for the creation of dynamic and complex data structures in Fortran applications. The examples provided here illustrate the basic principles, empowering the reader to explore more advanced techniques and applications. Proper memory management remains crucial to avoid leaks and ensure efficient memory usage throughout.

9.7 Memory Leaks and Garbage Collection

Memory leaks are a significant issue in programming, including Fortran, where dynamically allocated memory is not properly deallocated, leading to wasted resources and potential program failure. Garbage collection refers to the automated process of reclaiming memory that is no longer in use by the program. This section delves into identifying, preventing, and solving memory leaks, as well as understanding the concept and implementation of garbage collection in the context of Fortran.

Memory management in Fortran requires explicit actions from the programmer to allocate and deallocate memory. A memory leak occurs when a program allocates memory but fails to release it after it is no longer needed. Over time, this can exhaust the available memory, resulting in performance degradation or system crashes.

```
PROGRAM MemoryLeakExample
  INTEGER, POINTER :: leak_pointer(:)

  DO i = 1, 1000
    ALLOCATE(leak_pointer(10000))
    ! Some operations
    ! Forgot to deallocate memory leading to a memory leak
  END DO
```

```
END PROGRAM MemoryLeakExample
```

In the above example, the program continuously allocates memory for leak_pointer in a loop but fails to deallocate it using the DEALLOCATE statement. This oversight results in a memory leak.

To prevent memory leaks, it is crucial to ensure that every allocated pointer is paired with a corresponding DEALLOCATE statement.

```
PROGRAM FixedMemoryLeakExample
  INTEGER, POINTER :: leak_pointer(:)

  DO i = 1, 1000
    ALLOCATE(leak_pointer(10000))
    ! Some operations
    DEALLOCATE(leak_pointer)
  END DO
END PROGRAM FixedMemoryLeakExample
```

In the revised example, the DEALLOCATE statement ensures that the memory is released properly at the end of each iteration of the loop.

Garbage collection is not inherently built into Fortran as it is in some other programming languages like Java or Python. The responsibility falls on the programmer to manage memory manually. However, understanding the concept of garbage collection is beneficial for programming practices.

Garbage collection aims to identify and reclaim memory that a program is no longer using without requiring explicit commands from the programmer. Though Fortran lacks built-in garbage collection, some modern Fortran environments and libraries attempt to provide similar functionality indirectly by offering tools and utilities that help in detecting memory usage patterns and potential leaks.

For instance, Fortran programs can be analyzed using tools designed to detect memory leaks and improper memory management practices. Tools like Valgrind and Intel Inspector can be employed to monitor memory allocations, detect leaks, and identify coding patterns that lead to inefficient memory usage.

To demonstrate the use of Valgrind for detecting memory leaks, consider the compilation and execution of a Fortran program with memory leaks:

```
$ gfortran -o mem_leak MemoryLeakExample.f90
$ valgrind --leak-check=yes ./mem_leak
```

When run with Valgrind, the tool will provide detailed reports on memory usage, identifying allocations that were not properly released:

```
==12345== 40000 bytes in 1000 blocks are definitely lost in loss record 1 of 1
==12345==    at 0x4A078E3: malloc (vg_replace_malloc.c:270)
==12345==    by 0x4007B5: Main___ (MemoryLeakExample.f90:6)
==12345==    by 0x4006A4: main (MemoryLeakExample.f90:3)
```

The output shows where the memory leak occurred, guiding the programmer to the problematic part of the code. This aids in debugging and improving memory management.

Alongside using tools, some best practices can also aid in avoiding memory leaks:

- Always pair ALLOCATE with DEALLOCATE.
- Implement error handling for allocation failures.
- Use FINAL procedures in derived types to ensure deallocation.
- Regularly use static analysis tools to catch potential leaks during development.
- Adopt coding standards that emphasize meticulous memory management.

Advanced Fortran modules may provide utilities that mimic some aspects of garbage collection by encapsulating allocation and deallocation inside utility functions or modules. When crafting complex applications, modularize memory management to allow centralized deallocation procedures, thus reducing the risk of leaks.

Memory management remains a critical aspect of Fortran programming requiring diligent practices and, occasionally, the use of external tools to ensure efficient and effective use of system resources. By adhering to these principles, programmers can mitigate the risks associated with memory leaks and ensure robust application performance.

9.8 Best Practices for Memory Management

Memory management is a crucial aspect of developing efficient and robust Fortran programs. By following best practices, one can ensure proper utilization of memory resources, reduce the likelihood of memory leaks, and improve the overall performance of the application. The recommendations below provide guidance on efficient memory handling techniques.

- **Minimize Memory Usage:** Allocate only the memory that is necessary. Avoid allocating large blocks of memory unless required. This can be accomplished by carefully planning data structures and understanding the scope and lifetime of variables.

- **Use Automatic Arrays Where Possible:** Automatic arrays are allocated on the stack and are automatically deallocated when they go out of scope. They should be used when the size of the array is known at compile time or can be computed at procedure entry.

An example illustrating the use of automatic arrays:

```
program automatic_array_example
  implicit none
  integer, parameter :: n = 10
  real :: a(n)
  integer :: i

  do i = 1, n
    a(i) = i * 1.0
  end do

  print *, "Array elements: ", a
end program automatic_array_example
```

- **Explicitly Deallocate Allocated Memory:** Ensure that all allocated memory is deallocated as soon as it is no longer needed. This helps in preventing memory leaks. Use the deallocate statement for this purpose.

Example of explicit deallocation:

```
program explicit_deallocation
  implicit none
  real, allocatable :: array(:)

  allocate(array(100))
  ! Perform computations with array

  deallocate(array)
end program explicit_deallocation
```

- **Check Allocation Status:** Always check the status of allocation and deallocation to handle any errors promptly. This can be done using the stat parameter.

Example of checking allocation status:

```
program allocation_status_check
  implicit none
  real, allocatable :: matrix(:,:)
  integer :: stat

  allocate(matrix(50, 50), stat=stat)
  if (stat /= 0) then
    print *, "Allocation failed with error code: ", stat
    stop
  endif

  ! Use the matrix

  deallocate(matrix, stat=stat)
  if (stat /= 0) then
    print *, "Deallocation failed with error code: ", stat
  endif
end program allocation_status_check
```

- **Initialize Pointers to Null:** Ensure that pointers are initialized to null() upon declaration. This avoids undefined pointer states and helps in identifying unallocated pointers.

Example of pointer initialization:

```
program pointer_initialization
  implicit none
  real, pointer :: pArray(:)
  nullify(pArray)

  if (.not. associated(pArray)) then
    print *, "Pointer is not associated."
  endif
end program pointer_initialization
```

- **Use Pointers Judiciously:** Avoid excessive use of pointers. Use them only when dynamic memory allocation, deferred allocation, or dynamic data structures are essential.
- **Avoid Memory Fragmentation:** Consolidate memory allocation operations and deallocate memory blocks simultaneously, wherever possible, to reduce fragmentation. Fragmentation occurs over time with continuous allocation and deallocation of different-sized memory blocks.
- **Limit the Scope of Allocations:** Restrict the lifetime and visibility of allocated memory to the smallest possible scope by allocating and deallocating memory within modules or subprogram blocks and avoid long-lived global or module-level allocations.

- **Use Derived Types for Complex Data Structures:** When dealing with complex data structures or a combination of different types, use derived types. This provides better organization and management of related data and simplifies allocation and deallocation routines.

Example of using derived types with dynamic allocation:

```
module derived_type_example
  implicit none
  type :: matrix_type
    real, allocatable :: data(:,:)
  end type matrix_type
end module derived_type_example

program use_derived_type
  use derived_type_example
  implicit none
  type(matrix_type) :: A
  integer :: n, m

  n = 100
  m = 50

  allocate(A%data(n, m))

  ! Perform operations with A%data

  deallocate(A%data)
end program use_derived_type
```

Collectively implementing these practices ensures optimized and error-resistant memory management within Fortran applications. Consistent adherence to these guidelines fosters more sustainable and maintainable code.

9.9 Pointer Association and Disassociation

Pointer association and disassociation are fundamental concepts in Fortran that play a critical role in memory management. Understanding these concepts ensures the efficient use of memory and the avoidance of common pitfalls such as memory leaks and dangling pointers.

In Fortran, pointers are dynamic entities that can be associated or disassociated with target variables or arrays. The => operator is used to associate a pointer with a target, while the nullify intrinsic function disassociates the pointer from its target.

```
program PointerAssociations
   implicit none
```

```
    integer, target :: targVar = 10
    integer, pointer :: ptrVar

    ! Associating pointer with target
    ptrVar => targVar
    print *, 'Pointer value after association: ', ptrVar

    ! Disassociating pointer
    nullify(ptrVar)
    if (.not. associated(ptrVar)) then
        print *, 'Pointer is disassociated successfully.'
    endif
end program PointerAssociations
```

```
Pointer value after association:          10
Pointer is disassociated successfully.
```

The associated intrinsic function is used to check whether a pointer is currently associated with any target. This function returns a logical value: .true. if the pointer is associated and .false. otherwise.

```
program CheckPointer
    implicit none
    integer, target :: targArray(5) = (/1, 2, 3, 4, 5/)
    integer, pointer :: ptrArray(:)

    ! Check before association
    if (.not. associated(ptrArray)) then
        print *, 'Pointer is not associated yet.'
    endif

    ! Associating pointer with target array
    ptrArray => targArray
    if (associated(ptrArray)) then
        print *, 'Pointer is now associated with target array.'
    endif

    ! Output the associated array
    print *, 'Pointer Array Values: ', ptrArray

    ! Disassociating pointer
    nullify(ptrArray)
    if (.not. associated(ptrArray)) then
        print *, 'Pointer has been nullified.'
    endif
end program CheckPointer
```

```
Pointer is not associated yet.
Pointer is now associated with target array.
Pointer Array Values:          1          2          3          4          5
Pointer has been nullified.
```

In cases where pointers need to be dynamically allocated, memory management becomes crucial. The allocate and deallocate statements handle memory allocation and deallocation for pointers. It is important to properly disassociate pointers to avoid memory leaks.

```
program DynamicMemory
    implicit none
```

```
    integer, pointer :: dynArray(:)

    ! Allocate memory for pointer
    allocate(dynArray(10))

    ! Initialize the dynamically allocated array
    dynArray = 1
    print *, 'Dynamically allocated array: ', dynArray

    ! Deallocate memory and disassociate pointer
    deallocate(dynArray)
    if (.not. associated(dynArray)) then
        print *, 'Pointer is now disassociated after deallocation.'
    endif
end program DynamicMemory
```

```
Dynamically allocated array:            1           1           1           1           1
            1           1           1           1           1
Pointer is now disassociated after deallocation.
```

Proper disassociation of pointers also prevents the issue of dangling pointers, where a pointer still references a memory location that has been deallocated. Accessing this area causes undefined behavior.

When working with derived types, pointers are also associated and disassociated to specific components. This allows for advanced data structures and dynamic memory usage within user-defined types.

```
program DerivedTypePointers
    implicit none

    type :: Point
        integer :: x, y
        integer, pointer :: z
    end type

    type(Point) :: coord

    ! Allocate and associate pointer inside a derived type
    allocate(coord%z)
    coord%x = 1
    coord%y = 2
    coord%z => coord%x

    print *, 'Point Coordinates: ', coord%x, coord%y
    print *, 'Associated value: ', coord%z

    ! Disassociate the pointer
    nullify(coord%z)
    if (.not. associated(coord%z)) then
        print *, 'Pointer in derived type has been disassociated.'
    endif
end program DerivedTypePointers
```

```
Point Coordinates:            1           2
Associated value:            1
Pointer in derived type has been disassociated.
```

To avoid potential errors and ensure efficient management, it is crucial to keep track of pointer states. Pointers should be explicitly associated and properly nullified or deallocated. This practice prevents unintended behavior and contributes to the robustness of Fortran programs. This intricate understanding of pointer dynamics renders more effective and reliable memory management.

9.10 Advanced Pointer Features

Advanced pointer features in Fortran offer fine-grained control over memory and data structures, improving the efficiency and flexibility of complex applications. These features include polymorphic pointers, procedure pointers, and finalization of pointers. Each of these provides an additional layer of capability to Fortran's robust pointer capabilities.

Polymorphic Pointers

Polymorphic pointers in Fortran allow pointers that can reference objects of different types, provided those types are extended from a particular base type. To define a polymorphic pointer, the syntax includes the class keyword followed by parentheses containing the base type. Here is an example:

```
type :: base_type
    integer :: id
end type base_type

type, extends(base_type) :: derived_type
    real :: value
end type derived_type

class(base_type), pointer :: poly_ptr

type(derived_type) :: derived_obj
allocate(poly_ptr, source=derived_obj)
```

In the given code, poly_ptr is a polymorphic pointer that is allocated to reference derived_obj, an object of the derived type derived_type. This advanced feature is particularly useful in object-oriented programming within Fortran, enabling dynamic behaviors and flexible data handling.

Procedure Pointers

Procedure pointers enable the association of a pointer with a subroutine or function, facilitating dynamic procedure calls. This is similar to function pointers in other programming languages such as C. Declaration of a procedure pointer includes specifying the interface for the procedures the pointer can reference. Here is a concise example:

```
interface
    subroutine compute(x)
        integer, intent(inout) :: x
    end subroutine compute
end interface

procedure(compute), pointer :: compute_ptr

subroutine increment(x)
    integer, intent(inout) :: x
    x = x + 1
end subroutine increment

compute_ptr => increment
call compute_ptr(5)
```

In this example, compute_ptr is associated with the subroutine increment. When compute_ptr is called with argument 5, it effectively calls increment(5), demonstrating the flexibility of procedure pointers in managing dynamic procedure references.

Finalization of Pointers

Finalization in Fortran involves clean-up actions that need to be performed when a pointer is disassociated or a data object is deallocated. This is akin to destructors in object-oriented languages. To use finalization, define a final subroutine within a derived type. The final subroutine is automatically called during the deallocation of the derived type instance. Consider this example:

```
type :: my_type
    integer, pointer :: data(:)
contains
    final :: finalize_my_type
end type my_type

subroutine finalize_my_type(obj)
    type(my_type) :: obj
    if (associated(obj%data)) deallocate(obj%data)
end subroutine finalize_my_type

type(my_type) :: example
allocate(example%data(10))
! ... use the data
deallocate(example)
```

In this code, the finalize_my_type subroutine ensures that any dynamically allocated memory associated with the data pointer is properly deallocated when the example object is deallocated. This feature helps prevent memory leaks by ensuring proper clean-up.

Pointer Assignment Rules

When dealing with advanced pointers, it is essential to adhere to specific rules regarding pointer assignments, particularly concerning disassociated and nullified pointers. A pointer should be explicitly nullified using the nullify statement to prevent accidental use of uninitialized pointers:

```
class(base_type), pointer :: poly_ptr
nullify(poly_ptr)
```

Assessing the association status using the associated intrinsic function ensures that a pointer is not erroneously dereferenced:

```
if (associated(poly_ptr)) then
    ! Safe to use poly_ptr
endif
```

Using advanced pointer features judiciously can significantly enhance the robustness and flexibility of your Fortran applications. The following examples demonstrate how these features integrate into practical scenarios, yielding more modular and maintainable code structures.

9.11 Debugging Memory Issues

Debugging memory issues in Fortran is a crucial aspect of developing reliable and efficient applications. Memory bugs, such as leaks, corruption, and invalid accesses, can lead to erratic program behavior, crashes, or even subtle and hard-to-diagnose errors. This section delves into strategies and tools for identifying and resolving memory-related problems in Fortran programs, ensuring robust memory management practices.

Common Memory Issues

Memory issues often arise from improper allocation, deallocation, or usage of dynamically allocated memory. Some of the prevalent memory issues include:

- **Memory leaks**: Failure to release dynamically allocated memory results in unused memory that cannot be reclaimed.
- **Dangling pointers**: Pointers that reference a memory location that has already been deallocated.
- **Buffer overflows**: Accessing memory beyond the allocated boundaries.

- **Uninitialized memory**: Using memory before it has been initialized.
- **Memory corruption**: Inadvertently modifying memory due to erroneous pointer arithmetic or out-of-bounds accesses.

Identifying and rectifying these issues requires a systematic approach and the use of specialized debugging tools.

Using Debugging Tools

Several tools are available to help detect and debug memory issues in Fortran programs. Some of the most effective tools include:

- Valgrind
- Debugging with Compiler Options
- Memory Sanitizer

Valgrind is a powerful tool for detecting memory issues. It supports multiple tools for memory debugging, including memcheck, which can detect memory leaks, invalid memory access, and usage of uninitialized values. To use Valgrind with a Fortran program, compile your program with the -g flag to include debugging information and then run it under Valgrind:

```
$ gfortran -g -o my_program my_program.f90
$ valgrind --leak-check=full ./my_program
```

The output from Valgrind provides a detailed report on memory issues, including the location in the source code where the problem occurred.

Debugging with Compiler Options involves using compiler-provided flags to enable runtime checks and debugging information. Common flags include:

- -fbounds-check: Checks for array bounds violations.
- -fcheck=all: Enables various runtime checks such as array bounds, uninitialized variables, and null pointer dereferencing.

Compiling a Fortran program with these options enhances runtime error detection:

```
$ gfortran -g -fbounds-check -fcheck=all -o my_program my_program.f90
```

Memory Sanitizer is another tool for detecting memory issues. It can find uninitialized memory reads and other memory-specific bugs. Compiling with Memory Sanitizer requires specific flags:

```
$ gfortran -fsanitize=memory -o my_program my_program.f90
```

Running the program will then produce warnings and error messages if memory issues are detected.

Manual Code Review and Logging

While tools are indispensable, manual code review and strategic logging form essential parts of the debugging process. During code review:

- Carefully examine pointer allocation and deallocation logic.
- Ensure that pointers are set to NULL() after deallocation to avoid dangling pointer issues.
- Check array bounds and pointer arithmetic to prevent out-of-bounds accesses.

Strategically placed log statements can also help identify the point at which a memory corruption or leak occurs. For instance:

```
WRITE(*,*) 'Allocating memory for array A'
ALLOCATE(A(100))
! Add checks and log statements where appropriate
DEALLOCATE(A)
WRITE(*,*) 'Deallocated array A'
```

Reviewing logs can provide insights into where memory issues originate, especially in complex programs.

Case Study: Detecting a Memory Leak

Consider a scenario where a Fortran program is suspected of having a memory leak. The program allocates memory inside a loop but fails to deallocate it. We will demonstrate using Valgrind to detect this leak.

```
PROGRAM memory_leak_example
    REAL, POINTER :: ptr(:)
    INTEGER :: i

    DO i = 1, 10
        ALLOCATE(ptr(100))
        ! Memory allocated but not deallocated within the loop
    END DO
END PROGRAM memory_leak_example
```

Compile and run the program under Valgrind:

```
$ gfortran -g -o memory_leak_example memory_leak_example.f90
$ valgrind --leak-check=full ./memory_leak_example
```

The Valgrind output will indicate memory that was allocated but not freed, helping to pinpoint the issue. To fix the leak, ensure DEALLOCATE is called within the loop:

```
PROGRAM memory_leak_example
    REAL, POINTER :: ptr(:)
    INTEGER :: i

    DO i = 1, 10
        ALLOCATE(ptr(100))
        ! Perform operations
        DEALLOCATE(ptr)
    END DO
END PROGRAM memory_leak_example
```

Through the use of dedicated debugging tools and careful code review, memory issues in Fortran programs can be effectively identified and addressed. Adopting these practices enhances the overall reliability and efficiency of the applications.

9.12 Case Studies on Memory Management in Fortran

Memory management is a critical aspect of efficient Fortran programming. This section will present several case studies illustrating common practices, pitfalls, and advanced techniques for managing memory. Each case study includes snippets of code and their outputs, helping to contextualize the theoretical concepts discussed in the previous sections.

Case Study 1: Dynamic Memory Allocation in Arrays

Dynamic memory allocation allows arrays to be resized during runtime. Consider an application that reads data from a file and needs to adapt the array size according to the data volume.

```
program dynamic_array
  implicit none
  integer, allocatable :: data(:)
  integer :: n, i

  ! Determine the size of the array
  write(*,*) 'Enter the number of elements:'
  read(*,*) n
```

```
  ! Allocate array of size n
  allocate(data(n))

  ! Populate array
  do i = 1, n
    data(i) = i * 2 ! Example initialization
  end do

  ! Print array
  write(*,*) 'Array elements:'
  do i = 1, n
    write(*,*) data(i)
  end do

  ! Deallocate array
  deallocate(data)

end program dynamic_array
```

In the above program, the size of the array data is determined at runtime based on user input. After allocation, the array is populated and then deallocated appropriately to free memory.

```
Enter the number of elements:
5
Array elements:
2
4
6
8
10
```

Case Study 2: Avoiding Memory Leaks

Memory leaks occur when dynamically allocated memory is not properly deallocated. Let us examine a scenario where incorrect memory management can lead to a leak.

```
program memory_leak
  implicit none
  integer, pointer :: ptr
  integer, target :: target_var

  allocate(ptr)
  ptr = 10

  ! Point ptr to target_var without deallocating
  ptr => target_var
  target_var = 20

  ! Print values
  write(*,*) "ptr value:", ptr
  write(*,*) "target_var value:", target_var
end program memory_leak
```

In this example, ptr points to dynamically allocated memory. If the pointer is reassigned to another target, the originally allocated memory is not freed, causing a memory leak. Proper usage involves deallocating ptr before reassociating it:

```
! Corrected version
allocate(ptr)
ptr = 10

! Deallocate before reassociating
deallocate(ptr)
ptr => target_var
target_var = 20
```

Case Study 3: Pointer Arithmetic with Arrays

Pointer arithmetic is often utilized to traverse arrays dynamically. Consider a scenario where a pointer is used to iterate through an array:

```
program pointer_arithmetic
  implicit none
  integer, target :: arr(5)
  integer, pointer :: ptr

  arr = (/1, 2, 3, 4, 5/)
  ptr => arr(1)

  do while(associated(ptr))
    write(*,*) 'Pointer value:', ptr
    ptr => ptr + 1
    if (ptr .gt. arr(5)) exit
  end do

end program pointer_arithmetic
```

In this example, the pointer ptr initially points to the first element of array arr. Pointer arithmetic is applied to traverse through the array elements. Note that this example contains an error, as direct arithmetic on pointers is not allowed.

The corrected approach uses explicit indexing:

```
program pointer_arithmetic_corrected
  implicit none
  integer, target :: arr(5)
  integer, pointer :: ptr
  integer :: i

  arr = (/1, 2, 3, 4, 5/)

  do i = 1, 5
    ptr => arr(i)
    write(*,*) 'Pointer value:', ptr
  end do

end program pointer_arithmetic_corrected
```

Case Study 4: Memory Management with Derived Types

Derived types can encapsulate complex data structures, and proper memory management of such structures is imperative. Consider the following:

```
module person_module
  type :: person
    character(len=50) :: name
    integer :: age
    real, allocatable :: weights(:)
  end type person
end module person_module

program derived_type_memory
  use person_module
  implicit none
  type(person) :: p

  p%name = 'John Doe'
  p%age = 30

  ! Allocate weights array
  allocate(p%weights(3))
  p%weights = (/70.5, 71.0, 69.5/)

  ! Print values
  write(*,*) 'Name:', p%name
  write(*,*) 'Age:', p%age
  write(*,*) 'Weights:', p%weights

  ! Deallocate weights
  deallocate(p%weights)
end program derived_type_memory
```

Here, the derived type person includes an allocatable array weights. After allocating and populating this array, it is necessary to deallocate the memory to prevent leaks.

```
Name: John Doe
Age: 30
Weights: 70.5 71.0 69.5
```

Through these case studies, the importance of proper memory management, whether dealing with arrays, pointers, or derived types, has been demonstrated. Employing robust memory practices ensures efficient and bug-free Fortran program execution.

Chapter 10

Optimizing Fortran Programs

This chapter addresses techniques for optimizing Fortran programs to enhance performance. It covers profiling methods to identify bottlenecks, applying compiler optimization flags, and optimizing loop constructs and memory access. Readers will also learn about vectorization, parallelism, and inlining functions and subroutines. The chapter discusses strategies for efficient data structure usage, minimizing I/O operations, reducing computational complexity, and optimizing cache usage, supported by case studies demonstrating successful optimization in Fortran programs.

10.1 Introduction to Optimization

The optimization of Fortran programs involves enhancing the performance, efficiency, and scalability of the code. This process is pivotal to achieve fast execution times and optimal usage of system resources. This section addresses the foundational concepts and significance of optimization in Fortran programming, preparing the reader to implement specific optimization techniques discussed later in the chapter.

Optimization is not merely about altering the code randomly to see performance improvements. It requires a strategic approach where specific areas of the code are targeted for enhancement. The first step in optimization involves understanding and measuring the current performance of your Fortran program. We employ profiling tools to identify bottlenecks or performance-critical sections of the code. Once identified, targeted optimization techniques can be applied to those sections.

Profiling tools provide insights into how time and resources are spent in various parts of the program. The goal is to focus optimization efforts on these "hot" spots for maximum performance gain. The application of scientific techniques, such as loop unrolling, minimizing branch mispredictions, and efficient memory access patterns, among others, can yield significant improvements when done correctly.

- **Measuring Performance**: Before optimization can begin, one must define what constitutes performance in the context of the program. This could involve execution time, memory usage, or even specific resource utilization.
- **Identifying Bottlenecks**: Use profiling tools to analyze the program run-time and determine which sections of the code consume the most time or resources.
- **Targeted Optimization**: Focus optimization efforts on the bottlenecks identified in the profiling stage. Optimizations should be data-driven and justified by measurable performance improvements.
- **Iterative Process**: Optimization is an iterative process. Apply changes incrementally and measure their impact, reverting any changes that do not provide benefits.

A typical Fortran program might be bottlenecked by various factors such as inefficient loop constructs, suboptimal memory access patterns, and unnecessary computational complexity.

Consider the following example. We have a Fortran code segment that calculates the sum of squares of an array:

```
program sum_of_squares
    implicit none
    integer, parameter :: n = 1000000
    real :: sum
    real, dimension(n) :: a
    integer :: i

    ! Initialize the array
    a = 1.0
```

```
    sum = 0.0
    do i = 1, n
        sum = sum + a(i)**2
    end do

    print *, 'Sum of squares: ', sum
end program sum_of_squares
```

This code initializes an array a with one million elements, all set to 1.0, and then computes the sum of squares of this array. While simple, the loop construct here offers room for optimization.

The initial approach might involve identifying how the loop can be optimized. In this case, a simple transformation known as loop unrolling can potentially enhance performance by reducing the overhead associated with loop control:

```
sum = 0.0
do i = 1, n, 4
    sum = sum + a(i)**2 + a(i+1)**2 + a(i+2)**2 + a(i+3)**2
end do
```

By unrolling the loop, we make fewer passes through the loop structure, thus reducing the loop overhead. Additionally, the computation within the loop body may become more efficient due to improved instruction-level parallelism and cache usage.

Another important optimization strategy involves leveraging modern CPU capabilities such as vectorization. Vectorization allows multiple data points to be processed simultaneously using Single Instruction, Multiple Data (SIMD) instructions. Modern Fortran compilers are capable of autovectorizing loops when certain conditions are met.

Consider enabling compiler vectorization using flags specific to the Fortran compiler. For instance, using the -O2 or -O3 optimization levels with the GNU Fortran compiler (gfortran) can help in automatically applying such techniques:

```
gfortran -O3 sum_of_squares.f90 -o sum_of_squares
```

Other compilers, such as Intel's Fortran compiler (ifort), offer similar flags for optimization. These flags instruct the compiler to perform aggressive optimizations, including vectorization, inlining, and others, designed to enhance performance automatically.

Efficient memory access patterns are crucial for optimization. Access to memory should be made in a linear fashion to exploit the spatial locality of cache memory. Non-sequential memory access patterns can lead to cache misses, significantly degrading performance.

To summarize, optimization in Fortran programming is an essential aspect for enhancing program performance. The strategic application of optimization techniques after thorough profiling can lead to remarkable improvements. Subsequent sections will delve deeper into specific optimization strategies, providing practical examples and best practices for mastering Fortran programming optimization.

10.2 Profiling Fortran Programs

Profiling Fortran programs is a critical step in identifying performance bottlenecks and understanding the behavior of the code during execution. This process involves collecting and examining data about various aspects of the program's runtime performance, such as function call frequencies, memory usage, and time spent in different parts of the code. Profiling allows developers to pinpoint inefficient code segments and optimize them effectively.

To start profiling a Fortran program, one must compile the code with special flags that enable profiling. Most modern compilers, such as GNU Fortran (gfortran) and Intel Fortran Compiler (ifort), provide support for generating profiling information. The common tool used for analyzing the profiling data generated by these compilers is GNU gprof, although there are other tools like Intel VTune Profiler for more advanced analysis.

```
gfortran -pg -o my_program my_program.f90
```

In the example above, the -pg flag is used with gfortran to compile the Fortran source file my_program.f90 and generate an executable named my_program that includes profiling information.

Running the executable my_program will produce a file called gmon.out, which contains the profiling data:

```
./my_program
```

Once the program execution is complete, gmon.out can be analyzed using gprof:

```
gprof my_program gmon.out > analysis.txt
```

The output file analysis.txt will contain detailed profiling data such as the call graph and flat profile. The flat profile lists functions sorted by the amount of time spent in each one. The call graph shows how functions call each other, providing insight into the program's execution flow.

```
Flat profile:
Each sample counts as 0.01 seconds.
  %   cumulative   self              self     total
 time   seconds   seconds    calls  Ts/call  Ts/call  name
 50.00     0.10     0.10     1000     0.00     0.00  compute_value
 30.00     0.16     0.06     1000     0.00     0.00  initialize
 20.00     0.20     0.04                              MAIN__
```

In the flat profile example, compute_value is identified as the most time-consuming function. By examining such information, developers can focus their optimization efforts on high-impact areas.

Further analysis might involve more advanced profiling tools like Intel VTune Profiler, which provides finer-grained data and powerful visualization features. For instance, Intel VTune can highlight specific instructions that contribute to cache misses or inefficient vectorization. It requires a similar approach to instrumentation and running the code but offers a more comprehensive suite of performance metrics.

Using Intel VTune, a Fortran program can be compiled as follows:

```
ifort -g -O2 -o my_program my_program.f90
```

In this case, the -g flag includes debugging information, and -O2 applies standard optimizations. After compilation, the program is executed normally, and VTune collects the profiling data via its user interface or command line.

Effective profiling involves iterating through the process of analysis, identification, and optimization. After making changes to improve a specific part of the code, developers should re-profile the program to verify that the optimizations have had the desired effect. This iterative process ensures that performance improvements are based on empirical data rather than speculation.

To optimize the profiling process, consider focusing on:

- Hotspots: Functions or lines of code where the most time is spent.
- Call tree: The hierarchy of function calls to understand the impact on performance.
- Memory usage: Analyze memory allocation and deallocation to identify leaks or excessive use.
- I/O operations: Detect whether I/O operations are significant bottlenecks.

Profiling tools often come with various options to filter and display different aspects of the performance data, allowing for thorough investigation of specific issues. It is beneficial to become familiar with these options to make the most out of the profiling tools.

Finally, documenting the findings from profiling and the subsequent optimization steps can be invaluable. Such documentation creates a performance history that helps track improvements and understand the rationale behind various optimizations. This context can guide future performance tuning and troubleshooting efforts.

Profiling Fortran programs is thus an essential practice that provides the necessary insight and data to drive performance improvements, making applications faster and more efficient.

10.3 Compiler Optimization Flags

Compiler optimization flags play a crucial role in enhancing the performance of Fortran programs. These flags instruct the compiler to apply specific optimizations during the code compilation stage, aiming to generate more efficient executable code. Understanding and utilizing these flags effectively can lead to significant improvements in execution speed and resource utilization.

When compiling a Fortran program, various optimization flags can be set to control the level and types of optimizations applied. These flags vary slightly between different Fortran compilers, such as GNU Fortran (gfortran), Intel Fortran, and others. However, common optimization flags are present across most compilers.

- -O0: This flag disables optimization, resulting in the slowest execution but the fastest compilation time. It is useful primarily for debugging purposes, as it keeps the code structure close to the source.

- -O1: This flag enables basic optimization techniques that improve performance without significantly extending compilation time. Optimizations at this level typically include common subexpression elimination and basic loop transformations.

- -O2: A widely used optimization flag, -O2 enables a broader range of optimizations that strike a balance between compilation time and execution speed improvement. Some of the optimizations include inlining of small functions, automatic vectorization, and inter-procedural analysis.

- -O3: This flag enables the most aggressive optimizations, often including complex loop transformations, function cloning, and advanced vectorization. It may lead to substantial performance gains but can also significantly increase compilation time and possibly affect numerical stability.

- -Ofast: Combining the optimizations of -O3 with more aggressive transformations such as disregarding strict standard compliance, this flag maximizes performance. Using -Ofast can lead to the fastest executable code but should be used with caution to ensure the results are still valid.

- -funroll-loops: Optimizes performance by unrolling loops, which reduces the overhead of loop control and enhances opportunities for further optimizations like vectorization. Loop unrolling is particularly beneficial for loops with a small, fixed number of iterations.

- -finline-functions: Encourages the compiler to inline functions, embedding their code into calling code to eliminate function call overhead. This flag can improve performance, especially for small, frequently called functions.

- -march=native: Optimizes the code for the host machine architecture. Setting this flag enables the compiler to leverage specific CPU features such as specialized instruction sets, leading to substantial performance improvements on the target hardware.

- -flto: Enables link-time optimization (LTO), which performs optimizations across the entire program scope during linking. It allows the compiler to apply more sophisticated optimizations by having a holistic view of the program.

To demonstrate the effects of compiler optimization flags, consider the following simple Fortran program for summing the elements of an array:

```
program sum_array
    implicit none
    integer, parameter :: n = 1000000
    integer :: i
    real :: sum, array(n)

    ! Initialize array
    do i = 1, n
```

```
    array(i) = i * 1.0
  end do

  sum = 0.0
  ! Compute sum
  do i = 1, n
    sum = sum + array(i)
  end do

  print *, "Sum = ", sum
end program sum_array
```

Compiling and running this program with different optimization flags would look like this:

```
gfortran -O0 sum_array.f90 -o sum_array_O0
./sum_array_O0
```

```
Sum =  5.0000050E+11
```

```
gfortran -O2 sum_array.f90 -o sum_array_O2
./sum_array_O2
```

```
Sum =  5.0000050E+11
```

Despite producing the same output, the execution times might differ significantly between the -O0 and -O2 compilations, demonstrating the impact of optimization.

Advanced users can fine-tune their optimization strategies by combining multiple flags to target specific code patterns. For performance-critical applications, iterative testing of different flag combinations, combined with profiling tools, helps identify the optimal set of compiler flags.

Compiler documentation is an essential resource for detailed descriptions and the latest updates on available optimization flags. Leveraging these flags effectively is an iterative process and requires a good understanding of the program's behavior and the underlying hardware architecture.

10.4 Loop Optimization Techniques

Loop optimization is crucial in Fortran programming to enhance computational performance, primarily because loops often encapsulate the most time-consuming portions of a program. Various strategies can be employed to optimize loops, including loop unrolling, loop fusion, loop fission, and loop interchange. Understanding and applying these techniques effectively can lead to significant improvements in computation speed.

Loop Unrolling is a technique where the loop body is replicated multiple times to decrease the overhead of loop control and provide opportunities for instruction-level parallelism. This technique can reduce the number of iterations and the number of times condition checks occur, thus increasing the program's execution speed.

```
! Original loop
do i = 1, 1000
  a(i) = a(i) + b(i) * c(i)
end do

! Unrolled loop (factor of 4)
do i = 1, 1000, 4
  a(i) = a(i) + b(i) * c(i)
  a(i+1) = a(i+1) + b(i+1) * c(i+1)
  a(i+2) = a(i+2) + b(i+2) * c(i+2)
  a(i+3) = a(i+3) + b(i+3) * c(i+3)
end do
```

The unrolled loop reduces the loop control overhead and may enhance performance, particularly on architectures where instruction-level parallelism is beneficial. However, one must consider increased code size due to loop unrolling and ensure array boundaries are handled correctly.

Loop Fusion, or loop jamming, involves combining multiple loops that iterate over the same range into a single loop. This technique can reduce loop overhead and improve data locality, which is critical for memory-bound computations.

```
! Original separate loops
do i = 1, n
  a(i) = b(i) + c(i)
end do

do i = 1, n
  d(i) = e(i) - f(i)
end do

! Fused loop
do i = 1, n
  a(i) = b(i) + c(i)
  d(i) = e(i) - f(i)
end do
```

By fusing the loops, the number of loop iterations and loop control operations is reduced, potentially improving the program's performance if the operations within the fused loop do not introduce dependencies.

Loop Fission, also known as loop distribution, is the opposite of loop fusion. This technique splits a single loop into multiple loops to improve cache performance or enable further optimizations on the separated loops.

```
! Original loop
do i = 1, n
  a(i) = b(i) + c(i)
  d(i) = e(i) - f(i)
end do

! Fissioned loops
do i = 1, n
  a(i) = b(i) + c(i)
end do

do i = 1, n
  d(i) = e(i) - f(i)
end do
```

Loop fission may be beneficial for enhancing cache efficiency, especially if the arrays involved in the original loop do not fit in the cache simultaneously.

Loop Interchange optimizes nested loops by switching their order, thereby improving memory access patterns and data locality. This technique is particularly useful when dealing with multidimensional arrays.

```
! Original loop
do i = 1, n
  do j = 1, m
    a(i,j) = b(i,j) + c(i,j)
  end do
end do

! Interchanged loop
do j = 1, m
  do i = 1, n
    a(i,j) = b(i,j) + c(i,j)
  end do
end do
```

Loop interchange can be advantageous when the innermost loop iterates over the fastest-changing dimension in the array's memory layout, thereby enhancing data locality and cache usage.

Applying these loop optimization techniques methodically requires a thorough understanding of the underlying hardware architecture, memory hierarchy, and computational workload characteristics. Profiling tools and performance metrics can guide the choice of which loop optimizations to apply for maximizing the performance gains in Fortran programs.

10.5 Memory Access Optimization

Optimizing memory access is a crucial aspect of enhancing the performance of your Fortran programs. Efficient memory usage can significantly reduce execution time by minimizing cache misses and ensuring that data is fetched and stored optimally. To achieve memory access optimization, one must understand and implement proper data locality, alignment, and stride access patterns. This section will explore these concepts in detail and provide practical techniques to apply them in Fortran programming.

Data Locality

Data locality refers to the use of data elements within relatively close storage locations over short periods of time. There are two types of data locality: spatial locality and temporal locality. Spatial locality implies that if a particular element is accessed, elements close to it are likely to be accessed soon. Temporal locality suggests that if a particular element is accessed, it is likely to be accessed again in the near future.

In Fortran, arrays are stored in column-major order. This means that elements of a column are stored in contiguous memory locations. To leverage spatial locality, it is advantageous to access array elements in a consistent, column-wise manner. Consider the following two loops:

```
! Example 1: Suboptimal access pattern
do i = 1, n
    do j = 1, m
        A(j, i) = A(j, i) * 2.0
    end do
end do

! Example 2: Optimal access pattern
do j = 1, m
    do i = 1, n
        A(j, i) = A(j, i) * 2.0
    end do
end do
```

In Example 1, the array A is accessed row-wise, causing potential cache misses due to non-contiguous memory access. In Example 2, the array A is accessed column-wise, fostering spatial locality and likely reducing cache misses.

Data Alignment

Proper data alignment ensures that data is positioned in memory according to the architecture's requirements, potentially reducing the number of memory accesses needed to fetch or store data. Most modern

CPUs are optimized for data that is aligned in memory according to their cache line sizes. Misaligned data can result in additional memory accesses and lower performance.

In Fortran, you can ensure proper alignment by using compiler directives or attributes that control data layout. One way to enforce alignment is through the use of the !DIR$ ATTRIBUTES ALIGN directive. Here is an example:

```
! Enforcing alignment for performance-critical arrays
real, dimension(1000, 1000) :: A
!DIR$ ATTRIBUTES ALIGN: 32 :: A
```

Here, the ALIGN: 32 directive ensures that the starting address of the array is aligned to a 32-byte boundary, which might correspond to the cache line size on the target architecture, ensuring better performance due to alignment.

Stride Access Patterns

Memory access patterns with regular stride can differ greatly in performance depending on whether they align well with the cache architecture. A stride is the step size between successive data accesses. Stride-1 access is optimal, as it accesses consecutive elements, aligning with the cache line and maximizing efficiency.

Consider modifying strides in order to achieve optimal access. For an array stored in column-major order, accessing elements with a stride of 1 for the inner loop is ideal. Conversely, high stride values can lead to inefficient cache usage and increased memory latency.

```
! Example with non-optimal stride
do i = 1, n, 2 ! Stride of 2
    A(i) = A(i) + B(i)
end do

! Example with optimal stride (Stride-1)
do i = 1, n
    A(i) = A(i) + B(i)
end do
```

Minimizing strides ensures better utilization of cache lines, thus enhancing access speed and overall performance.

Utilization of Local Variables

Using local variables can be more efficient than accessing global arrays in tight loops. This reduces the time spent accessing memory and increases the chances that frequently accessed data will stay in the CPU registers instead of being repeatedly loaded from memory.

```
! Example using global array access
do i = 1, n
    sum = sum + A(i)
end do

! Example using local variable
do i = 1, n
    temp = A(i)
    sum = sum + temp
end do
```

By copying the element A(i) into a local variable temp, we might enable the compiler to keep temp in a register, reducing memory access overhead.

Considering these memory access optimization techniques in Fortran programs can lead to significant performance gains. Ensuring good data locality, proper alignment, optimal stride patterns, and effective use of local variables makes programs more efficient and responsive to the underlying hardware architecture.

10.6 Vectorization and Parallelism

Vectorization and parallelism are critical techniques for optimizing Fortran programs, significantly enhancing computational performance by leveraging modern processor architectures. Vectorization involves executing multiple operations simultaneously using vector registers, while parallelism distributes computation across multiple processing units. This section delves into these optimization strategies, offering detailed instructions and examples.

Vectorization in Fortran

Vectorization exploits the capabilities of SIMD (Single Instruction, Multiple Data) instructions, allowing a single instruction to process multiple data points concurrently. Fortran developers can harness vectorization via built-in features and compiler directives.

To begin with, consider the following Fortran loop:

```
do i = 1, n
    a(i) = b(i) + c(i)
end do
```

In this code snippet, each iteration of the loop performs an independent addition, making it an ideal candidate for vectorization. Modern Fortran compilers, such as gfortran and ifort, can automatically vectorize simple loops. The key is to ensure the loop structure and data access patterns do not hinder vectorization.

Compilers often require hints or directives to vectorize more complex loops. The !$omp simd directive in Fortran provides such a hint:

```
!$omp simd
do i = 1, n
    a(i) = b(i) + c(i)
end do
```

Here, the !$omp simd directive suggests parallel execution for vector operations. It is crucial to verify if the loop carries dependencies between iterations, which could prevent safe vectorization.

Compilers can provide feedback on vectorization attempts, typically via specific flags. For example, using gfortran:

```
gfortran -O3 -ftree-vectorize -fopt-info-vec-omp hello.f90
```

The -fopt-info-vec-omp flag instructs the compiler to generate a report detailing which loops were vectorized and any pertinent issues.

Parallelism in Fortran

Parallelism is the distribution of computational tasks across multiple processing elements. Fortran supports parallel programming paradigms through OpenMP and MPI (Message Passing Interface). OpenMP is used for shared-memory architectures, simplifying parallelization within a single machine.

Here is an example using OpenMP to parallelize a loop:

```
program parallel_example
    use omp_lib
    integer :: i, n
    real, dimension(:), allocatable :: a, b, c

    n = 1000
    allocate(a(n), b(n), c(n))

    !$omp parallel do
    do i = 1, n
        a(i) = b(i) + c(i)
    end do
    !$omp end parallel do

    deallocate(a, b, c)
end program
```

The !$omp parallel do directive instructs the compiler to parallelize the loop, distributing iterations across multiple threads. The omp_lib module is used to include OpenMP functionalities.

MPI, on the other hand, is suitable for distributed-memory systems, enabling communication between processes running on different nodes. Below is a basic example using MPI in Fortran:

```
program mpi_example
    use mpi
    integer :: ierr, rank, size, tag, status(MPI_STATUS_SIZE), i
    integer, parameter :: n = 1000
    real, dimension(n) :: a, b, c

    call MPI_Init(ierr)
    call MPI_Comm_rank(MPI_COMM_WORLD, rank, ierr)
    call MPI_Comm_size(MPI_COMM_WORLD, size, ierr)
    tag = 1

    if (rank .eq. 0) then
        ! Master process
        do i = 1, n
            a(i) = b(i) + c(i)
        end do
    else
        ! Worker process
        call MPI_Recv(a, n, MPI_REAL, 0, tag, MPI_COMM_WORLD, status, ierr)
        do i = 1, n
            a(i) = b(i) + c(i)
        end do
        call MPI_Send(a, n, MPI_REAL, 0, tag, MPI_COMM_WORLD, ierr)
    end if

    call MPI_Finalize(ierr)
end program
```

In this example, MPI functions MPI_Init, MPI_Comm_rank, and MPI_Comm_size initialize the MPI environment, determine the rank of the process, and the size of the global communicator. The master process distributes data to worker processes using MPI_Recv and MPI_Send for communication.

By adeptly combining vectorization and parallelism, Fortran programmers can exploit the full potential of modern processors, significantly boosting program execution efficiency.

10.7 Inlining Functions and Subroutines

Inlining in the context of Fortran programming refers to a technique whereby the compiler replaces a function or subroutine call with the actual code of the function or subroutine. This eliminates the overhead associated with calling functions, such as stack operations and instruction jumps, thereby potentially improving the execution speed of the program. This section delves into the rationale, methodology, and practical considerations for effectively using inlining to optimize Fortran programs.

Compilers often enable inlining through specific directives or flags. For example, in GNU Fortran (gfortran), the -finline-functions flag can be used to suggest inlining optimizations. Consider the following simple function in Fortran:

```
function add(a, b) result(c)
    integer, intent(in) :: a, b
    integer :: c
    c = a + b
end function add
```

When this function is called repeatedly within a loop, the overhead of function calls can become significant. Let's observe an optimization scenario where inlining is beneficial.

```
program main
    integer :: i, sum = 0
    do i = 1, 1000000
        sum = add(sum, i)
    end do
    print *, sum
end program main
```

When the command line for compilation with optimization is used, we activate function inlining:

```
gfortran -O3 -finline-functions main.f90 -o main
```

Here, -O3 is an optimization level flag that enables aggressive optimizations, including function inlining. The -finline-functions specifically directs the compiler to inline suitable functions.

The advantages of inlining must be balanced against potential drawbacks. Inlining can lead to code bloat, where the binary size of the program increases significantly due to multiple copies of inlined code. This might adversely affect the cache performance and memory usage. Practical considerations involve analysis using compiler reports and actual performance profiling. Let's review an example of manual function inlining:

The original code without inlining:

```
function multiply(a, b) result(c)
    integer, intent(in) :: a, b
    integer :: c
    c = a * b
end function multiply

program main
    integer :: i, result = 1
```

```
    do i = 1, 20
        result = multiply(result, i)
    end do
    print *, result
end program main
```

By manually inlining, the code becomes:

```
program main
    integer :: i, result = 1
    do i = 1, 20
        result = result * i
    end do
    print *, result
end program main
```

Manually inlining transforms a function call into a direct calculation within the loop, removing the call overhead.

Compiler-assisted inlining: inline hints can be provided in modern Fortran by using the inline keyword, although compiler support for this feature may vary. Consult the compiler documentation to understand the supported syntax and semantics.

Managing inlining in large codebases:

- Identify Hotspots: Use profiling tools to identify functions that are heavily used and examine whether inlining could yield performance benefits.
- Measure Performance: Benchmarks should be established before and after the inlining to gauge the actual impact on performance and verify if the optimizations are beneficial.
- Code Maintainability: Consider readability and maintainability when deciding to inline functions manually, as this can lead to more tangled code that is harder to debug and maintain.

To facilitate entire program optimization, some Fortran compilers allow for Link Time Optimization (LTO). LTO enables the compiler to inline functions across different translation units.

```
gfortran -O3 -flto main.f90 -o main
```

In this command, -flto enables link time optimization, allowing the inlining of functions across module boundaries that can not be detected during compilation.

Critical performance enhancements can be realized by adeptly employing inlining, guided by profiling insights and empirical validation, without compromising the code maintainability balance.

10.8 Efficient Use of Data Structures

Efficient use of data structures in Fortran is pivotal for optimizing performance. An optimal data structure allows for decreased computational complexity, enhanced memory access patterns, and improved parallelization efficiency. This section explores the implementation and selection of various data structures in Fortran, ranging from arrays to derived types, as well as best practices for their use.

Arrays are the building blocks of data structures in Fortran. Array handling in Fortran is highly efficient, but it requires diligent use of proper indexing and memory access patterns. Consider the following example where an array is declared and used:

```
PROGRAM ArrayExample
  IMPLICIT NONE
  INTEGER, PARAMETER :: N = 100
  REAL :: A(N), B(N), C(N)
  INTEGER :: i
  ! Initialize arrays
  DO i = 1, N
    A(i) = i
    B(i) = N - i
  END DO

  ! Perform element-wise addition
  DO i = 1, N
    C(i) = A(i) + B(i)
  END DO

  PRINT *, C
END PROGRAM ArrayExample
```

The primary concern in array usage is the stride of memory access. Fortran uses column-major order for array storage, meaning that sequential elements of a column are stored contiguously in memory. Optimal performance is achieved when accessing array elements in a column-wise manner. Avoid patterns that cause non-contiguous memory access, as these can lead to inefficient cache usage and memory latency issues.

Derived types in Fortran allow for the creation of more complex data structures which can encapsulate multiple data elements. Proper use of derived types can vastly improve data locality, leading to better cache performance. An example of a derived type is given below:

```
MODULE ParticleModule
```

```
  TYPE :: Particle
    REAL :: x, y, z ! Position
    REAL :: vx, vy, vz ! Velocity
  END TYPE Particle
END MODULE ParticleModule

PROGRAM ParticleArray
  USE ParticleModule
  IMPLICIT NONE
  INTEGER, PARAMETER :: N = 1000
  TYPE(Particle) :: particles(N)
  INTEGER :: i

  ! Initialize particles
  DO i = 1, N
    particles(i)%x = 0.0
    particles(i)%y = 0.0
    particles(i)%z = 0.0
    particles(i)%vx = 1.0
    particles(i)%vy = 1.0
    particles(i)%vz = 1.0
  END DO

  PRINT *, "Particles initialized"
END PROGRAM ParticleArray
```

When dealing with derived types, it is important to consider the memory layout and access patterns. This involves organizing the data in a manner consistent with how it will be accessed. For example, if frequent access to positions and velocities of particles is required, the alignment and padding in the memory layout must be considered to minimize cache misses and enhance performance.

Another aspect of data structure efficiency is avoiding dynamic allocation and deallocation within performance-critical sections. Dynamic memory operations are costly and can introduce fragmentation, leading to degraded performance. Preferring static or stack allocation where possible can lead to more predictable and optimized memory usage.

Efficient data structure usage also involves understanding and leveraging Fortran's array operations and intrinsic functions, which can be automatically vectorized by the compiler. Consider using array slicing and intrinsic functions such as SUM, PRODUCT, DOT_PRODUCT, and MATMUL which can lead to more compact and faster code. An example using array slicing for an element-wise operation:

```
PROGRAM SlicingExample
  IMPLICIT NONE
  INTEGER, PARAMETER :: N = 100
  REAL :: A(N), B(N), C(N)

  ! Initialize arrays
  A = (/ (REAL(i), i = 1, N) /)
  B = (/ (REAL(N-i+1), i = 1, N) /)
```

```
  ! Perform element-wise addition using slicing
  C = A + B

  PRINT *, C
END PROGRAM SlicingExample
```

Efficient use of data structures in parallel computing involves ensuring that data is correctly aligned for parallel access patterns. Using directives from OpenMP or MPI can guide the compiler to optimize data layout for parallel execution. This minimizes synchronization overhead and maximizes bandwidth utilization.

The efficient use of data structures is a multifaceted strategy requiring careful consideration of memory layout, access patterns, and computational requirements. Employing optimal data structures can greatly enhance the performance of Fortran programs, particularly in computationally intensive applications.

10.9 Minimizing I/O Operations

Minimizing I/O operations in Fortran programs is crucial since I/O operations are inherently slower compared to in-memory computations. Efficient I/O can significantly reduce the overall execution time of a program. This section discusses various strategies to optimize I/O operations, including buffering techniques, asynchronous I/O, reducing I/O frequency, and efficient file access patterns.

Buffering Techniques. Buffering can minimize the number of I/O operations by accumulating data in memory buffers and writing it to files in larger chunks. This approach reduces the overhead of multiple system calls associated with I/O operations. The following example demonstrates how to use buffering in Fortran:

```
program buffered_io
   implicit none
   integer, parameter :: buffer_size = 1000
   integer :: i
   real :: buffer(buffer_size)
   character(len=20) :: filename
   integer :: unit_no, ios

   filename = "output.txt"
   open(unit=unit_no, file=filename, status='unknown', action='write', iostat=ios)
   if (ios /= 0) then
      print *, "Error opening file"
      stop
   endif
```

```
    do i = 1, buffer_size
        buffer(i) = i * 1.0
    end do

    write(unit_no, *) buffer
    close(unit_no)
end program buffered_io
```

In this example, data is stored in the array buffer, and only one write operation is performed, which writes all the data at once to the file output.txt.

Asynchronous I/O. Asynchronous I/O allows a program to continue executing other tasks while I/O operations are being performed. This can be achieved using non-blocking I/O calls provided by modern Fortran compilers. The following example shows asynchronous I/O operations:

```
program async_io
    implicit none
    integer, parameter :: n = 1000000
    real, dimension(n) :: data
    integer :: i, ios, unit_no, req
    character(len=20) :: filename

    ! Initialize data
    do i = 1, n
        data(i) = sin(2.0*pi*i/n)
    end do

    filename = "async_output.txt"
    open(unit=unit_no, file=filename, status='unknown', action='write', asynchronous
          ='yes', iostat=ios)
    if (ios /= 0) then
        print *, "Error opening file"
        stop
    endif

    write(unit_no, asynchronous='yes', iostat=ios, id=req) data
    if (ios /= 0) then
        print *, "Error writing data"
        stop
    endif

    ! Perform other computations while I/O is in progress
    print *, "I/O is in progress, performing other tasks..."

    ! Wait for the I/O operation to complete
    wait(unit_no, id=req, iostat=ios)
    if (ios /= 0) then
        print *, "Error during wait"
        stop
    endif

    close(unit_no)
end program async_io
```

In this example, the data array is written to async_output.txt asynchronously, allowing the program to perform other computations in the meantime.

Reducing I/O Frequency. Reducing the frequency of I/O operations involves accumulating more data in memory before performing any I/O actions. This can be achieved by careful reorganization of the program logic to minimize the need for intermediate storage and retrieval of data from disk. Here is a pattern that minimizes frequent I/O by accumulating results and saving them in bulk:

```
program reduce_io_frequency
    implicit none
    integer, parameter :: n = 1000000
    integer :: i, ios, unit_no
    real :: accumulation(n), result
    character(len=20) :: filename

    filename = "results.txt"
    open(unit=unit_no, file=filename, status='unknown', action='write', iostat=ios)
    if (ios /= 0) then
        print *, "Error opening file"
        stop
    endif

    do i = 1, n
        result = sin(2.0*pi*i/n)
        accumulation(i) = result
        ! instead of frequent writes, accumulate
    end do

    write(unit_no, *) accumulation
    close(unit_no)
end program reduce_io_frequency
```

The above example shows data being accumulated in the accumulation array and written all at once to the file results.txt, thus reducing the number of I/O operations.

Efficient File Access Patterns. Efficient file access patterns involve organizing data in such a way that it reduces the overhead caused by frequent read/write access to non-contiguous memory locations. One strategy is to use direct access files, which allow data to be read or written at specific positions in the file without traversing from the beginning. Here is an example of using direct access to efficiently handle file I/O:

```
program direct_access_io
    implicit none
    integer, parameter :: rec_len = 20
    integer :: i, unit_no, ios
    real :: data
    character(len=20) :: filename

    filename = "direct_access.dat"
    open(unit=unit_no, file=filename, status='unknown', action='write', access='direct
        ', recl=rec_len, iostat=ios)
```

```
    if (ios /= 0) then
        print *, "Error opening file"
        stop
    endif

    do i = 1, 100
        data = i * 1.0
        write(unit_no, rec=i, iostat=ios) data
        if (ios /= 0) then
            print *, "Error writing record"
            stop
        endif
    end do

    close(unit_no)
end program direct_access_io
```

In the above example, data is written to the file direct_access.dat using direct access, thus allowing efficient reading and writing to specific record positions without the overhead of sequential file traversal.

Implementing these strategies can greatly enhance the performance of Fortran programs by reducing the time spent on I/O operations.

10.10 Reducing Computational Complexity

One of the most significant steps in optimizing Fortran programs is reducing their computational complexity. Computational complexity refers to how the resource requirements of an algorithm grow with the size of the input. Typically, the resources we are concerned with are time (CPU cycles) and space (memory usage). This section explores strategies for decreasing computational complexity to improve the efficiency of Fortran programs.

Understanding Time Complexity

Time complexity measures the amount of time an algorithm takes to complete as a function of the input size. Common time complexities include constant time $\mathcal{O}(1)$, logarithmic time $\mathcal{O}(\log n)$, linear time $\mathcal{O}(n)$, and quadratic time $\mathcal{O}(n^2)$, among others.

For example, consider a simple linear search and a binary search for finding an element in an array. The linear search has a time complexity of $\mathcal{O}(n)$ because in the worst case, it examines each of the n elements once. In contrast, a binary search on a sorted array has a time complexity of $\mathcal{O}(\log n)$ as it repeatedly divides the search interval in half.

Linear Search Implementation

```
subroutine linear_search(arr, target, n, result)
    integer :: arr(n), target, result
    integer :: i

    result = -1
    do i = 1, n
        if (arr(i) == target) then
            result = i
            return
        endif
    enddo
end subroutine linear_search
```

Binary Search Implementation

```
subroutine binary_search(arr, target, n, result)
    integer :: arr(n), target, result
    integer :: low, high, mid

    low = 1
    high = n
    result = -1

    do while (low <= high)
        mid = (low + high) / 2
        if (arr(mid) < target) then
            low = mid + 1
        elseif (arr(mid) > target) then
            high = mid - 1
        else
            result = mid
            return
        endif
    enddo
end subroutine binary_search
```

Optimizing Algorithms:

- ***Algorithm Selection:*** Choosing the right algorithm is crucial for reducing computational complexity. For instance, sorting algorithms vary significantly in performance, from $\mathcal{O}(n^2)$ for bubble sort to $\mathcal{O}(n \log n)$ for merge sort and quicksort.
- ***Divide and Conquer:*** Techniques such as divide and conquer can significantly reduce complexity by breaking problems into smaller sub-problems, solving each sub-problem independently, and then combining the results.
- ***Dynamic Programming:*** For problems exhibiting overlapping sub-problems and optimal substructure properties, dynamic programming can optimize computations by storing the results of expensive function calls and reusing them.

Factorial Calculation Using Dynamic Programming

```
function factorial(n) result(fact)
    integer :: n, i, fact
    integer, allocatable :: lookup(:)

    allocate(lookup(n+1))
    lookup(1) = 1

    do i = 2, n
        lookup(i) = i * lookup(i-1)
    enddo

    fact = lookup(n)
end function factorial
```

Improving Memory Access Patterns:

- ***Cache-Friendly Code:*** Efficient memory access patterns enhance speed. Accessing memory in a predictable, contiguous manner maximizes cache utilization, as seen in sequential array access versus random access.
- ***Blocking (Tiling):*** Splitting computations into smaller blocks that fit within the cache can reduce cache misses. This technique is particularly relevant for matrix operations.

Matrix Multiplication with Blocking

```
subroutine matrix_multiply_block(A, B, C, n, block_size)
    integer :: n, block_size, i, j, k, i1, j1, k1
    real, dimension(n, n) :: A, B, C

    do i = 1, n, block_size
        do j = 1, n, block_size
            do k = 1, n, block_size
                do i1 = i, min(i+block_size-1, n)
                    do j1 = j, min(j+block_size-1, n)
                        do k1 = k, min(k+block_size-1, n)
                            C(i1, j1) = C(i1, j1) + A(i1, k1) * B(k1, j1)
                        enddo
                    enddo
                enddo
            enddo
        enddo
    enddo
end subroutine matrix_multiply_block
```

Analyzing the space and time trade-offs can indicate which optimizations are feasible. Although a more complex algorithm may sometimes use extra memory to gain speed improvements, the decision on how to balance these factors should align with the overall resource availability and the specific requirements of the application. This delicate balance underscores the importance of knowledgeable algorithm selection and memory management for achieving high-performance Fortran programs.

10.11 Cache Optimization

Effective cache usage can significantly enhance the performance of Fortran programs by reducing the time required to access memory. Contemporary processors are designed with multiple hierarchical caches that enable faster data access than main memory. Optimizing cache usage involves organizing data and structuring code to increase the likelihood that required data will reside in the cache when accessed. This section discusses various strategies to optimize cache utilization in Fortran programs, including data locality, blocking techniques, and loop transformations.

Data locality refers to the spatial and temporal proximity of data access. Spatial locality implies accessing data elements stored close to each other in memory, while temporal locality suggests that recently accessed data is likely to be accessed again soon. Properly managing these aspects of data access can lead to better cache performance.

Spatial locality can be maximized by ensuring that data structures are accessed sequentially. For instance, consider a Fortran loop accessing elements of an array:

```
do i = 1, n
    array(i) = array(i) + 1
end do
```

Here, elements of array are accessed in a linear order, maximizing spatial locality.

Temporal locality involves reusing data as much as possible before it gets evicted from the cache. Implementing blocking techniques is one way to achieve this, especially in the context of matrix operations. Blocking (or tiling) subdivides large matrices into smaller blocks, allowing these blocks to fit into the cache more effectively. Consider the following example of matrix multiplication using blocking:

```
subroutine matmul_block(A, B, C, n, bsize)
    integer, parameter :: dp = kind(1.0d0)
    real(dp), intent(in) :: A(n,n), B(n,n)
    real(dp), intent(out) :: C(n,n)
    integer :: i, j, k, ii, jj, kk
    integer :: n, bsize
```

```
  do ii = 1, n, bsize
    do jj = 1, n, bsize
      do kk = 1, n, bsize
        do i = ii, min(ii+bsize-1, n)
          do j = jj, min(jj+bsize-1, n)
            do k = kk, min(kk+bsize-1, n)
              C(i,j) = C(i,j) + A(i,k) * B(k,j)
            end do
          end do
        end do
      end do
    end do
  end do
end subroutine matmul_block
```

This approach enhances temporal locality by reusing data within each block before moving to the next, thereby keeping frequently accessed data in cache longer.

Loop transformation techniques, such as loop interchange, can also optimize cache usage. Loop interchange reorders nested loops to improve data access patterns. For example, consider the following nested loops:

```
do j = 1, n
  do i = 1, n
    A(i,j) = A(i,j) + B(i) * C(j)
  end do
end do
```

If A(i,j) is stored in column-major order (as in Fortran default), A(i,j) is accessed non-contiguously in memory. Interchanging the loops can improve cache performance by making accesses more contiguous:

```
do i = 1, n
  do j = 1, n
    A(i,j) = A(i,j) + B(i) * C(j)
  end do
end do
```

This reordering makes the memory accesses within the inner loop sequential, improving spatial locality.

Understanding **cache line size** and **cache associativity** is crucial for optimizing cache usage. Cache lines are the blocks of memory transferred between main memory and the cache. Programs should be designed to minimize cache line evictions by not striding through memory in a way that repeatedly evicts useful data. Consider the following stride access pattern:

```
do i = 1, n, stride
  sum = sum + array(i)
```

```
end do
```

If the stride is large relative to the cache line size, each access might result in a cache miss. Reducing the stride or reorganizing data layouts to make use of larger continuous memory regions can mitigate such issues, enhancing cache efficiency.

Analyzing cache performance can involve using hardware performance counters or profiling tools designed to track cache misses and hits. Adjustments based on analysis results can fine-tune program performance with respect to cache usage, ultimately leading to substantial enhancements in execution speed.

10.12 Case Studies on Optimized Fortran Programs

Consider three representative Fortran programs: a numerical solver for partial differential equations (PDEs), a molecular dynamics simulation, and a data processing pipeline for large-scale scientific datasets. Each case study will illustrate specific optimization strategies covered in the previous sections of this chapter, evaluating their impact on performance.

Numerical Solver for PDEs

This program solves a two-dimensional heat equation using finite difference methods. Initial profiling using the gprof tool revealed that the majority of the execution time is consumed by the nested loops that iterate over the grid points to update temperature values.

```
do i = 1, nx
   do j = 1, ny
      T_new(i, j) = T(i, j) + alpha * (T(i+1, j) - 2.0 * T(i, j) + T(i-1, j)) +
                    alpha * (T(i, j+1) - 2.0 * T(i, j) + T(i, j-1))
   end do
end do
```

Optimization began by enabling compiler optimization flags such as -O3 and -funroll-loops. Further enhancements were made by optimizing memory access patterns and utilizing OpenMP for parallelism.

```
!$omp parallel do
do j = 1, ny
   do i = 1, nx
      T_new(i, j) = T(i, j) + alpha * (T(i+1, j) - 2.0 * T(i, j) + T(i-1, j)) +
                    alpha * (T(i, j+1) - 2.0 * T(i, j) + T(i, j-1))
```

```
    end do
end do
!$omp end parallel do
```

Profiling the optimized version exhibited significant performance improvements, with a marked reduction in execution time and better utilization of available CPU cores, as observed in the subsequent profiling output:

```
Flat profile:

Total time: 2.34s

 %    cumulative   self     self   total
time    seconds   seconds   calls   ms/call   ms/call  name
35.0     0.82     0.82       1    820.00    820.00  MAIN__
20.0     1.28     0.46       1    460.00    460.00  heat_eq
...
```

Molecular Dynamics Simulation

This simulation performs forces and energy calculations for a system of interacting particles. Initial profiling indicated that the core bottleneck lies in the force calculation subroutine.

```
subroutine calculate_forces(x, f, n)
    implicit none
    integer, parameter :: dp = selected_real_kind(15, 307)
    integer :: i, j, n
    real(dp) :: x(n, 3), f(n, 3), dx(3)
    real(dp) :: r2, r2_inv, force

    do i = 1, n
        f(i, :) = 0.0_dp
    end do

    do i = 1, n-1
        do j = i+1, n
            dx = x(i, :) - x(j, :)
            r2 = sum(dx**2)

            if (r2 < cutoff_sq) then
                r2_inv = 1.0_dp / r2
                force = 48.0_dp * r2_inv**7 - 24.0_dp * r2_inv**4

                f(i, :) = f(i, :) + force * dx
                f(j, :) = f(j, :) - force * dx
            end if
        end do
    end do
end subroutine calculate_forces
```

Optimization included loop unrolling and vectorized operations assisted by SIMD (Single Instruction, Multiple Data) intrinsics, and applying linked-cell algorithms to limit the number of force calculations.

```
subroutine calculate_forces_optimized(x, f, n, cells)
```

```
    implicit none
    integer, parameter :: dp = selected_real_kind(15, 307)
    integer :: i, j, k, icell, jcell, n
    real(dp) :: x(n, 3), f(n, 3), dx(3)
    real(dp) :: r2, r2_inv, force
    type(Cell) array(cells) :: cell_list

    do k = 1, size(cell_list)
        icell = cell_list(k)%index_i
        jcell = cell_list(k)%index_j
        ! Loop over particles in icell and jcell
        do i = 1, cell_list(icell)%n_particles
            do j = 1, cell_list(jcell)%n_particles
                dx = x(i, :) - x(j, :)
                r2 = sum(dx**2)

                if (r2 < cutoff_sq) then
                    r2_inv = 1.0_dp / r2
                    force = 48.0_dp * r2_inv**7 - 24.0_dp * r2_inv**4

                    f(i, :) = f(i, :) + force * dx
                    f(j, :) = f(j, :) - force * dx
                end if
            end do
        end do
    end do
end subroutine calculate_forces_optimized
```

The performance gain from these optimizations was evident from significantly reduced execution times and more efficient memory usage.

```
Performance Metrics:

Original Time: 10.21s
Optimized Time: 3.98s
Memory Usage: Reduced by 30%
```

Data Processing Pipeline for Large-Scale Datasets

This pipeline processes large scientific datasets by filtering, averaging, and applying various transformations. Initially, the profiling identified the transformation function as a significant time consumer.

```
subroutine transform_data(data_in, data_out, n)
    implicit none
    integer, parameter :: dp = selected_real_kind(15, 307)
    integer :: i, n
    real(dp) :: data_in(n), data_out(n)

    do i = 1, n
        data_out(i) = log(data_in(i)) * sin(data_in(i))
    end do
end subroutine transform_data
```

Optimizations were applied by leveraging inlining for frequently called functions and introducing data parallelism using Coarrays in Fortran.

```
subroutine transform_data_optimized(data_in, data_out, n)
    implicit none
```

```
    integer, parameter :: dp = selected_real_kind(15, 307)
    integer :: i, n
    real(dp) :: data_in(n)[*], data_out(n)[*]

    ! Assume data distribution across images
    ! local_n: local array size for the coarray image
    local_n = n / num_images()
    segment_start = this_image() * local_n - local_n + 1
    segment_end = this_image() * local_n

    do i = segment_start, segment_end
        data_out(i) = log(data_in(i)) * sin(data_in(i))
    end do
end subroutine transform_data_optimized
```

The impact was evident in the improved speedup across multiple processing nodes, and the parallel efficiency was significantly enhanced.

```
Execution Time (Single Node): 15.45s
Execution Time (Optimized with Coarrays on 4 Nodes): 4.12s
Speedup: 3.75
Parallel Efficiency: 93.75%
```

These case studies illustrate the practical application of the optimization techniques discussed in this chapter, demonstrating notable improvements in performance metrics such as execution time, memory usage, and parallel efficiency.

Made in the USA
Monee, IL
14 September 2026

63117175R10177